Social Work with Lesbians, Gays, and Bisexuals

Social Work with Lesbians, Gays, and Bisexuals

A Strengths Perspective

Katherine van Wormer
University of Northern Iowa

Joel Wells
University of Northern Iowa

Mary Boes
University of Northern Iowa

Allyn and Bacon
Boston ▪ London ▪ Toronto ▪ Sydney ▪ Tokyo ▪ Singapore

Series Editor, Social Work and Family Therapy: *Judith Fifer*
Vice President, Editor-in-Chief, Social Sciences: *Karen Hanson*
Editorial Assistant: *Julianna M. Cancio*
Marketing Manager: *Jackie Aaron*
Production Editor: *Christopher H. Rawlings*
Editorial-Production Service: *Omegatype Typography, Inc.*
Composition and Prepress Buyer: *Linda Cox*
Manufacturing Buyer: *Julie McNeill*
Cover Administrator: *Jenny Hart*
Electronic Composition: *Omegatype Typography, Inc.*

A Pearson Education Company
160 Gould Street
Needham Heights, MA 02494

Internet: www.abacon.com

Library of Congress Cataloging-in-Publication Data

van Wormer, Katherine
Social work with lesbians, gays, and bisexuals : a strengths perspective / Katherine van Wormer, Joel Wells, Mary Boes.
p. cm.
Includes bibliographical references and index.
ISBN 0-205-27931-7
1. Social work with lesbians. 2. Lesbians—Services for. 3. Social work with gays. 4. Gay men—Services for. 5. Bisexuals—Services for. I. Wells, Joel. II. Boes, Mary. III. Title
HV1499.W67 2000
362.8—dc21 98-41567
CIP

Printed in the United States of America

10 9 8 7 6 5 4 3 2 1 04 03 02 01 00 99

To my daughter, Flora, whose coming out letter is included in these pages and whose joy in her lesbianism is an inspiration to us all.
Katherine van Wormer

To my son, Brett, with love and admiration.
Joel W. Wells

For Virginia without whom, so much less.
Mary Boes

CONTENTS

PREFACE

The primary job that any writer faces is to tell you a story out of human experiences—I mean by that, universal mutual experience, the anguishes and troubles and griefs of the human heart, which is universal, without regard to race or time or human condition. He wants to tell you something that has seemed to him so true, so moving, either comic or tragic, that it's worth preserving.

—William Faulkner, 1962

As team teachers involved in offering a course in gay/lesbian studies at the University of Northern Iowa, we searched together and separately for a text that would somehow tackle biological, psychological, and cultural aspects of gayness and lesbianism. What we were looking for was a textbook that would incorporate social work's person-in-the-environment approach, a conceptualization that views the individual and environment in constant and dynamic interaction. More specifically, we wanted our students to recognize how society's norms for heterosexuality are internalized by all of us, sometimes with devastating results. We also felt the need for a source that was sufficiently up-to-date to counter some of the right-wing, antigay, antilesbian rhetoric with which we have all grown familiar in recent years. Finally, as members of the helping professions, we sought a positive, strengths-based focus so that individuals (both our students and their future clients) could be empowered to take charge of their personal lives and to reach out in partnership to communities within which to achieve their highest potential.

Indeed, there are a great many books on lesbian, gay, and bisexual existence, enough to fill whole libraries. At the level of the popular press, issues relating to sexual orientation—for example, same-sex marriage, gays and lesbians in the military—have become more and more prominent in public discourse. Social scientific research on homosexuality has been prolific as well. But, apart from anthologies, no contemporary volume offering an integrated, social work approach had appeared. Why not draw up a tentative chapter outline, we thought, to see if the holism of the social work perspective could effectively address, in a dozen chapters or less, the complexity of issues across the homosexual/heterosexual spectrum? We did; the arrangements seemed to work, and the challenge was on. Once the structure was laid out and operationalized, the only remaining task was to fill in the content: the science (research, data, findings) and the art (poetry, commentaries, and the wealth of human experience). Consistent with the aims of the profession most committed to serving oppressed groups in our society, this book offers an overview of social work and related theory on lesbian, gay, and bisexual identities across the life span. Our focus is influenced by the perceived need.

The shaping and writing of *Social Work with Lesbians, Gays, and Bisexuals: A Strengths Perspective* was made possible through the collaboration of three feminist, pro-gay/lesbian social activists, each with a separate counseling and/or research expertise.

Katherine van Wormer, MSSW, Ph.D., a member of Gay and Lesbian Issues Committee of Iowa NASW, PFLAG (Parents, Families, and Friends of Lesbians and Gays), and NOW (National Organization for Women) is the author of *Alcoholism Treatment: A Social Work Perspective* and *Social Welfare: A World View,* both published by Nelson-Hall. Her dissertation, *Sex Role Behavior in a Woman's Prison,* was published by R & E Publishing Company.

Joel Wells, MA, Ph.D., teaches courses on human sexuality each semester and conducts workshops on homophobia for teachers and gay/lesbian organizations. Additionally, he has conducted extensive empirical research on homophobia and published numerous articles on his findings. The proud father of a gay son, Joel Wells is a member of the AIDS Coalition of Northeast Iowa, Planned Parenthood, and the American Association for Marriage and Family Therapy.

Mary Boes, MSW, MPH, DSW, is a member of Gay and Lesbian Issues Committee of Iowa NASW, who brings to her writing eight years of emergency room social work at an inner-city Philadelphia hospital. The hospital specialized in treating end-stage AIDS patients.

We share responsibility for this book as a whole and each chapter is a collaborative effort of all three authors. However, initial responsibility for the Preface, Chapters 1, 2, 9, 11, Glossary, and Resources was taken by Katherine van Wormer, Chapters 4, 5, 6, 7, and 8 by Joel Wells, and Chapters 3 and 10 by Mary Boes.

Our manageably sized volume is designed for either a specialized course or as a supplementary resource for the standard practice course curriculum.

The writing of a social work practice text on counseling gays, lesbians, and bisexuals brings up problems, questions, and controversies. What is homosexuality? Is it sexuality and/or a social identity? Even more problematic, what is heterosexuality? Are people born with a predisposition for attraction to the opposite sex? Or are many of them forced into heterosexuality in much the same way that left-handed people were once forced into right-handedness? To the extent that gays and lesbians can be singled out, what percentage of the population are they? And how common is bisexuality? For all the voluminous writing on these matters, the questions remain unanswered. Although as freelance historian Neil Miller (1995) points out, "There is clearly more coherence in the modern period than in the homosexual worlds of the more remote past. But there are difficulties that any writer has to take into account" (p. xix).

Social work with lesbian, gay, and bisexual clients incorporates complexities that transcend meeting the immediate personal needs of individual clients. Such social work practice is delivered in a climate characterized by increasing hostility and antigay/lesbian hysteria. In 1994, for instance, there were 2,064 reported incidents of harassment of sexual minorities, according to a recent federal government report on hate crimes. This physical violence is matched by political attacks on openly gay and lesbian teachers, Boy Scout leaders, and members of the clergy, among others.

This current criminal and political activity offers a significant challenge to affirmative perspectives on lesbian, gay, and bisexual identity. In such a climate of oppression and self-righteousness, it is imperative that those of us who are truly committed to improving social work practice with lesbians and gay men work together to develop strategies to motivate social work students to confront covert and institutionalized heterosexism. It is toward this end that this book is written.

Foundations

One of the primary rationales for gay/lesbian studies, as for ethnic and women's studies, is in the advancement of knowledge, especially in areas in which knowledge has been willfully hidden or distorted. To know about the lives of one's fellow citizens and to understand their history and culture are essential if we are to have a humane and just society; it is especially affirming to those populations whose very existence and contributions have been so consistently overlooked.

A major goal of this book, then, is to bring together in one work essential knowledge for effective and affirmative social work practice with gays, lesbians, and bisexuals who are coping with all the usual crises of everyday life in addition to concerns related to their individual uniqueness. During the coming-out stage and committed relationship stage, social work intervention can be especially helpful. The secondary goal, on the macro level, is to incorporate this knowledge under an ecosystem-interactionist framework for a multidimensional understanding of the many complexities and nuances of lesbian, gay, and bisexual orientations. The ecological approach, in its person-in-the-situation conceptualization, successfully integrates the components of sexual/affectual relations. These components are biological, psychological, and environmental. Especially helpful to the study of homosexuality is ecosystems' holistic framework for viewing reality. There is no either/or with this formulation—either you are a homosexual or you're not—but rather, the individual is perceived in terms of all his or her biopsychosocial complexity. Relevant to our purposes, instead of polarizing sexuality into mutually exclusive opposites—straight and gay, "us" and "them"—we can be aware of shades of gray and of sexual orientation as a complexity of constellations of feelings and identities that may fluctuate in intensity over time. Imagining homosexuality on one side of this constellation and heterosexuality on the other, we can say that most of us probably would find ourselves somewhere in the middle. Such is one of the assumptions of this book.

A second major assumption, related to the first, is the notion that our society is predicated on *heterosexual privilege.* Heterosexual privilege entails access to the taken-for-granted institutional arrangements including having respected love role models, validation from the culture in your relationships, marriage with all the legal rights bestowed thereof, and acceptance in respected social roles such as adoptive parent, teacher, or member of the clergy. Gaining heterosexual privilege: This is what "being in the closet" and adopting a facade are all about.

Some of the other basic assumptions that underlie this presentation are as follows:

- The causes of homosexuality cannot be understood apart from knowing the causes of heterosexuality.
- Homophobia, or the irrational fear of homosexuality, is pervasive in Anglo American culture and it affects not only some of us but all of us.
- Homophobia is closely related to fear of sexuality or erotophobia.
- The growth of homophobia paralleled the heightened awareness of sexuality generated by Freudian psychology; gay and lesbian identity and culture are a modern Western phenomenon as well.
- The bond among gay men and lesbians, the brother/sister bond, is a little noted but striking phenomenon and source of considerable social support and political unity.
- To encourage a people to remain invisible and keep their private lives to themselves is to effectively disempower them. Oppression and silence are integrally interconnected.

- The strengths of the gay/lesbian community to organize for social change and social helping can be seen in its response to AIDS, violence, and discriminatory legislation.
- Because variation in sexual orientation is universal, the economic and cultural diversity of this group is pronounced. Learning about the lesbian and gay population must include differential experiences on the basis of age, class, ethnicity, gender, and disability.
- Open and nonjudgmental attitudes by social workers are essential to the development of supportive practice environments for lesbian and gay clients; same-sex relationships are potentially as healthy (or unhealthy) as opposite-sex relationships.

A Proud History

Consistent with the strengths approach, our perspective is influenced by the need to look at possibilities as well as problems and at the special strengths that emerge out of lesbian and gay identity and experience. In this volume, homosexuality—gayness/lesbianism—is viewed as an Anglo American historical construction developed out of the late nineteenth century's heightened awareness of sexuality. The notion of normal human development, which presupposes the development of opposite-sex attachments, is viewed as of little or no use in addressing diversity across the life span. Of more use is the notion steeped in Native American tradition of homosexuality as a special gift allotted to only a few, a gift that entailed social roles and spiritual attributes. Central to our conceptualization is the use of a positive vocabulary. In the body of this text, we will use words such as *gays* but usually *gay males* to refer to men with same-sex orientation and *lesbian* to women with same-sex orientation. *Homosexual* as a noun we do not use; however, *homosexuality* and *gayness/lesbianism* are sometimes used to refer to lesbians, gays, and bisexuals collectively. Despite the appeal of brevity in using *gay* as a generic adjective for homosexuality in both genders, we have chosen not to do so, and have added the term *lesbian* when referring to both genders. We realize the word *queer,* as in queer art or queer culture, is being reclaimed by the gay and lesbian community, but as use of this term appears to lack sensitivity, at least on the surface, we will avoid it apart from reference to the work of others. An undeniable advantage of this usage is aesthetic: Queer art simply sounds better than gay, lesbian, and bisexual (and transgender) art and meets the same need for a generic term that *gay* did in the 1980s.

Equally problematic are the words *orientation* and *lifestyle. Sexual orientation* will be used to denote one's sexual attraction—whether this is to the same or opposite gender or both. *Lifestyle* we will use only reluctantly for want of a better word to denote a positive identity, and, in fact, a whole way of life.

Judy Grahn (1990) detects a vibrant gay culture common to both sexes:

> Gay people have a history because Gay culture has histories that give us a continuity with the past and that give us connections with Gay people in other cultures and countries, places, and times. We're the inheritors of a distinct cultural background with very long roots, long buried to be sure. (p. 18)

And Mark Thompson (1987:78) articulates "the gay spirit" accordingly:

> "Being gay is about being in the world in a different and essential way. Androgyny permits all things," said a lesbian psychic. "There's something about gay people that goes beyond sexual orientation. All throughout history we've been very different from heterosexual people. I believe there is something about gay people that is profoundly religious," said a shaman. "A gay person cannot live an unexamined life," concluded a poet. (p. 78)

Thompson's words, a tribute to gay/lesbian legacy and uniqueness, are meaningful to social workers preparing to work with this clientele and who wish to adopt a strengths perspective. The strengths model—actually more of an approach than a theoretical model—empowers and validates lesbian and gay clients in a social climate characterized by homophobia and hostility, on the one hand, and by the triumph of gay identity and community, on the other. In encouraging social workers to reframe their perspective from the negative (problem centered) to the positive, the strengths perspective is grounded in the premise that "each person already carries the seeds for his or her own transformation" (Weick, 1992, p. 25). Not only does the client learn from the social worker, but for social workers there is so much to learn from the rich vein of autobiographical and semiautobiographical material devoted to lesbian and gay experience. There is so much to learn also about the developmental stages across the life span for individuals who identify themselves along various points of the heterosexual–homosexual continuum.

This book is designed to help practitioners acquire an affirmative, relevant framework for working with diverse sexual and family arrangements. Greater understanding must be supported by sound research to rebut some of the public rhetoric and discriminatory public policy reported in the media. Knowledge of what it means to live (as gay or straight or in between) in a fiercely heterosexist society is essential for human service workers if we are to succeed in intervening in both the personal and political realms to help lesbians and gay males live a psychologically healthy life.

Organization

Social Work with Lesbians, Gays, and Bisexuals is divided into three parts. The three chapters comprising Part One concern the social and cultural context of lesbian, gay, and bisexual experience. These chapters, roughly speaking, follow the 1994 Council on Social Work Education (CSWE) mandate to include in the social work curriculum information about populations at risk such as sexual minorities and to emphasize the impact of discrimination, economic deprivation, and oppression on these groups. In order to elucidate the more specific material that follows, Chapter 1 sets forth the theoretical framework of the book and of social work as well—the ecosystems approach—and a rationale for the strengths as opposed to pathology perspective. Definition of important terms pertaining to lesbian, gay, and bisexual phenomena lays the groundwork for the treatment issues that follow.

Chapter 2 explores the dynamics of homophobia, gay/lesbian baiting, and denial of one's selfhood in a heterosexist society. Homophobia is viewed individually and institutionally, historically, and globally. On a far more upbeat note, Chapter 3 reveals the light in the darkness—the gay/lesbian cultural contribution and also the largely hidden subculture that has sustained gay life and sensitivity over the generations.

Part Two takes us across the life span—from growing up to growing old—and reviews social scientific research pertinent to variations in sexual behavior, family forms and civil rights issues affecting living arrangements, and handling of predictable crises. Throughout this section, keen attention is paid to racial and ethnic diversity. Chapter 4 is concerned with gay/lesbian youth, with emphasis on the coming-out experience—coming out to oneself and others. The range of intense social and personal pressures facing gay and lesbian adolescents is discussed. This chapter highlights the all-American junior and senior high school experience.

Chapter 5 delves into sexuality in considerable depth. Data from extensive surveys concerning attitudes toward various male-specific and female-specific sexual practices are presented. Looming over this whole issue is the universal question: Is sexual orientation a choice? Reference to recent empirical research provides some interesting considerations if not definitive answers. That we are an erotophobic society is a major theme of this chapter. The detailed and graphic information provided should be especially helpful for mental health counselors.

Chapter 6 explores issues, both economic and legal, pertaining to the workplace and the family respectively. Workers' rights, health insurance, child custody battles, and adoption are among the matters discussed. Chapter 7 concludes this section by providing information on the meaning of old age, first for gay men and then for lesbians. Advantages and pitfalls of gay and lesbian aging are highlighted.

Part Three is practice focused. In this section, we provide firsthand case material to demonstrate effective strategies for intervention. The strengths model shapes interventions so that negative self-perceptions are challenged. Attention is paid to both individual and family therapy.

Chapter 8 views the general counseling needs of sexual minorities, what brings them into treatment, and what makes their efforts to resolve issues worthwhile. Key practice questions are addressed such as, should gay/lesbian clients have gay/lesbian therapists? Should gay/lesbian therapists practice self-disclosure?

Because of the scope and intensity of health care issues, which range from the ordinary acute and chronic diseases to sexually transmitted diseases such as AIDS, two chapters provide special attention to this topic. Chapter 9 gives an overview of critical health care concerns for lesbians, whereas Chapter 10 surveys the needs of gay male clients. Both chapters address the unique health care needs and issues from a biopsychosocial perspective.

Chapter 11 applies gay and lesbian affirmative perspective to family (including couples) counseling. Children growing up with one gay or lesbian, or even two bisexual, parents and parents who have discovered they have gay or lesbian children are the subjects of this final chapter. It is important that therapists be aware of the ways in which routine life stressors may be intensified for individuals who are outside the mainstream of society.

From a general education standpoint, the study of gay/lesbian populations offers an opportunity for critical thinking on a topic often infused with emotionalism and politically charged mythology. To understand the reasons for homophobia in individuals or in the wider society is to understand the nature of oppression against minority groups and backlash against group members who fight for their rights. The personal and social attitudes of prejudice inevitably must be viewed as intertwined. We believe that, taken together, these chapters will enable social work practitioners to take an active, transformative role for the twenty-first century. The social work profession, in fact, can learn a great deal about new family forms and incredible resilience in the face of adversity from work with this often invisible population whose only wish is to have the kind of acceptance that others take entirely for granted.

Acknowledgments

The authors' appreciation goes to the following reviewers for their comments on the manuscript: Linda E. Jones, University of Minnesota; and Marion Wagner, Indiana University. Special thanks is extended to Darlys Hansen for her invaluable support in the preparation of this manuscript. Thanks is also extended to Tami Huff who, as a student assistant, diligently and thoughtfully typed numerous handwritten rough drafts of the original effort. The authors would like to recognize Judy Fifer, the series editor, for cheerfully and bravely overseeing the project from start to finish, and the staff at Omegatype Typography for their help and patience in securing difficult-to-get copyright permissions. Additionally, Katherine van Wormer thanks the University of Northern Iowa for providing financial support in the form of a summer research grant.

References

Grahn, J. (1990). *Another mother tongue: Gay words, gay worlds.* Boston: Beacon Press.

Miller, N. (1995). *Out of the past: Gay and lesbian history from 1869 to the present.* New York: Vintage Books.

Thompson, M. (1987). *Gay spirit: Myth and meaning.* New York: St. Martin's Press.

Weick, A. (1992). Building a strengths perspective for social work. In D. Saleebey (Ed.), *The strengths perspective in social work practice* (pp. 18–26). New York: Longman.

Social Work with Lesbians, Gays, and Bisexuals

CHAPTER 1 Social Work Mission and Policies

Our difference is our strength.

—Audre Lorde, 1984

In mythology the many-colored veil of the Egyptian goddess Isis symbolized the creative spirit clothed in material forms of great diversity, the ever-changing form of nature (Shepherd, 1993). The political symbols of gay/lesbian identity—the rainbow and the color lavender (a blending of blue and pink)—are a reminder of the versatility and multiplicity of nature. They are also a reminder of the tendency in Western culture to engage in hierarchical, dichotomous thinking, which leads naturally into that ultimate division between *us* and *them.*

Among mental health professionals, the tendency to dichotomize has been played out as a tendency to juxtapose the bad and the good, or more commonly, the sick and the well. Lesbianism and gayness, accordingly, are still described largely in psychological language. Unlike other oppressed groups, the members of which are rarely thrown into treatment on the basis of their minority identity, gays and lesbians are frequently referred to mental health agencies. Their individual strengths and collective contributions to the wider American culture are rarely considered. Yet a denial of a people's culture is a denial of their very being.

Today the cost of denying one crucial portion of humanity and the interconnectedness of all humanity is paid in oppression at every level of society—on the school playground, in the courts, in the military ranks. The vision of wholeness—what Shepherd (1993) terms "the Feminine in each of us" (p. 1)—the part of us that sees life in context, the relatedness of everything—can help heal wounds in a society that so often enforces conformity along painfully narrow lines. In order to survive, as Lorde (1984) points out, those of us for whom oppression is as American as apple pie have always had to be watchers, to become familiar with the language and manners of the oppressor, sometimes even adopting them for some illusion of protection. Lesbians and gay men must learn to function in two cultures: the gay/lesbian community and mainstream society. In contrast to members of ethnic minority groups who first become socialized within their own group and then later by the dominant culture, lesbians and gay men are first socialized by the dominant culture and later identify with the member group (Rothblum, 1997). And sometimes the schizophrenic existence of people who are required to be what they cannot be, compounded with the ordinary problems of living, brings gays and lesbians to seek help from clinicians. Many others, however, will back off or delay until too late in getting the help they need due to the reputation of mental health establishments, a reputation for conventionalism and nonawareness of alternative living arrangements. To some extent it is deserved, but to a large extent this reputation is a legacy from the past, from a time when homosexuality was designated as a mental disorder and therapeutic intervention was directed accordingly.

This introductory chapter presents the strengths-based perspective as an alternative to social work's traditional problem-solving approach to working with gays and lesbians. The purpose of this chapter is to provide an overview of gay/lesbian issues and also to set the stage for later chapters concerning heterosexism and homophobia, the gay/lesbian cultural contribution, issues of sexual identity across the life span, and the counseling challenge. A discussion of contemporary mass media images introduces this chapter. Then, following a brief presentation of the demographic facts of gayness, lesbianism, and bisexuality and an analysis of the political context of liberation, we will review the historical approaches to the phenomenon of homosexuality. A section on the nature versus nurture debate pertinent to the causes of sexual orientation follows.

At the heart of this chapter is the strengths perspective. In sharp contrast to the traditional deficit approach, the strengths perspective offers a framework for affirmatory practice that represents the nearest expression of the ethics and values of the social work profession. Following a summary of gay/lesbian terminology and a definition of terms (e.g., *heterosexual privilege* and the *sexuality continuum*), we will delve into the fundamentals of the strengths perspective. The chapter will close with a discussion of social work's mission (as defined by the Council on Social Work Education), a mission characterized by the pursuit of such relevant goals as the enhancement of human well-being and the alleviation of poverty and oppression.

Mass Media Images

People are at once fascinated and repelled by their awareness of sexual diversity. The American ambivalence toward sexuality—*erotophobia*—plays into this paradox. Divergent sexuality has enormous mass media appeal and even entertainment value. More and more, today, news stories of notable and notorious gay and lesbian personalities fill the airwaves and newspaper headlines.

In the spring of 1997, for instance, the world read of a charismatic cult leader who led thirty-nine people into a mass suicide. The leader, according to newspaper accounts, was torn between his homosexuality and Presbyterian background: A minister's son with one year of seminary experience, the cult leader was drawn to deny his sexuality and ultimately life itself. "Deeply ashamed of his homosexual urges," stated the article, "at some point Marshall Herff Applewhite had himself castrated, an action many of his followers emulated" (*The Washington Post,* 1997, p. 1A). Of special interest to our readers was Applewhite's reported treatment in a psychiatric hospital where he was to be "cured" of his homosexuality. His cult activity, in fact, sprang directly out of this ill-guided treatment experience.

And on April 2, 1997, Amendment B, popularly known as the "fidelity and chastity amendment," was adopted by the Presbyterian Church (USA). This amendment excludes self-affirming gays and lesbians from full participation in the church. Many congregations have pledged open defiance of this action (Mills, 1997). As the summer rolled on, however, the strict wording was watered down.

Astoundingly, within the same month, and on a celebratory rather than tragic note, the nation was inundated with news reports on the coming out of the television character, Ellen. Although the show was destined to be curiously short-lived, this occasion marked the first time in television history that a lead character on television was a lesbian or gay person. This historic moment was paralleled by the actress's simultaneous coming out on national talk shows. Meanwhile, all across the United States, other news stories concerned the uproar over the possibility of same-sex marriage. Surveys of public attitudes, however, consistently showed a majority favored protection against discrimination at work. In the fall of 1998, television audiences were introduced to *Will and Grace,* a new gay-inclusive sitcom depicting the often lifelong relationships between gay men and straight women.

Lest we get too complacent, professors of gay and lesbian studies cringed as the CBS television show *60 Minutes* highlighted college courses that focused on "butch-femme" lesbian sex, sadomasochistic relationships, anal sex, and masturbation. The topic was queer studies; the implication left by interviewer Mike Wallace was that the offering of gay/lesbian studies courses made a mockery of academics (*Chronicle of Higher Education,* 1998).

Demographic Facts

A popular gay/lesbian activist button commonly seen at rallies simply displays the number 10. This 10 percent figure, which is so often quoted as the percentage of the population reported to be gay or lesbian is, in fact, a misinterpretation of the data presented in Kinsey's two landmark reports (Witt, Thomas, & Marcus, 1997). This figure is derived from the famous Kinsey reports on human sexual behavior (Kinsey, Pomeroy, & Martin, 1948; Kinsey, Pomeroy, Martin, & Gebhard, 1953) that indicated, based on interviews of more than 12,000 men and 8,000 women, that approximately 10 percent of the population (13 percent of men and 7 percent of women) has been exclusively homosexual for an extended period of time. Only 4 percent of the males identified themselves as exclusively homosexual compared to less than 3 percent of the females. Far more, however (37 percent of men and 19 percent of women), reported having had same-sex relations at some time in their adult lives. Statistically and methodogically reliable data on sexual behavior remain hard to obtain because they are so politically charged (Vaid, 1995). Probably the best numerical estimate, in that it was based on a random sample, comes from the National Opinion Research Center (1994), which concluded that 9 percent of men and 4 percent of women reported having same-sex contact since puberty.

Detracting from our ability to come up with estimates of the homosexual population is the confusion abounding on two levels—basically, over *what* homosexuality is and *who* the participants are. Ambiguity over what constitutes homosexuality (is it behavior? desire? identity?) as distinguished from heterosexuality complicates the research design and findings. Moreover, the fact that sexual minorities, unlike most other minority members, can "pass" confounds the experts and other observers in their attempts to learn who among them is gay, lesbian, or bisexual. Many are married and remain safely inside the system of heterosexual respectability. Societal pressure to remain hidden is symbolized in the military's "don't ask, don't tell" policy punishing only those who refuse to conceal their homosexuality. Such publicly enforced silencing effectively keeps the personal from becoming political, the powerless from becoming empowered. Significantly, 48 percent of persons questioned in a *U.S. News & World Report* survey indicated that they did not personally know anyone who was gay or lesbian (Shapiro, 1993). Widely cited in the literature, the survey also revealed that personal acquaintanceship with someone gay or lesbian was associated with support of full gay and lesbian equality. According to a more recent *USA Today*/CNN/Gallup poll, 59 percent of Americans believe homosexuality is morally wrong versus 34 percent who believe it is not wrong (Bash, 1997).

Social workers and others in the helping professions are, of course, susceptible to absorbing the attitudes and biases of mainstream society. A recent study by Berkman and Zinberg (1997) measured the extent of homophobia and heterosexist bias among a cohort of 187 practicing social workers. Although only 10 percent of respondents were found to be homophobic (defined by the authors as a very extreme form of prejudice against homosexuals), a large majority were found to believe that only heterosexuality was natural and that it was superior to homosexuality. The social workers expressed more prejudice against gay males than lesbians. Religiosity was associated with negative attitudes whereas having personal contact with gays and lesbians and having been in psychotherapy were associated with more positive attitudes toward this population. Although the reasons for this latter correlation are not clear, one can speculate that a heightened self-awareness by persons who have undergone therapy is responsible for this finding. This study reinforces the importance of social contact among people of diverse sexual orientations.

In order to increase knowledge of lesbians and gay men as people, sometimes professors in the social sciences encourage students to attend panel discussions in which lesbians, gays, and bisexuals talk about themselves and their lives. Such experiences are helpful not only in the coming-out process for the speakers but can be a real eye-opener for all members of the audience. The significance of exposure to gay/lesbian speakers, openly lesbian and gay faculty, and content in the social work classroom in terms of changing attitudes has been documented (Aronson, 1995; Cramer, Oles, & Black, 1997). See Box 1.1 for one student's unsolicited and refreshingly honest response to her first encounter with openly gay and lesbian speakers.

BOX 1.1

A Social Work Student Attends a Gay/Lesbian Panel

I was a little apprehensive at first about attending this discussion. I don't think that I'm a homophobic by any means; however, I have had such limited contact with the group that I was unsure of what to expect. Will there be angry people there? Will Christian Fundamentalists come to accuse the panel of grave sin? Will anyone show up?

I went about 20 minutes early and sat outside the room waiting for the doors to be unlocked. Gradually more and more people joined me. I was surprised at the large turnout. I noticed a group of guys goofing around outside the doors and thought nothing at first. But when the doors opened and the crowd funneled through the doors, I noticed the same guys moving their chairs to the front, facing the crowd.

"These men are gay?" I found myself thinking. And it was there that I realized my stereotypical image of a gay man. As if I should be able to tell just by looking at them what their sexual preference was. I cringed as I had to admit my ignorance.

The panel answered audience questions after they introduced themselves. They said that for the most part they experienced little harassment on campus, but were unsure what to expect now that UNIGLO (University of Northern Iowa Gay/Lesbian Organization) meetings are public. I was surprised when the panel announced the weekly meetings to us and encouraged us to come and show our support. One of the main issues discussed was the recent denial of a bill in the U.S. Congress that would have made firing a person because they are homosexual illegal; the bill lost 50–49.

Personally I can't understand anyone who would be against this becoming law. I may have my stereotypes but I recognize that they are humans just like the rest of us. They should not be denied rights and privileges that other Americans enjoy. Sexual preference should not be an issue, period.

As I looked at the four men and one woman in front of me, I really felt for them. Here they were in a world where they can't legally marry the person they love, where they could be fired based on what gender they choose to love. And to all of the people on the panel this really isn't a choice, it's an inborn feeling, genetic.

How can our society treat these people this way? Wasn't America based on the principle "freedom for all"? Why is this group excluded? What threat could they possibly pose? Although we came to question the panel, we were the ones being questioned, only we had no answers.

Source: By Rachel Wilson; printed with permission of Rachel Wilson.

The Political Context

Same-sex behavior is as old as desire itself, but the categories of homosexual and heterosexual are twentieth-century inventions (Vaid, 1995). A heightened awareness of sexuality as an outgrowth and concomitant of public morality campaigns at the turn of the century paved the way for a clear-cut distinction between conduct that was considered normal and conduct that was not (Katz, 1996). In her analysis of the sociopolitical context of gay and lesbian liberation, Vaid lists six stages in the evolution of gay/lesbian consciousness: (1) the pre–World War II era in which homosexual desire in men—"fairies"—was seen as a kind of gender role inversion as was the butch-femme arrangement in women; (2) the post–World War II period, marked by the emergence of the minority status model that followed the landmark Stonewall police raid and riot of 1969; (3) gay and lesbian liberation strongly influenced by feminism in which the personal became political and coming out was seen as essential; (4) gay and lesbian identity politics; (5) the eighties, marked by AIDS, an antigay backlash, and internal conflict over racial identity; and (6) the present period of virtual equality in which the intransigence of the radical right defines the issues. Two basic themes that emerge from this cavalcade of history are first, the strong influence of American puritanism over sexuality and especially diverse sexuality and second, from within the movement, the borrowing of concepts and methods from feminism. Kushner (1995) captures the first theme in the following commentary:

> Lesbian and gay kids will have less trouble accepting their homosexuality not when the Gay Pride Parade is an orderly procession of suits arranged in monogamous pairs but when people learn to be less horrified by sex and its complexities. (p. 28)

And of the feminist/lesbian link we learn from Vaid (1995):

> AIDS dramatically changed the composition of the gay and lesbian movement. . . . Men who had never been political, never considered coming out of the closet, never attended a gay or lesbian fundraising event, began to do so in large numbers. Lesbians who had shunned the mixed gay movement, choosing to work on women's rights, grew alarmed at the exploitation of AIDS by the right, and decided to confront the homophobia of the medical, political, and legal systems. (p. 89)

The lesbian/feminist link no doubt enhanced the flow of ideas as well as the particular strategies employed. The AIDS service organizations, for example, adopted feminist critiques to challenge health care's discriminatory practices. The AIDS issue itself united men and women in what was then called the gay liberation movement to help build a social service apparatus throughout the country and to lobby for AIDS patients' rights at every level of health care.

Ridiculed for years, *transgenders,* or persons who identify with or dress like members of the opposite sex, are emerging as the newest group to demand equality (Cloud, 1998). At least 25,000 Americans have undergone sex-reassignment surgery. Many transsexuals, however, express their sexuality through clothing, hormone treatments, or with partial surgery only. Their political focus is on hate crimes, child custody, and job discrimination. Although their presence was considered an embarrassment in the 1970s, increasingly their interests are embraced by gay, lesbian, and bisexual organizations. Throughout North America, the transgender political movement is building. Lawyers with the Transgender Law Conference have helped pass statutes in at least 17 states allowing transexuals to change the sex designation on their birth certificates. In Britain, however, the government refuses to let transsexuals have their birth certificates altered; the European Court of Human Rights, in a recent decision, refused to find that the British government had acted improperly (Gibb, 1998).

Models of Homosexuality

Despite the fact that the term *homosexuality* was not differentiated from *heterosexuality* until 1869, moral proscriptions against same-sex eroticism are ages old. The tendency for society to regulate sexuality is universal; the forum that the regulation takes has important implications for power relationships (intimacy breeds influence) and familial/reproductive issues (for example, who is father to the son). Thus, even in ancient Greece where sexual activity between men and adolescent boys was a social institution endowed with cultural, spiritual, and educational significance, there were strict norms pertaining to the contexts within which such love affairs were approved. Strict controls were imposed on "effeminate" homosexuality in mature men, for example (Conrad & Schneider, 1992). Surveying history, over the past 2,000 years, therefore, we can conclude that although definitions of natural and unnatural behavior have varied by time and place, moralism has always been with us.

The evolution of attitudes toward homosexual conduct has gone from perceiving same-sex conduct as sinful, criminal, sick, a normal variation, and back to sinful again. The conceptualizations are not necessarily chronological but exist as recurring themes throughout the centuries. Whether homosexuality is viewed as a result of nature or nurture is central to the sanctions society provides and to the effort exerted to "correct" the offending behaviors.

Sin

The road from badness to madness starts with the religious proscriptions of the ancient Hebrews and early Christians. The only fully approved standard, as Conrad and Schneider indicate, was heterosexual procreative intercourse. Influences of ancient Judaism prohibiting sex for pleasure were incorporated into Christianity, and as this new religion was accepted in the Roman Empire, canon law forbade same-sex contact, which came to be both morally and legally forbidden throughout the Western world (O'Neill & Naidoo, 1990). Medieval church theologians such as Thomas Aquinas argued that same-sex intimacy was selfish and pleasure seeking and, therefore, sinful (Mondimore, 1996). All kinds of "unnatural" sexual acts came to be defined as instances of sodomy and strictly condemned. Religious beliefs, in short, have been used to justify intolerance of homosexuality down to the present day.

Crime

Throughout the Middle Ages, homosexual behavior and other acts of sodomy were elevated to "crimes against nature" and proscribed by law. Punishments were provided, first of an ecclesiastical nature, but gradually, over time, sexual sins became transgressions against the state. This was seen most notably in the Spanish Inquisition of the thirteenth and fourteenth centuries. In England, homosexuals along with Jews, Muslims, and disabled persons were scapegoated following the devastation of society by the catastrophic Black Death of 1348. Interestingly, following the cruel defeat of World War I and financial hardship in its aftermath, Germany sought out virtually the same groups to exterminate (van Wormer, 1997). This persecution under Nazism was the more startling in consideration of the fact that twentieth-century Germany had been the home of a great awakening of consciousness in the 1920s, the mother of what was probably the first homosexual civil rights movement in the world. The awakening disintegrated, however, with the swift return of fascism: Tens of thousands of homosexual men and a small number of lesbians were imprisoned during the Holocaust (Mondimore, 1996). We do not know how many survived. Today, the pink triangle that homosexual males were forced to wear is often used as a symbol of defiance.

In the Anglo-Saxon world, similarly, the tradition of criminalization, which culminated in sixteenth century English statutes making "the crime against nature" a capital offense, survives today. Its legacy prevails in the United States where approximately half of the states retain antisodomy laws on their books. Attempts at reform are not without well-organized opposition.

Sickness

In 1810 the Napoleonic Code decriminalized homosexual conduct between consenting adults in private. New scientific theories of health and illness during this period warned against deviant sexual activity as detrimental to one's health. Badness thus became sickness, as Conrad and Schneider argue. In the latter half of the nineteenth century, sodomy, the sin, was transformed into homosexuality, the medical category. And now attention was turned to the sexual proclivities of women as well as men.

Congenital invert was the term applied to masculine females and feminine males by sexologists (primarily physicians) who began writing about nonnormative sexuality. Like their predecessors, these writers were often motivated by the moral vision of their day (Faderman, 1991). The subjects of their research were regarded as degenerates whose problems stemmed from a physiological basis. In lesbians, one noted a male hair pattern; in men a feminine flexibility of the wrists prevailed, according to these "scholars."

At first, according to Faderman (1991), working-class women whose hard work, rough lives, and ambitions perhaps drove them to seek masculine attire or mannish ways got the attention of the sexologists. But as the turn-of-the-century feminist movement grew, it was not long before the middle- and upper-class feminists found themselves branded as acting inappropriately to their gender. Feminism, in fact, was seen in medical circles as a cause of "inversion."

A horror of masturbation and other "unnatural" sex acts believed to be the cause of poor mental health filled the air (Conrad & Schneider, 1992). Allegations about certain unhealthy practices at English boarding schools were rampant during the Victorian era. By the turn of the century, however, the focus was off masturbation and on principles of heredity and evolution.

Homosexuality, a term coined by a Hungarian physician in 1869, was seen as a throwback to a previous, more-primitive evolutionary state of pathology. Freud's contribution to medical research was to introduce a new, more progressive theory of homosexuality, which he perceived as an incomplete or arrested psychosexual development. His belief was that bisexuality was a latent predisposition in all of us. Because the condition of homosexuality is not likely to be cured, it must be accepted. Later psychoanalysts, however, ignoring Freud, looked to many varieties of intervention in a frenzy to find a cure. Characteristically, blame was placed on overprotective or unconsciously hostile mothers who were married to weak, ineffectual fathers.

Until 1976 the American Psychiatric Association (APA) considered homosexuality a sexual deviation, a listing shared with voyeurism and child molestation in the *Diagnostic and Statistical Manual of Mental Disorders* (*DSM*). Then, after extensive lobbying by homophile organizations and in response to scientific research showing that gays and lesbians are no more prone to mental illness or personality disorders than the rest of the population, the APA omitted homosexuality from its famed list of disorders.

Nevertheless, the current edition of the *DSM IV* (APA, 1994) contains reference to a curious disorder in children under the diagnosis of gender identity disorder:

> In children, the disturbance is manifested by four (or more) of the following:
> (1) repeatedly stated desire to be, or insistence that he or she is, the other sex
> (2) in boys, preference for cross-dressing or simulating female attire; in girls, insistence on wearing only stereotypical masculine clothing
> (3) strong and persistent preferences for cross-sex roles in make-believe play or persistent fantasies of being the other sex
> (4) intense desire to participate in the stereotypical games and pastimes of the other sex
> (5) strong preference for playmates of the other sex. (p. 537)

This conceptualization is strangely reminiscent of the early pathologizing of feminine males and masculine-appearing, liberated females. The International Gay and Lesbian Human Rights Commission is trying to get the APA to remove this diagnosis from the next edition of the *DSM*.

Perhaps the most frightening development, one actively condemned by the National Association of Social Workers (NASW), is the resurgence in reparative or conversion therapies for lesbians and gay men. False claims by therapists of documented success stories in converting people to heterosexuality can lead to severe emotional damage, whether through the claims or through the treatments (NASW, 1992). Interestingly, reparative therapy concerns itself, according to Mondimore (1996), almost exclusively with males. The theory behind the treatment is that if a boy's father did not provide him with an authentic masculine identity, the boy would come to eroticize men. Anecdotal stories of "cures" through psychotherapy constitute the only available proof of the efficacy of this questionable treatment modality.

Normal Variation

A growing number of social science studies on same-sex conduct and Kinsey's extensive research on human sexuality combined to create a countertrend to the stigmatizing and repression of homosexuality. But it took the social activism of the late sixties for gays and lesbians to define themselves as a sexual minority, fully deserving of all the rights and benefits of any ethnic or cultural minority group. The minority group model helped move homosexuality from the domain of illness and sociopathic deviance into the public domain of civil rights (Vaid, 1995).

Stonewall (the violent police raid on a gay bar in Greenwich Village in 1969) marks the turning point in gay/lesbian consciousness. The Stonewall riots and the raid that precipitated them would have been fairly routine except for one fact: A well-organized band of gay and lesbian activists was in place to galvanize a movement. One of the most far-reaching consequences of this movement, and of special interest to social workers, was the political notion that coming out and pursuing gay and lesbian visibility held the key to freedom (Vaid, 1995). Simply put: In silence there is only pain, pain without recourse.

Another aspect of the gay/lesbian movement worthy of comment is the unlikely blending of gender-based attitudes concerning the actual dimension of the gay/lesbian discrimination. Duberman (1991) recalls how earlier male/female tension within one political organization gradually gave way as members became persuaded by angry feminists to redefine the organization's purpose. The proposal that finally passed stated that the group's primary purpose was "to combat oppression against women." Gender nonconformity was thus recognized, at least for the moment, as the uniting bond between gay men and lesbian women. Despite some prejudice on both sides of the gender issue, concludes Duberman, a sense of camaraderie emerged over time.

Back to Sin

The U.S. Catholic bishops' recent urging of parents to love and accept their gay and lesbian children is a welcome although limited overture by an unexpected source (*The Washington Post,* 1997). The bishops, in their pastoral letter, asserted that homosexual orientation is deep-seated and that parental rejection can lead to substance abuse or suicide. Although homosexual orientation was not rejected by the church, homosexual *activity* was. Generally, in recent years, a backlash response to the gay/lesbian militance has been reinforced by a palpable resurgence of the Christian fundamentalist right. Often initiated, supported, and financed by the Christian Coalition, the civil rights of gay and lesbian citizens have been put on the ballot all over the United States. The far right's code words—for example, "pro-family," "the gay agenda," and "traditional values"—offer a cloak to suppress difference. The "love the sinner, hate the sin" refrain is commonly voiced on college campuses. We learn from the following social work major's journal (Mogard, 1997), which is quoted at length with the permission of the writer, of an attitude that is hard to dispel:

> "No man should lie down with another. . . ." I think that the Bible clearly states what the Lord thinks about homosexuality. It goes against His design for human sexuality.
>
> Although homosexuality is a sin, it is not an unforgivable sin. All sins are forgivable. Those who engage in these sorts of unacceptable lifestyles, just like alcoholics or materialists, should come before God in confession and repentance and ask for His forgiveness and His healing. God loves homosexuals just as much as he loves other sinners.
>
> We as Christians have to be tolerant of homosexuals and show them the love that Jesus showed us. We need to try to help them see the right way of life. There is no way that homosexuals will listen to our witness if we are mean and degrading to them. That has been a hard thing for me to come to terms with. I used to be a homophobic, but after learning that God loves all sinners just the same (I am a sinner), I realized I should have a loving attitude toward them. Also, my best friend has a roommate who is a bisexual. She is really nice. At first I was a little afraid, but now I can talk to her freely. She's a great person, but she just needs Jesus in her life.
>
> I just felt that I needed to comment on our class discussion. We didn't have time in class, and I wanted to state my opinion. (pp. 1–2)

Embedded in much of this rhetoric are several basic assumptions that are offensive to lesbians, gay males, bisexuals, and to those who love them. First is the notion of homosexuality as a conscious choice, a choice to indulge in bad behavior, to sin. The solution is repentance and a changed sex life.

Second, and equally objectionable, is the notion that a person's sexuality (the sinful part) is separable from the rest of his or her being. The love that the Christian deigns to grant, therefore, is only granted condescendingly. The fundamentalist's patronizing and condemning creed thus makes a mockery of the whole spirit of religion, which is centered on acceptance and love. Equally discredited in the sentiments of the social work student quoted earlier are the central tenets of social work practice, namely, nonpossessive warmth, empathy, not to mention appreciation of diversity. The student's words echo the kind of narrow theology that is gaining ground today, itself a reflection no doubt of economic and political forces in the wider American society. Additionally, the new visibility of gays and lesbians in the cultural and political arenas renders this group vulnerable to a conservative backlash. Many of our student viewpoints, therefore, cannot be understood apart from a recognition of the bombardment of antigay/lesbian prejudice pronounced from the pulpit in evangelical churches and broadcast on Christian radio and television stations all across the United States. The fundamentalist doctrine concerning sexual mores is strident and unequivocal. The variety of ministry known as "ex-gay ministry" and delivered by converts to heterosexuality is an all-too familiar sight on college campuses. Modeled after self-help groups, such religious ministries fight the "evil" of homoerotic behavior by exposing individuals to be "saved" to a tirade of verbal abuse. False claims are made of conversion to heterosexuality of persons who have sought forgiveness and surrendered to God (Mondimore, 1996). Change of sexual orientation is one that, as yet, cannot be delivered. Under the circumstances, the risk of suicide in the recipient of this (unwanted) attention is very real. For a moving and upbeat description of a spontaneous event that took place in an African American Southern Baptist church, see Box 1.2.

Vaid (1995) groups opponents of gay and lesbian rights into three categories: the concerned, the ignorant, and the hostile, or more glibly, the good, the bad, and the ugly. *Concerned* people are those who are uncomfortable with homosexuality but who mean well and can be reached by the gay and lesbian movement through subduing their fears with accurate information. *Ignorant* opponents, in contrast, are those who accept at face value the myths imparted by the religious right and other "authorities." These individuals seek guidance for how they should think from political and religious leaders. The best means of getting through to them is indirectly by enlisting the support of major religious and political leaders.

The third category of opponents Vaid labels the openly *hostile.* Little hope of persuasion exists here. To the extent that these individuals are religious, they preach a moralistic, exclusionary message that advocates a fusion of church and state. Gay and lesbian clergy and their followers can best challenge this doctrine in revealing themselves as morally upstanding persons. The foremost barrier to this happening, however, comes from the persistence of gay and lesbian invisibility, the secrecy of the closet.

Many crimes and injustices have been committed against sexual minorities in the name of religion: In her response to critics who cite biblical sources for their equation of homosexuality with sin, Vaid urges us not to condemn the condemners but, rather, to uphold and make known the morality, ethics, and spiritual values engendered in the gay and lesbian community. "The amazing truth," notes Vaid (p. 378), "is that, despite the hostility to traditional religion, the rejection by our families, the shame and stigma that we all must overcome to accept our true natures, gay and lesbian people are a profoundly moral people." Embodied in the "queer moral vision" of which Vaid speaks is a strong sense of justice, commitment to honesty (the coming-out process), commitment to community, and last but not least, an acquaintance with joy.

BOX 1.2

No More Music Today

For centuries, closeted gay and lesbian people have been *implicitly* protesting the false stereotypes about them, the blatant, even haughty, self-righteous discrimination and the hateful rhetoric. They have been implicitly protesting the isolation, the silence, the ignorance, and the indifference (the ultimate form of hatred).

Because gay and lesbian people have been taught the same misinformation about same-gender oriented people as everyone else has been taught, this implicit protest has traditionally been in the form of self-destructive behaviors. They have dropped out of school. They have abused alcohol and other drugs. They have engaged in promiscuous behaviors. They have committed suicide. And, worse, they have lived entire lifetimes of lies and deceit. Every such self-destructive act has been an *implicit* protest. It has hurt the individual gay and lesbian person, and it has hurt society as a whole. It has resulted in endless days of anguish and sleepless nights for themselves and those who love them. It has resulted in the loss of their energy, their creativity, their productivity, their self-confidence, their taxes, and their intellectual and artistic contribution to society.

And it is changing, thank God Almighty.

It is changing with men who are willing to join and participate in a gay men's breakfast club that meets in broad daylight once a month with prominent community opinion leaders, the largest breakfast club in the state of Iowa. It is changing with men and women who do nothing more daring than drive around with a rainbow or triangle bumper sticker on their cars. It is changing with some businesses and some governmental subdivisions adopting policies assuring nondiscrimination employment environments for all persons regardless of gender orientation. As self-respect grows, there is daily less self-destructive *implicit* protest.

Recently, a black Baptist preacher in the South was waxing eloquent in his condemnation of gay and lesbian children of God. He was really getting into it in the tradition and spirit of Pat Robertson, Jerry Falwell, and our local version of Professor Harold Hill, Bill Horn. Suddenly, in the middle of the sermon, the gay choirmaster stood up and raised his hands high in the air. Surprised, the preacher fell silent, and the choirmaster announced in a resonant voice, "There will be no more music today." He then walked out of the sanctuary and the entire choir and most of the congregation followed.

It happened. Things are changing, thank God Almighty. If every gay male church organist elected on the same Sunday not to "play," there would be very little music that day and a powerful point would be made.

Such explicit protest is healthy, productive, and utterly effective. It is a great improvement over *implicit,* self-destructive protest. It is where we are heading and it promises tremendous progress in the very near term for enlightenment, tolerance, personal empowerment, and equality.

Source: Jonathan C. Wilson, Des Moines, Iowa, *Des Moines Register,* Monday, November 3, 1997. Reprinted with permission of Jonathan Wilson, attorney.

Nature versus Nurture

Related to the notion of sin, although not unambiguously, is the issue of causation. The way in which one reconciles the nature/nurture controversy has a lot to say about the kind of judgment that is made of individuals whose practices are contrary to the norm. If sexual minorities are born, not made, or "made by God," even the most ardent fundamentalist is hard put to cast blame. Moreover, the hysteria over the possible spread of "diverse" sexuality falls to the wayside should a characteristic such as homosexuality be deemed innate.

An extensive study of about 1,000 lesbians and gay men whose characteristics were compared to 477 heterosexual women and men revealed that gender nonconformity in childhood was a significant forerunner of later homosexuality, especially in males (Bell, Weinberg, & Hammersmith, 1981). Gender nonconformity is measured in terms of boys who hate rough and tumble play and who like to play house or play with dolls and girls who exclusively play with trucks and GI Joe action figures rather than Barbie dolls. This research indicates that sexual orientation develops early in life and is not solely a matter of choice (Zastrow & Kirst-Ashman, 1997). The study also indicates that sexual orientation includes a whole range of behaviors only indirectly related to sexuality but stemming, at least in part, from a biological predisposition.

The biological school holds that there is something fundamental, unchanging, and biologically wired in lesbians, gay males, and straight people that causes their differences. The psychosocial or learning school, on the other hand, holds that variation in human sexuality is largely a product of cultural forces operating at crucial moments in one's life. Interactionist theory considers both nature and nurture as key ingredients in sexual orientation and thus combines the biological and psychosocial positions into a holistic approach.

Biological theories of homosexuality can be clustered under three kinds of research; these pertain to the brain, genes, and hormones, respectively. We will review studies under each category briefly.

Brain Research

The most frequently cited of the brain studies is LeVay's (1991) research on the brains of nineteen gay men who died of AIDS, sixteen heterosexual men, and six heterosexual women. Findings indicated that the anterior hypothalamus in gay men was approximately half the size of that in the other men.

A second study by Gorski and Allen (cited in the *Los Angeles Times,* 1992) examined brains obtained from autopsies from ninety homosexual and heterosexual men and heterosexual women. They found that an important structure connecting the right and left sides of the brain, known to be larger in women than in men, is larger still in gay men. Due to the obvious sample bias, as in the foregoing study, results are by no means generalizable to male homosexuals as a whole. Nevertheless, one could theorize from the findings that something unusual happens when the brain is being formed in the fetus, something with enduring consequences for one's later sexuality. Future research should help confirm or refute these preliminary results and help unravel mysteries pertaining to lesbians, a population largely ignored in empirical research. What we do know is that when asked, gay males tend to attribute their homosexuality more to biology and lesbians more to situational factors (Mondimore, 1996). Several of the genetic studies of sexual orientation in men examined by Mondimore do indicate that men tend to be more exclusively gay or straight whereas women are more fluid in their orientations.

Genes

The best means of getting at hereditary factors is to study differences between identical and fraternal twins. Identical, unlike fraternal, twins develop from a single fertilized egg, yet both types of twins when raised together inhabit similar environments. Comparisons of characteristics among the more genetically similar and less genetically similar sets of twins can provide evidence of a genetic link. Bailey and Pillard (1991) recruited by means of advertisements in gay publications gays or bisexuals who had twin siblings. Results showed that when one brother was gay, 52 percent of the time, the identical twin was gay also. This compared to 22 percent of the fraternal twins. In a later study involving sisters, the concordance rate was 48 percent in identical twins and 16 percent for non-identical twins (Bailey & Pillard, 1993). These results support the theory of a genetic link in homosexuality, but they also indicate that environmental factors play a role as well. Otherwise the concordance rate would be 100 percent for the identical twins. An alternative explanation would be to speculate that if one twin is gay or lesbian, the other twin may be overcoming natural tendencies to pass as straight.

Hormonal Factors

In humans, the study of rare medical conditions (e.g., pregnant women who were exposed to a synthetic hormone) indicates that prenatal hormonal events can influence human behaviors. Animal studies, likewise, reveal the potency of prenatal influences. Testosterone-treated female rats, for example, are shown to have better navigational ability than untreated rats (Mondimore, 1996).

In general, hormonal studies involving humans are extremely contradictory (Zastrow & Kirst-Ashman, 1997). The greatest likelihood is that such effects as there are occur prenatally rather than later in life. Hormonal therapies for medical conditions unrelated to sexuality have shown no effects on altering sexual orientation or behavior (Furr, 1997).

Many feminist lesbians are troubled by the implications of the biological explanation of homosexuality. Because women perhaps, as we will see, tend to be more flexible in their sexual orientation (some women prefer the term *preference*) than men, the notion of homosexuality as an inborn trait is less relevant to their personal experience. Jeffreys (1996) does not mince her words on this point:

> This regression to biologism has come from gay male researchers in particular. In the queer politics of the 1990s there is much evidence of a return to the values of the 1890s. . . . Biological arguments, arguments from nature, could be used to assert the rightness and inevitability of women's subordination, of racial inequality, of heterosexual hegemony and of drugs and institutions for those suffering from mental ill health. . . . My choice of lesbianism is a source of considerable pride and sense of achievement and not something I wish to relegate to biology. (pp. 90–91)

Duberman (1991), author of the autobiography *Cures: A Gay Man's Odyssey,* goes one step further. He refutes the missionary fervor with which Western science pursues the causes and cures of homosexuality. If the causes of shifting social *reactions* to supposed sexual deviations had been pursued with anything like the same fervor, he writes, we might have had some relief from punitive laws and misguided moralism.

Interaction Theory

A close reading of the biological reports gives credence to the nature *and* nurture argument. Whether or not it is politically acceptable to say so, it does appear that same-sex experiences during a crucial stage in one's life can alter a person's sexual identity. The process of being or becoming heterosexual is surely a combination of both innate predisposition and socialization history. For both social and physical scientists, the debate should no longer center on nature versus nurture, but on the contributions that each makes and how they interact.

The evidence on what kind of socialization patterns are correlated with homosexuality is lacking. As we will see in Chapter 11, the children reared by gay and/or lesbian parents tend overwhelmingly to be heterosexual. And as most commentators would argue, as a general rule, gays and lesbians are born, not made. There are exceptions, however—instances in which one's sexual identity is altered through cruel or unusual circumstance. One such scenario occurs in the rigid unisexual environment within prison walls.

Prison Socialization

The prison environment, enclosed and unisexual, is an ideal laboratory from which to contemplate developing sexual consciousness. The *postprison* experience is an even better indicator of the socialization component in homosexual identity. Once homosexually initiated men return to the world of men and women, to what extent do their learned behavior patterns remain with them? Does the process vary based on whether the inmate was the aggressor or victim, on the top or bottom, during sexual intercourse?

There are in a male prison the victims (or involuntary recruits) and the voluntary aggressors (Earley, 1992). The involuntary recruit is younger and smaller than those who are not targeted. The aggressors are older and tougher. Insertion is an act of absolute masculinity (Sagarin, 1976; van Wormer, 1997). The Sagarin postprison study on nine gay ex-convicts revealed a striking difference in sexual identity. Subjects studied were all jail turn-outs; that is, none came to prison with previous homosexual experience. Whereas the five aggressors all resumed a postprison heterosexual pattern (but a violent pattern toward women), none of those who had been forcibly "turned out" and used as punks resumed their previous heterosexual life (Sagarin, 1976).

Sagarin's study (1976) best describes the process involved in the making of a homosexual. Those who were assaulted were told by their rapists that no one could have forced them if they had not liked it and that they would come to beg for such sexual activity later. The predictions indeed became a self-fulfilling prophecy. The assaulted individuals began to play the roles they had been recruited and forced to play. They came to define themselves as others defined them (van Wormer, 1984).

Sagarin's data confirm not that all men who forcibly become homosexual in prison remain homosexual, but that some do so; therefore, homosexual identity *may* be acquired in certain instances. Heterosexuals may become homosexuals because they learn to like what they have experienced, even though initially the acts were painful to them. On the other hand, the aggressors—who saw themselves as "men's men," and who made "women" out of other men—did not alter their postprison behavior thereby. "Why would I want a fairy when I can get a broad?" remarked one such ex-con (Sagarin, 1976).

The process behind the making of a homosexual is thus an internalization of a role that was played for reasons having nothing to do with latent homosexuality but solely related to factors such as size, youth, and being streetwise.

In women's prisons, this kind of sexual coercion, apart from grade B Hollywood movies, is not the norm (Struckman-Johnson, Struckman-Johnson, Rucker, Bumby, & Donaldson,

1996). Women are concerned with emotional commitment, and when prison violence occurs, it is usually due to jealousy over a third party. Generally speaking, femmes are fighting over the scarce commodity—the masculine inmates or butches.

Although the majority of women who participate in prison homosexuality abandon their practices when they reenter society, many do not. Yet, once women have discovered each other—women who have often suffered tremendously at the hands of men, women who have gotten involved in crime through men, women who have been beaten by men and then deserted—often do not wish to return to men.

Classical studies on women in prisons, such as that of Ward and Kassebaum (1965), quote women who claim that sexual experiences between *women* were more satisfying than heterosexual experiences. Vedder and King (1967) refer to the "unwholesome environment" that is prison. If one tried to plan an institution perfectly designed to produce sexual delinquency, they write, the end result could well be the typical prison. Women in prison may have tried men, but they often find they like women better.

Former inmate Lee Massey Wright, herself strongly reproachful of the behavior of "queers," provides this account (Wright, 1980):

> Judy Jones was a white girl, sentenced from Montgomery County for embezzlement. When Judy came here she was very quiet; she had kind of a masculine appearance in the true sense of the word. She dressed neat and just looked like a kind of an athletic-type person. I asked her when I interviewed her when she came in if she had any homosexual tendencies at that time or maybe I skirted the question in explaining some of the problems that she might have. She was not a homosexual in any way and never had been.
>
> Tina Hall—Tina had kind of played games around the institution, but we had never decided if she was a homosexual or just playing games. But later Judy and Tina got together. Judy told me she had written her family that she had finally come to the conclusion that she was homosexual even though she had tried all those years to act if she were normal. And she had found her true love in life and that they were going to become man and wife at some time or other, in their carryings-on. (p. 1)

From the research and firsthand reports, we have seen that those who begin by *playing* parts sometimes come to *be* the parts they are playing. Over time, the self-concept adjusts to absorb the new behavior. Reports from co-correctional institutions (where both men and women are held) reveal that the homosexual pattern among women transferred from traditional prisons persists (Propper, 1997). Even when men are present, those women "turned on" to homosexuality continue in the pattern. One could speculate that homosexuality is more personally satisfying for these women, for whatever reason, than heterosexuality.

Beyond anecdotal reports, however, there is no empirical evidence of widespread socialization into homosexuality or heterosexuality, for that matter. What happens in prison, nevertheless, does reveal the potential of the human organism.

Other Psychosocial Theories

Storms (1981) has proposed a theory—the early sexual maturity hypothesis—that focuses more specifically on the interaction of biological predisposition and elements in the environment. His theory links early sexual maturation to homosexuality. Because early maturing adolescents are at an age of close same-sex bonding, sexual interest may become centered on members of the same sex. The theory is not without some plausibility, but as yet it is more at the level of speculation than of definitive proof.

Psychosocial theories concerning dysfunctional family constellations (such as a domineering mother and a weak, passive father) are based on studies that are seriously flawed (Furr, 1997). Similarly, claims that childhood trauma, such as rape or incest or seduction by a homosexual adult, is a causative factor in the development of same-sex attraction have not been substantiated (Rothblum, 1997).

The safest conclusion we can draw at this time is to say that a combination of biological predisposition and sex-related socialization experiences determines a person's sexual orientation and that in women, at least, the orientation can shift over time. As Vaid (1995) captures the diversity of the gay/lesbian scene:

> Some of us are probably born gay—have known it since we were children and are finally living the lives we imagined. Others of us may have chosen to be gay or lesbian or bisexual. Still others may have fallen in love with a man and later with a woman; what does that make us? (p. 288)

The situation, in short, is not nature *or* nurture but nature *and* nurture. The biopsychosocial formulation of social work provides a fit that is probably as good as any for explaining sexual orientation. Even as scientific research advances our knowledge, we will still be hard pressed to separate the roles of choice, happenstance, cultural conditioning, and nature in shaping our sexuality.

As with alcoholism, the evidence of a hereditary factor in homosexuality has enormous political implications. A generation ago, as an article in *U.S. News and World Report* points out, the gay/lesbian community was at war with organized psychiatry, arguing that sexual orientation was a lifestyle choice and ought to be deleted from the manual of disorders (Herbert, 1997). Recently, some activists are latching on to the "biology is destiny" position for the civil rights benefits that this position engenders in opposition to religious zealots who insist that homosexuality is a choice. And there is every indication that the members of the general public are more accepting of lesbians and gay men if they believe that such people are "born that way" rather than having chosen to lead such a lifestyle (Gelman, Foote, Barrett, & Talbot, 1992). Some gays and lesbians, meanwhile, fear the genetic argument may lead to a genetic solution—abortion of gay and lesbian fetuses—should such a determination ever be possible. Whatever the political implication of the biological findings may be—and the implications are vast—we do know studies will continue and that the nature/nurture controversy probably will never be resolved to everyone's satisfaction. In unraveling the mysteries of sexual attraction, gay, lesbian, and heterosexual research, like any social scientific endeavor, ultimately leads only toward the ineffable and inexplicable.

Definition of Terms

Power is more than an authoritative voice in decision making; its strongest form may well be the ability to define social reality through language. Words carry connotations that shape attitudes. Denial of the use of language as enforced silencing is another aspect of social control discussed in the following chapter.

The terms defined in this section are those not otherwise defined in later sections of the book. Terms pertaining to homophobia, for example, are defined in Chapter 2 whereas language relevant to sexuality appears in Chapter 5. A glossary of terminology defines these and other words commonly used within and outside of gay and lesbian circles.

For a historical understanding of the etymology of words that are connected to gay/lesbian culture, Grahn (1990) provides the most readable and intriguing source. From her book, *Another Mother Tongue: Gay Words, Gay Worlds,* accordingly, we learn that the term *gay* for years was an insider term with the advantage that when outsiders heard it they assumed another meaning entirely; that the color *lavender* had a multiple significance as the formed gay/lesbian color—a mixture of female pink and male blue and a symbol of dawn and dusk, life and death; that *dyke* for masculine lesbians comes from the goddess Dike of Greece who provided a balance of forces.

General Terminology

Sexual orientation refers to the inclination of an individual toward sexual or affectional partners of the same sex, opposite sex, or both sexes. The term *sexual orientation* is favored over *sexual preference* because the latter term denotes choice (Queralt, 1996). The assumption is made by the general public that one's sexual orientation is heterosexual if there are no indications otherwise. *Heterocentrism* is the term, parallel to ethnocentrism (as applied to ethnicity), to express this phenomenon of viewing the world through the eyes of the dominant group. Heterosexism is evidenced everywhere, in advertisements, counseling sessions, conversations, workshops, lectures, and ministers' sermons. The notion of *heterosexual privilege* refers to the rights and advantages that heterosexuals have and take for granted every day, the right to marry a single person of the opposite sex, for example, or the informal privilege of holding hands in public.

Homosexuality refers to sexual attraction between members of the same gender, often but not always accompanied by sexual behavior. As stated in the preface, the terms *gay* and *lesbian* are used in this book as parallel and equal terms to refer to male and female homosexuality, respectively. It is recognized, however, that gay is often used as a generic term as it has been historically. As an insider generic term, *queer* is being reclaimed—as in, for example, queer art, queer theory. The advantage of this term is it can encompass all sexual minorities. The disadvantage is obvious.

Activist organizations sometimes use the abbreviation *lgbt* to indicate inclusiveness of membership. Lgbt stands for lesbian, gay, bisexual, and transgender people. Of these terms, *bisexual* and *transgender* are the most problematic.

As alluded to in the previous section, *bisexuality* may be used in one of two senses. One is to indicate individuals who are neither strongly heterosexual nor strongly homosexual when their inclinations are measured on a scale such as the Kinsey scale. On the Kinsey scale, zero represents an absolute attraction to members of the opposite sex and six represents absolute same-sex attraction. Interestingly, several of the genetic studies indicate that in terms of behavior, fantasy, and self-identification, a large majority of men can be rated at either one end of the Kinsey scale or the other (Mondimore, 1996). Adolescent males, however, often pass through a transitional bisexual stage. In contrast to men, women of all ages tend to score in the middle or bisexual range on this scale. The term *bisexual* used in this way as in the sentence, "Most women are bisexual by nature," refers to a biological given and potentiality, but not to an identity.

As used politically, bisexuality refers to those individuals who can be attracted to either men or women or as they say, to a person, not a gender, but who, unlike the preceding group, identify themselves with the label, *bisexual* or *bi.* Their demand is to be included in civil rights organizations and in academic research on sexual orientation. This group has suffered discrimination by the general public who perceive them as promiscuous and within lesbian/feminist groups who regard women bisexuals as sometimes "sleeping with the enemy" and being wishy-washy in their affiliations. *Biphobia,* or fear and rejection of bisexuality, is discussed in Chapter 2.

Transgender is a term that has come to be used to encompass several different types of sexual identities and sets of behaviors that involve taking on the attributes of the opposite sex: individuals who believe they are of the opposite sex but are in the wrong body—*transsexuals*—and who may even consider surgery to make the anatomy fit the image, and individuals who dress in clothing of the opposite gender (cross-dressers) but who identify with their own gender—*transvestites* (Mondimore, 1996). Only recently has the transgender rights movement come into its own voice within the gay/lesbian organizations. An issue that we will be hearing more about in the future is the American Psychiatric Association's aforementioned categorization of gender identity disorder as a mental disorder (Gallagher, 1996).

One fact that emerges from this maze of definitions is the wide variety of sexuality represented. Consistent with Kinsey's findings (Kinsey, Pomeroy, & Martin, 1948), we can conceive of sexuality not as dichotomous but, as with other human attributes, in terms of a spectrum. The concept of the *sexual continuum* is useful in its recognition that we are not all alike and that the potential for diversity is very great. It is also useful in differentiating male homosexuality, which, as Mondimore suggests, is more centered on genital activity (at least initially), from the female variety, which is decidedly more complex, usually focused on the relational aspects of sex such as intimacy and emotional involvement. The old joke—"What does a lesbian bring to a second date? A U-Haul"—depicts the female proclivity for bonding.

Years ago, in her classic book, *The Second Sex* (1953/1971), de Beauvoir underscored the distinction of lesbian love:

> For all these reasons it is erroneous to distinguish sharply between the homosexual and the heterosexual woman. Once past the uncertain period of adolescence, the normal male no longer permits himself homosexual amusements; but the normal woman often returns to the amours—platonic or not—which have enchanted her youth. Disappointed in man, she may seek in woman a lover to replace the male who has betrayed her. (p. 393)

Another interpretation of a married woman's attraction for other women is provided by Adrienne Rich who, in her widely cited essay on compulsory heterosexuality, boldly states that far from being a mere refuge from male abuse, lesbianism represents an electric and empowering charge between women that is its own reward. Here the institution of enforced heterosexuality is problematic, keeping many women from their natural best.

There is a wide range of behavior; in short, much same-sex activity, especially among youth, but the significance, as always, comes not from the act itself—most people at one time or another "mess around," as Vidal (1996) declared—but from the meaning attached to the act or acts. Coming to terms with one's sexuality is a way of answering the most basic of questions: Who am I? Only when this is addressed is one ready to pursue or follow through with a relationship of intimacy. Because of the importance in our society attached to one's sexuality and the pervasive tendency to want to categorize people, the possibly false dichotomy of homosexuality versus heterosexuality is reified in the mind's eye. The individual often wrestles with his or her sexual identity, the resolution of which may pit the person against society, against family, against peers. In the absence of role models, one would expect that bisexuals would have the most difficulty in this regard. Referring to our tendency toward a binary, either/or way of thinking, Vidal (1996) writes with a characteristic bluntness:

> Good team: hetero. Bad team: homo. Straight versus gay. Either one or the other; no Mr. In-Between. This division has led to endless trouble for many men and women while giving vast joy to the rulers of those lands that accept these unnatural categories—for they can proscribe the bad team, thus maintaining control over much of the population. (pp. ix–x)

For all orientations, in short, the sexual continuum paradigm is infinitely more helpful as a frame of reference than the simplistic gay/straight dichotomies. The concept that one's position on the continuum changes over time provides a flexibility that accurately mirrors the reality of one's biopsychosocial being.

The Strengths Perspective

Things defined as real are real in their consequences.

—W. I. Thomas and D. Thomas, 1928

A presumption of health over pathology, a focus on self-actualization and personal growth, and a recognition that the personal is political, and the political, personal: These are among the key tenets of the strengths approach. Pertaining to groups and communities as well as individuals, the strengths perspective can help reveal the light in the darkness and provide hope in the most seemingly dismal of circumstances. As articulated by Bricker-Jenkins (1991), the social work goal is to promote self-actualization, to help people who ask for help find their strengths, frame their choices, take steps to empower themselves, and support others to do the same. Given the societal barriers that obstruct one's vision and keep women and other oppressed groups from achieving their potential, all practice is necessarily political. In work with lesbian, gay, and bisexual clients, for example, attention would be focused not merely on the dynamics of heterosexism in particular but on the dynamics of oppression and scapegoatism generally.

Filtering out the major themes from the strengths perspective relevant to gay/lesbian sensitive practice, the following guidelines emerge:

> *Seek the positive* in terms of people's coping skills and you will find it; look beyond presenting symptoms and setbacks, and encourage clients to identify their talents, dreams, insights, and courage.

Listen to the personal narrative, the telling of one's own story in one's own voice, a story that ultimately may be reframed in light of new awareness of unrealized personal strength.

Validate the pain where pain exists; reinforce persistent efforts to alleviate the pain (of themselves and others) and help people recover from the specific injuries of oppression, neglect, and domination.

Don't dictate: collaborate through an agreed upon, mutual discovery of solutions among helpers, families, and support networks. Validation and collaboration are integral steps in a consciousness-raising process that can lead to healing and empowerment (Bricker-Jenkins, 1991).

Move from self-actualization to transformation of oppressive structure, from individual strength to a higher connectedness.

At both the macro and micro levels, the focus on strengths leads us toward the pluses, away from the minuses of the problem-solving approach. The pitfalls of the strengths approach, however, are several, mainly related to the imperfect fit between the vocabulary of personal helping and the bureaucratic mandates. In conformity with the standardized reimbursement schemes and in the tradition of the medical model, the diagnosis shapes the treatment, as does the need for task-oriented paperwork. With assessment tools, paperwork, and reliance on the *DSM IV*'s classification scheme for diagnosis of pathology, the strengths perspective is rendered a strange anomaly. Such a concentration on client deficits as prescribed by the system often impairs the practitioner's best intentions of promoting client growth and awareness of inner strengths and resources. The relationship between client and worker, similarly, is impaired when pathology-based assessment becomes pathology-based treatment, when instead of partnership and client self-determination, emphasis is on the profession-as-expert. Often a tug of war with the reluctant recipient of the attention ensues. The pitfall for the client strengths proponent comes in relationship to colleagues utilizing the normative approach. "You are letting the clients manipulate you" or "you will learn . . ." are warnings to the worker who strives to be positive in a decidedly negative work milieu. Such accusations will continue to plague us—we who embrace the language of strength—until the walls of the deficits approach come tumbling down.

The counseling chapters to follow (Chapters 8 and 11) will apply the principles underlying the strengths perspective to lesbians, gays, and bisexuals who request counseling for a variety of reasons often related to the difficulties of functioning in a heterosexist society, difficulties related to school, work, family, parenting, and partner relationships. How helpful it is to be provided with hope and a sense of perspective in the midst of so much negativism!

Whereas mainstream Anglo American culture views gay men as less than men and lesbians as lacking the desirable female traits, the positive approach (such as that once held by many Native American tribes) perceives gays and lesbians as having more to offer, not less, as uniquely able to identify with both genders and to "straddle the fence" between groups often considered to be polar opposites. As an outgrowth of this difference, and pride in this difference, has arisen an astonishing cultural contribution. In the world of art, film, theater, music, and literature, the contribution has sometimes been (as in Michelangelo's art or Tennessee Williams's plays) to humanity as a whole, and sometimes to an autonomous realm. The gay and lesbian subculture, at least the flamboyant part, is most evident to outsiders through the annual "gay pride" parades and rallies across the country each June. Quieter forms of gay and lesbian culture are found in churches and synagogues, sports leagues, musical bands, writers' groups, recovery support groups, cruise lines, and professional associations (Vaid, 1995). The richness of gay/lesbian cultural expression, in short, represents strength at the community level—strength in a consciousness of kind, resilience against the forces of persecution, pride in a lively and vital cultural history. In a social climate fighting to maintain the illusion of universal heterosexuality, access to what Grahn (1990) calls "the world of the Gay underground" (p. 18) and to the body of knowledge contained therein may be elusive, especially to closeted youth. The informed professional, however, can lead the way to discovery of the rich cultural heritage of the past as well as to the vibrant activity of the present.

Within the clinical context, through the medium of a caring relationship, the practitioner seeks to boost the lesbian, gay, or bisexual client through the aforementioned five steps to strengths-based practice: Seek the positive; hear the narrative; feel the pain; don't dictate, collaborate; and pave the way for further growth through helping others. What lesbians and all sexual minorities have to overcome, along with their practitioners as well, is the long conspiracy of silence that has served to keep generations of people from sharing their truths about their lives and their loves. "What has not been told, even in the clinical research and practice literature, which has itself undergone profound changes in focus in just a few years, is a story of strength and resilience, a story of private satisfaction and public success" (Laird, 1994, p. 197).

Social Work's Mission

The history of social work largely overlaps with the history and public works of "women-identified women" who around the turn of the century lived in lifelong, intimate companionship with each other (Faderman, 1991; Laird, 1994). Although their family arrangements closely parallel those of lesbians today, these so-called "Boston marriages" were not defined in terms of sexuality, and there was no stigma attached to them. This was before women who partnered other women were defined as a threat to the male establishment and to what was later characterized as the norm of compulsory heterosexuality. In any case, those founding mothers in social work were the leaders of social reform movements of their day; in every area of social life—health, child welfare, women's suffrage, immigration, labor rights—these women were at the forefront of political change. Social work as a profession claims its beginnings in the proud and controversial work of these formidable advocates for social justice. Today, as the impetus toward mass reform has been superseded by a focus on individual therapy, the profession sometimes needs a reminder of its roots (see Sprecht & Courtney, 1994). But we must never lose sight of the fact, as Laird cautions, that our individual stories take shape in a powerful sociopolitical context. And as we adopt a strengths perspective, emphasizing the myriad ways gays and lesbians have managed to survive with grace, humor, and good will, we should never lose sight of the harsh reality of living under the shadow of constant moralistic assault and taunting aimed at diverse sexuality. Writing of African American survival strategies in *Killing Rage,* bell hooks's words apply equally well to the gay and lesbian experience (1995):

> Only as African Americans break with the culture of shame that has demanded that we be silent about our pain will we be able to engage holistic strategies for healing that will break this cycle.
>
> Without surrendering the meaningful legacy of triumph over adversity that has been such a dynamic aspect of black experience in the United States, we must always make a place for the acknowledgement of unresolved, recurring psychological pain. (p. 144)

Where is social work in addressing this pain? Where is social work in remedying it? The profession's historic mission, way before it was a profession, has been to work on behalf of the despised, the downtrodden. Until recently, the training of social work, like that of other mental health professions, included virtually no consideration of the knowledge and skills needed to work with gays and lesbians. To the extent that the needs of this highly invisible population were recognized at all, the focus was on causation and pathology. The change effort was directed toward "the sexual deviant"; various forms of cures were tried. In recent years, as we have seen, social work has moved with psychiatry away from a view of homosexuality as an illness to be cured to a view of homosexuality as a viable alternative orientation. In large measure, due to contemporary gay/lesbian militance and the vital participation of feminists as researchers and therapists, the focus has shifted to appreciation of the uniqueness and inclusiveness of all minority groups. Consistent with its longstanding civil rights activism, the National Association of Social Workers (NASW) and its sister organization, the Council on Social Work Education (CSWE), through their committees on lesbian and gay issues, provide a forum to ensure that gay/lesbian concerns are addressed by social work practitioners and educators. CSWE's recommendation (passed in 1977 following years of heated discussion) that content on diverse sexuality be included in the social work curriculum has now (as of 1994) been strengthened to a requirement. Whether or not to grant an exemption to conservative religious colleges, however, is a controversy that has been fraught with divisiveness and irresolution (van Soest, 1996). Jones (1996) correctly takes the profession to task for the compromised ethical standards and inherent contradiction in its willingness to accredit social work programs within a host setting in which homosexuality is declared a sin. The validity of these arguments is evident in a perusal of NASW's (1994) own policy statement on lesbian and gay issues, which articulates the ethical position of the profession as follows:

> The National Association of Social Workers (NASW) recognizes that homosexuality and homosexual cultures have existed throughout history. Homosexuals have been subject to long-standing social condemnation and discrimination. It is the position of NASW that same-gender sexual orientation should be afforded the same respect and rights as opposite-gender orientations. NASW asserts that discrimination and prejudice directed against any group are damaging to the social, emotional, and economic well-being of the affected group and of society as a whole. NASW affirms its commitment to work toward full social and legal recognition of lesbians and gay people. To this end, NASW shall support legislation, regulation, policies, judicial review, political action, changes in social work policy statements, the *Code of Ethics,* and any other means necessary to establish and protect the equal rights of all people without regard to sexual orientation. Specific activities include, but are not limited to, working for the adoption of policies and legislation to end all forms of discrimination based on homophobia at the federal, state, and local levels, in all social institutions, and in both the public

> and private sectors. NASW will work toward the elimination of prejudice, both inside and outside the profession. (p. 163)

No institution, as Jones argues, has an automatic right to an accredited social work program. If programs of social work are housed in religious colleges that discriminate against openly gay, lesbian, and bisexual students and faculty, then CSWE is legitimizing the enforced invisibility of this population. This silencing, as Jones further suggests, is the most devastating societal weapon in the oppression of homosexuals. Discrimination against any other minority group, including African Americans and women, would never be tolerated.

Despite this divisive issue that pits religious freedom against social work ethics, the American social work accreditation standards lead the world in terms of mandating that gay/lesbian content be included in the curriculum. In compliance with this requirement, the major textbooks for the core courses—for example, in social services, practice, and human behavior—typically include chapters on sexual orientation. No other discipline has a comparable requirement.

In the United Kingdom, social work accrediting authorities require competencies in antidiscriminatory practice but rarely is antiheterosexist content included in this agenda (Trotter & Gilchrist, 1996). In Canada, there is a complete absence of accreditation requirements to address sexual orientation in policies and programs, and curriculum schools of social work typically avoided gay/lesbian issues altogether (O'Neill, 1994). In June, 1998, new standards for social work education were introduced by CASSW (Canadian Association of Schools of Social Work) to address multiple bases of oppression including sexual orientation. In the end, however, according to personal correspondence from CASSW representatives, the General Assembly backed off from any specific reference to sexual orientation.

Conclusion

Adherence to our social work mission and values demands that the profession and those who represent it take a strong and proactive position on the individual, organizational, and educational levels on gay/lesbian issues (Hartman, 1993). In compliance with the strengths perspective, the goal we, in the helping professions, are working toward is not mere acceptance or toleration but *appreciation* of the strengths of this largely invisible minority, strengths that, at least to some extent, come from living both within society and apart from it. Like members of other groups rendered invisible in a patriarchal and highly puritanical society, gay men and lesbians have unique histories (both individually and as a whole), creative family forms, gender role flexibility, and vast social networks. And the gay/lesbian contribution to underground culture as well as mainstream arts—art, music, dance, and literature—has been incalculable. To social work practitioners the challenge is to discover and reinforce the special insights and resiliencies that have developed out of the uniqueness of lesbian and gay experience.

Social workers can build on these strengths even as they help individuals surmount their difficulties, not the least of which is minority group membership in a group the very existence of which has to be explained. Simply put: First you have to explain the nature of homosexuality, then your own experience of it, then why you are telling all these things in the first place.

A second major difficulty unique to this population pertains to their dual citizenship, first, in mainstream society in which the norm of silence prevails and, second, in the home community in which the pressure to be open, to come out of the closet, may be relentless. This need to conform almost simultaneously to two conflicting sets of values is familiar to people of color in Anglo American culture and to feminist women living in a male-dominant world. The challenge that Goffman (1959) once described so graphically is in keeping the two worlds, the audiences, separate; otherwise a disturbing role conflict ensues. In this complex situation, as Bricker-Jenkins (1991) reminds us, the therapeutic task is to depathologize, to establish that the client and his or her community have competence, "and to reinforce the client's need, ability, and right to 'name the world' for herself" (p. 293).

Within the strengths approach, the goal is through mutual exploration of ideas and possibilities to help clients move from doubtfully or shamefully homosexual to affirmatively gay and lesbian. This approach builds intervention on what clients are already doing that works. The collaborative principle, "together we can," replaces the hierarchical struggle characteristic of traditional models of treatment. This principle likewise logically opens the door for advocacy for social and civil rights and work with individuals and groups toward social and political transformation of all people. Lorde (1984) gloried in this unity of difference:

> Those of us who stand outside the circle of this society's definition of acceptable women; those of us who have been forged in the crucibles of differences—those of us who are poor, who are lesbians, who are Black, who are older—know that *survival is not an academic skill.* It is learning how to stand alone, unpopular and sometimes, reviled and how to make common cause with others identified as outside the structure in order to define and seek a world in which we can all flourish. It is learning how to take our differences and make them strengths. *For the master's tools will never dismantle the master's home.* (p. 112)

Starting with contemporary mass media images and moving to a look at the professional literature, this opening chapter has provided a brief overview of many of the issues pertinent to lesbians, gays, and bisexuals. We have seen how the high visibility in the one area—the popular realm—is countered by an alternating neglect and pathology-based treatment in the other—psychology. In modern times, homosexuality has been regarded as a deviation from normal, a malady to be explained and, if possible, overcome. Accordingly, themes were filtered out from the literature, themes that have shaped the treatment models for viewing homosexuality. More or less approaching chronological order, these models are sin, crime, sickness, normal variation, and back to sin. Treatment seems to have come full circle. Is homosexuality biological or is it learned behavior? The nature versus nurture controversy, discussed in some depth in this chapter, seems to have come full circle as well. Recent empirical research, as formerly, focuses on biological causation. The historic journey has thus been from sin to sin (again) and from the old nature versus nurture dispute to a new one. The treatment formation that is the most consistent with this book is the "homosexuality as natural variation" approach and, regarding etiology, homosexuality is viewed interactively in terms of a biopsychosocial framework.

Before highlighting the strengths perspective, we took a brief excursion into a discussion of basic terminology of gay/lesbian studies to consider such diverse concepts as transgender, heterosexism, and the sexual continuum. This excursion was not a mere side trip, however. For only through knowing the language can we gain entrance to the client's moral and social universe. We have seen how various terms for aspects of sexual diversity, such as *homosexual, gay, lesbian, transgender person,* do not denote immutable characteristics of individuals but rather that they are emergent and shifting social categories, categories that can and do become the objects of intense political struggle. The positive terms of today may be a reclaiming of the negative terms of yesterday and vice versa. For example, consider the words *queer* and *dyke.* Familiarity with the nuances of word usage of the day brings a kind of rapport vital for therapeutic communication.

The significance of attention to gay/lesbian terminology parallels the potency of the language of strengths used here and throughout this book. Inasmuch as our use of language both reflects and shapes how we view the world, the worker's role in the helping process will be affected accordingly. If we think in terms, for instance, of the jargon of pathology that sometimes passes for professionalism, we are distancing ourselves from those who look to us for hope and vision.

A major purpose, then, of this opening chapter has been to introduce the health or strengths perspective as an approach that is absolutely essential in working with lesbians, gays, and bisexuals and their families. Central to this approach is the belief, as quoted in the strengths perspective section, that things defined as real are real in their consequences. The labels society bestows on sexual minorities—for example, with reference to gays, lesbians, or transsexuals—are overwhelmingly and unequivocally negative. Heterosexism and homophobia are so widespread in the dominant culture, in fact, and so pervasive across most ethnic and religious minority groups that the negativism is internalized by members of the divided and maligned group. This internalization is exacerbated in all probability by the secrecy and duplicity entailed for most gays and lesbians in living a closeted life. There is no power in invisibility and, accordingly, mainstream society demands that it be so. Even the profession of social work for all its liberalism and historic stand for truth and justice has, at times, colluded in the conspiracy of silence. "Shut up and we'll hardly know you're there": This seems to have been the message until recently.

A strong argument for a strengths focus has been presented, in short, in an attempt to bridge the gap between social work theory stressing listening to clients and "meeting them where they are" and agency-regulated practice, which requires extensive problem-oriented documentation. Many concerned social workers, of course, are cognizant of this incongruity between teaching and practice and go out of their way to rectify the situation. If they have been trained in a pathology perspective, however, they may define homosexuality (not heterosexism or erotophobia) as the problem and provide a treatment that does more harm than good. Although individual workers in the mental health field may fail their lesbian and gay clients, the social work profession continues through policy to recognize that heterosexism is embedded in our society and that unless we identify its roots, and work to eliminate them, we are part of the problem. The challenge is to bring social workers to conscious awareness of sexual diversity, which in its hiddenness and the mainstream social workers' discomfort with it, may be entirely overlooked. The challenge is to recognize the strength in difference, sexual and otherwise. Again we can learn from Lorde (1984) of this challenge:

> In our world, divide and conquer must become define and empower. . . . Racism and homophobia are real conditions in our lives in this place and time. *I urge each one of us here to reach down into that deep place of knowledge inside herself and touch that terror and*

loathing of any difference that lives there. See whose face it wears. Then the personal as the political can begin to illuminate all our choices. (pp. 112–113)

The "real conditions of our lives in this place and time" of which Lorde speaks are the subject of Chapter 2. Hate crimes, denial of custody to lesbian and gay parents, the enforced secrecy policy of the military, and the ranting and raving of the religious right are just a few of the many examples of heterosexism discussed in the pages to follow. Without careful attention to the sociopolitical context from which gay and lesbian kinship and culture have emerged, an observer could easily overlook the essence of gay/lesbian experience and the need for both individual and collective coming out of isolation, but above all else, the need for acceptance.

REFERENCES

American Psychiatric Association. (1994). *Diagnostic and statistical manual of mental disorders* (4th ed.). Washington, DC: Author.

Aronson, J. (1995). Lesbians in social work education: Processes and puzzles in claiming visibility. *Journal of Progressive Human Services 6* (1), 5–26.

Bailey, J. M., & Pillard, R. (1991). A genetic study of male sexual orientation. *Archives of General Psychiatry 48,* 1089–1096.

Bailey, J. M., Pillard, R. C., Neale, M. C., & Agyei, Y. (1993). Hereditable factors influence sexual orientation in women. *Archives of General Psychiatry 50,* 217–223.

Bash, A. (1997, April 25). Lesbian lead doesn't faze most. *USA Today,* p. 3D.

Bell, A., Weinberg, S., & Hammersmith, S. K. (1981). *Sexual preference.* Bloomington: Indiana University Press.

Berkman, C., & Zinberg, G. (1997). Homophobia and heterosexism in social workers. *Social Work 42* (4), 319–332.

Bricker-Jenkins, M. (1991). The propositions and assumptions of feminist social work practice. In M. Bricker-Jenkins, N. Hooyman, & N. Gottlieb (Eds.), *Feminist social work practice in clinical settings* (pp. 271–303). Newbury Park, CA: Sage.

Cloud, J. (1998, July 20). Trans across America. *Time,* 48–49.

Conrad, P., & Schneider, J. (1992). *Deviance and medicalization: From badness to sickness.* Philadelphia: Temple University Press.

Cramer, E., Oles, T., & Black, B. (1997). Reducing social work students' homophobia: An evaluation of teaching strategies. *Aretê 21* (2), 36–49.

de Beauvoir, S. (1953/1971). *The second sex.* New York: Bantam Books.

Duberman, M. (1991). *Cures: A gay man's odyssey.* New York: Dutton.

Earley, P. (1992). *The hot house: Life inside Leavenworth Prison.* New York: Bantam Books.

Faderman, L. (1991). *Odd girls and twilight lovers: A history of lesbian life in twentieth century America.* New York: Columbia University Press.

Footnotes. (1998, April 3). *Chronicle of Higher Education,* p. A12.

Furr, L. A. (1997). *Exploring human behavior and the social environment.* Boston: Allyn and Bacon.

Gallagher, J. (1996, December 10). The transgender. *The Advocate,* pp. 49–51.

Gelman, D., Foote, A., Barrett, T., & Talbot, M. (1992, February 24). Born or bred? *Newsweek,* pp. 46–53.

Gibb, F. (1998, July 31). Sex change pair lose battle for recognition. *The Times,* 10.

Goffman, E. (1959). *The presentation of self in everyday life.* Woodstock, NY: Overlook Press.

Grahn, J. (1990). *Another mother tongue: Gay words, gay worlds.* Boston: Beacon Press.

Hartman, A. (1993). Out of the closet: Resolution and backlash. *Social Work 38* (3), 245–246.

Herbert, W. (1997, April 21). Politics of biology. *U.S. News and World Report,* pp. 72–80.

hooks, bell (1995). *Killing rage: Ending racism.* New York: Henry Holt.

Jeffreys, S. (1996). The essential lesbian. In L. Harne & E. Miller (Eds.), *All the rage: Reasserting radical lesbian feminism* (pp. 90–113). New York: Teachers College Press.

Jones, L. (1996). Should CSWE allow social work programs in religious institutions an exemption from the accreditation nondiscrimination standard related to sexual orientation? No. *Journal of Social Work Education 32* (3), 304–310.

Katz, J. (1996). *The Invention of Heterosexuality.* New York: Penguin.

Kinsey, A. C., Pomeroy, W. B., & Martin, C. E. (1948). *Sexual behavior in the human male.* Philadelphia: W. B. Saunders.

Kinsey, A. C., Pomeroy, W. B., Martin, C. E., & Gebhard, P. H. (1953). *Sexual behavior in the human female.* Philadelphia: W. B. Saunders.

Kushner, T. (1995). *Thinking about longstanding problems of virtue and happiness:* Essays, a play, two poems, and a prayer. New York: Theatre Communications Group.

Laird, J. (1994). Changing women's narratives: Taking back the discourse. In L. Davis (Ed.), *Building on women's strengths: A social work agenda for the twenty-first century* (pp. 179–210). New York: Haworth.

LeVay, S. (1991). A difference in hypothalamic structure between heterosexual and homosexual men. *Science 253,* 1034–1037.

Lorde, A. (1984). *Sister outsider: Essays and speeches.* Trumansburg, NY: Crossing Press.

Los Angeles Times (1992, August 2). More differences found between brains of gay, heterosexual men. *Waterloo–Cedar Falls Courier,* p. A4.

Mills, R. P. (1997). Amendment B approved; Opponents pledge defiance. *The Presbyterian Layman 30* (3), 1, 8.

Mogard, J. (1997, Spring). Personal reaction. Unpublished student reaction paper submitted to instructor, University of Northern Iowa.

Mondimore, F. (1996). *A natural history of homosexuality.* Baltimore: Johns Hopkins University Press.

National Association of Social Workers. (1992). Position statement: "Reparative" or "conversion" therapies for lesbians and gay men. Washington, DC: Author.

National Association of Social Workers. (1994). Lesbian and gay issues. *Social work speaks* (3rd ed., pp. 162–165). Silver Spring, MD: Author.

National Opinion Research Center. (1994). *General social survey.* Chicago: University of Chicago/Author.

O'Neill, B. J. (1994, May). Canadian social work education from the standpoint of gay men. Unpublished dissertation, Wilfrid Laurier University, Waterloo, Ontario.

O'Neill, B. J., & Naidoo, J. (1990). Social services to lesbians and gay men in Ontario: Unrecognized needs. *The Social Worker 58* (3), 101–104.

Propper, A. (1997). Lesbianism in female and coed correctional institutions. *Journal of Lesbian Studies 1* (1), 97–107. A reprint of an article from 1978.

Queralt, M. (1996). *The social environment and human behavior: A diversity perspective.* Boston: Allyn and Bacon.

Rich, A. (1980). Compulsory heterosexuality and lesbian existence. *Signs: Journal of Women and Society 5* (41), 631–660.

Rothblum, E. (1997). Introduction: What are "classics" in lesbian studies? *Journal of Lesbian Studies 1* (1), 1–7.

Sagarin, E. (1976). Prison homosexuality and its effect on post-prison sexual behavior. *Psychiatry 39,* 245–257.

Shapiro, J. (1993, July 5). Straight talk about gays. *U.S. News and World Report,* pp. 42–48.

Shepherd, L. (1993). *Lifting the veil: The feminine face of science.* Boston: Shambhala.

Sprecht, H., & Courtney, M. (1994). *Unfaithful angels: How social work has abandoned its mission.* New York: The Free Press.

Storms, M. D. (1981). A theory of erotic orientation development. *Psychological Review 88,* 340–353.

Struckman-Johnson, C., Struckman-Johnson, D., Rucker, L., Bumby, K., & Donaldson, S. (1996). Sexual coercion reported by men and women in prison. *Journal of Sex Research 33* (1), 67–76.

Thomas, W. I., & Thomas, D. (1928). *The child in America.* New York: Alfred A. Knopf, p. 572.

Trotter, J., & Gilchrist, J. (1996). Assessing Dip SW students: Anti-discriminatory practice in relation to lesbian and gay issues. *Social Work Education 15* (1), 75–82.

Vaid, U. (1995). *Virtual equality: The mainstreaming of gay and lesbian liberation.* New York: Anchor Books.

van Soest, D. (1996). The influence of competing ideologies about homosexuality on nondiscrimination policy: Implications for social work education. *Journal of Social Work Education 32* (1), 53–64.

van Wormer, K. (1984). Becoming homosexual in prison: A socialization process. *Criminal Justice Review 9* (1), 22–27.

van Wormer, K. (1997). *Social welfare: A world view.* Chicago: Nelson-Hall.

Vedder, C., & King, P. (1967). Problems of homosexuality in corrections. Springfield, IL: Charles C. Thomas.

Vidal, G. (1996). Foreword. In J. Katz, *The Invention of Heterosexuality* (pp. vii–xi). New York: Penguin.

Ward, D., & Kassebaum, G. (1965). *Women's prison: Sex and social structure.* Chicago: Aldine.

The Washington Post. (1997, March 30). Portrait of a cult leader. *Waterloo–Cedar Falls Courier,* pp. A1, A9.

The Washington Post. (1997, October 1). Bishops urge acceptance of gay children. *Waterloo-Cedar Falls Courier,* p. A7.

Witt, L., Thomas, S., & Marcus, E. (1997). Where do they get the numbers? In L. Witt, S. Thomas, & E. Marcus (Eds.), *Out in all directions: The almanac of gay and lesbian America* (pp. 363–366). New York: Warner Books.

Wright, L. M. (1980). *Mating stories.* Unpublished manuscript, Julia Tutweiler Prison for Women, Wetumpka, Alabama.

Zastrow, C., & Kirst-Ashman, K. (1997). *Understanding human behavior and the social environment.* Chicago: Nelson-Hall.

CHAPTER

2 The Heterosexist Society

When I was in the military, they gave me a medal for killing two men, and a discharge for loving one.

—Leonard Matlovich, inscription on gravestone, 1988

The degree of hatred and hostility generated toward gay males, lesbians, and nonnormative sex role behavior is daunting. Until fairly recently, the basis for heterosexuals' hostility toward those perceived as sexually deviant was little noted or studied; homosexuality was the condition to be studied and explained. But once homosexuality was depathologized, at least in medical (psychiatric) circles, attention began to shift from the victimized to the victimizers. In 1972, a term for the irrational fear of homosexuals—*homophobia*—was introduced. More recently, the term *heterosexism* was added to the vocabulary to refer more specifically to the overt and covert mistreatment of lesbians and gay males. Little empirical research has been done on these phenomena, however, beyond simple correlational studies. And there is still so much left to learn concerning the dynamics of antigay/lesbian hostility.

Utilizing a social psychological perspective, this chapter views attitudes—such as hostility toward an out-group—as strategies for meeting psychological and social needs. Such an analysis can provide meaning to otherwise incomprehensible behavior. We are speaking here, remember, not of homosexuality but of the intense emotional response sometimes generated by homosexuality. What we might call the heterosexual problem is, in essence, a problem with *differentness,* a problem that is institutionalized throughout society and that has political as well as cultural and psychological overtones. Oppression and the climate of oppression hurt everyone but especially those defined as sick, queer, or just plain inferior. Society's animosity is expressed variously as rejection, job loss, imprisonment, forced treatment, and horrific hate crimes.

This chapter views the persecution of sexual minorities both historically and in a global context. After defining and differentiating the terms *heterosexism* and *homophobia,* we trace the roots of antigay and antilesbian prejudice in the United States and consider biological, psychological, and cultural explanations for these attitudes. Then we turn our attention to hate crimes perpetuated against gays and lesbians across the world. The relationship among sexism, racism, anti-Semitism, and homophobia will be explored. Because gays and lesbians from fundamentalist religious backgrounds are especially prone to internalized self-hatred sometimes culminating in suicide, a special section on religious doctrine, especially

Judeo-Christian ideology, is included. Two other areas on which we focus our attention are the military and prison establishments. Finally, because social workers are likely to encounter in the course of their practice both the victims of homophobia and their perpetrators, implications for social workers are considered.

Definition of Terms

A perusal of the literature indicates considerable disagreement over use of the term *homophobia.* The conventional definition and the one used here is that homophobia is the irrational fear of homosexuals or of homosexuality (Barker, 1995). To this we would add the fear of sexuality in same-sex friendships. The reluctance of American men to express their affection for each other or to share living arrangements can be construed as instances of homophobia. Fear of what others would think or say, of others' homophobic reactions, in other words, has a strong inhibiting effect on close relationships. Introduced by Weinberg (1972), the term *homophobia* encompasses a spectrum of behaviors ranging from mild derision to lethal assault and battery. Fear of same-sex closeness is seen to be at the heart of such negativism. Pellegrini (1992), however, is critical of use of the term. The latter half of the word—*phobia*—he observes, implies a problem in the psyche of the individual while overlooking the institutional aspect of compulsory heterosexuality.

Writing in the *Encyclopedia of Homosexuality,* the author of the entry *homophobia* objects to the notion that prejudice against homosexuality is an irrational fear altogether. "Care should be taken," Herek (1990) suggests, "to identify homophobia as a prejudice comparable to racism and anti-Semitism, rather than an irrational fear similar to claustrophobia or agoraphobia" (p. 552). In the popular press, similarly, the notion of homophobia is often equated with antigay prejudice. An article in *Newsweek* (Leland, 1994), for instance, makes the following statement, "We've all known homophobes. They're the ones who hurl epithets or worse at gays, who discriminate in housing or employment" (p. 42). Earlier, Herek (1984) argued that we should move beyond a unidimensional construct and distinguish various varieties of homophobia such as those arising from inner conflicts or as a result of cultural conditioning.

One response to the need for more scope is to conceive of homophobia in terms of its original, almost literal meaning and to employ another word entirely, *heterosexism,* to highlight the *social* context of antigay prejudice, to depict a worldview in which the reference point is distinctly heterosexual. *Heterosexism* was advanced as a term by Morin (1977) to refer to beliefs and attitudes that favor opposite-sex over same-sex partnerships.

Accordingly, in this book we will distinguish homophobia from heterosexism, *homophobia* to refer to individuals and reference groups within the society who feel personally threatened by diverse sex role behavior or sexuality, and *heterosexism* to indicate the broader societal response. *Heterosexism* in the dictionary sense is prejudiced attitudes or discrimination practices against homosexuals by heterosexuals (*Random House Dictionary,* 1993). This word refers to negative treatment of the gay, lesbian, and bisexual minority. Compared to homophobia, however, this term is more inclusive and concerns itself with external behavior rather than motivation.

Institutional heterosexism is a term we will use to indicate the often unintentional obliviousness to the needs and concerns and even the very existence of nonheterosexual members of the society. Typical examples of institutional heterosexism are the use of school forms for children to fill out that assume the presence in the home of one mother and one father; insurance policies with no coverage for same-sex partners; health care providers who, striving to be sexually neutral, presuppose that sexual means heterosexual; inclusion in the fourth edition of the *Diagnosis and Statistical Manual for Mental Disorders* (*DSM IV*) (APA, 1995) of the category "gender identity disorder" for girls who resist wearing dresses and boys who "avoid rough-and-tumble play" (p. 537); and the omission of sexual orientation as a category in national probability health samples. The consequences of such multilevel oversight is to make the provisions of services useless to all but the most conventional of participants.

Use of the concept of *institutional heterosexism* offers an important conceptual framework for our understanding of gay/lesbian oppression. The usage shifts attention away from the human psyche, a clinical conceptualization, onto the social realm in which it belongs. It shifts responsibility for the hostility away from the recipients of mistreatment onto the collective violators. It prepares us to grasp the link among sexism, racism, and heterosexism in the cultural enforcement of gender roles and power relations. Oppression, after all, is all about power, about, as Pellegrini (1992) suggests, "the power to enforce a particular worldview; the power to deny equal access to housing, employment opportunities, and health care; the power alternately to define and to efface difference; the power to maim, physically, mentally, and emotionally" (p. 54).

The phrase *internalized homophobia* refers to the phenomenon of gays and lesbians absorbing the fears and prejudices of the society and turning these fears and prejudices within. Weinberg's (1972) classic definition of homophobia is broad enough to include this internalized dimension also: "Homophobia is the revulsion toward homosexuals and often the desire to inflict punishment as retribution . . . and in the case of homosexuals themselves, self loathing" (p. 133).

Related to the process of internalizing homophobia is *externalizing* homophobia. This eventuality occurs when in anticipation of negative reactions in people, one almost provokes such reactions. In the autobiographical novel, *Iowa* (Moore), for instance, the hero lashes out at a friendly elderly neighbor as follows: "I'm the fairy with AIDS that lives up the street. Actually, I don't have AIDS yet, but I probably will because I liked getting . . ." (p. 213). Vulgarities complete the sentence. The narrator is attacking before he can be attacked. We can conceive of this behavior pattern as *reverse heterosexism* or more simply *homosexism.* It involves a hostility born out of hurt and pain that has culminated in bitterness.

Cultural Context

Oppression and persecution have marked the history of gays and lesbians since at least the beginning of modern times. Chapter 3 explores the historical dimensions of homosexuality in some depth; for the present discussion, a brief overview will suffice.

Homosexuality is a universal occurrence characteristic of all cultures and social groups. The conflict generated by homosexuality, however, is culturally variable. In many times and places there has been no conflict at all; elsewhere the issue has been surrounded with ambivalence and turmoil. Homosexuality has been variously honored (among certain Native American tribes), tolerated (in Scandinavia), prescribed (in ancient Greece among male scholars), and proscribed (throughout the modern Anglo-Saxon world).

Research in both men's studies and gay and lesbian history indicate that homophobia is not biologically determined but prompted by learned cultural behavior (Lichtenberg, 1995; Rotundo, 1993). Many societies and periods in history have been condoning and accepting of homosexual activities. Gramick (1983) characterized attitudes in the Far East as historically benevolent. In Japan, for instance, during the feudal period, male homosexual love was considered more "manly" than heterosexual love. In premodern China where male brothels were common, boys were trained for prostitution by their parents. More rigid attitudes, however, were held by the Hindus of India. The same was true of the ancient Greeks and Romans. Some Native American tribes had special, culturally prescribed roles for effeminate gay men and masculine-acting women. This custom, which so astonished European explorers and delighted anthropologists, was known as the *berdache.* Today, in acknowledgment of the existence of people whose spirit is neither entirely male nor entirely female, the term *two spirit* is preferred by many Native Americans and Canadians (Tafoya & Wirth, 1996).

Any attempt at a worldwide perspective has to take into account vast differences in European American and Eastern approaches to sexual orientation. Whereas the contemporary European American model dichotomizes people as straight and gay, in countries such as Egypt, China, Korea, Japan, and Thailand, men can have sex with other men as a sexual outlet devoid of connotations of identity or lifestyle. The Latino tradition (including Filipino societies) in addition to the European pattern, assigns male homosexual identity only to the person assuming the receptive-passive sexual role. The "masculine" men are not belittled in any way within their own society (Longres, 1996). Lesbianism, seemingly, is unrecognized. In his survey of homosexuality around the world, Miller (1992) makes the interesting observation that countries that were once colonized by Britain had a heightened awareness of homosexuality; antisodomy laws are still on the books in many of the former colonies today. However, the role of the West has done a turnabout: Europe and North America are now the world's leading exporters of the ideas of gay and women's liberation. Countries cut off from this influence—for example, China, Cuba, and Iran—regard homosexuality with great hostility.

Taking a historical perspective, sociologists perceive a relationship between catastrophic events in history and persecution of members of the out-groups. In the aftermath of the horrendous loss of life wrought by the Black Death or great plague of 1348, a frantic populace scapegoated Jews, Moslems, women, and homosexuals with a vengeance. Similarly, lynching of blacks by frenzied mobs in the South and Midwest occurred during periods of economic depression. And interestingly, following the cruel defeat of World War I and financial hardship in the decades that followed, Germany sought out Jews, disabled persons, and homosexuals among others to persecute and even eliminate.

Like other forms of mass hatred, homophobia distracts individual citizens from focusing on economic and political problems in society. This inaccuracy is classic during tough economic times when people tend to latch onto the rhetoric of hate (often masked as serving some greater good such as saving America, saving the family, or saving marriage). Displaced aggression against gays and lesbians can be perceived as the ultimate distraction by a people who are economically and socially insecure.

Homophobia and Heterosexism

Gays, lesbians, bisexuals, and transgendered persons increasingly are making their presence known in every area of social life. Yet concurrent with the prominent spot that gay rights has won on the national agenda, gays and lesbians are finding that increased visibility is a double-edged sword (Leland, 1994). Bolstered by mass media attention, a salient backlash has ensued directed at the society's most basic social institutions: the church, the school, the military, the family. A culture that in its religious and ethnic heritage exclusively promotes heterosexuality is also inclined to reject, debase, and punish same-sex attractions. Western society, accordingly, controls sexuality by imposing harsh sanctions on those who are not discreet in their allegiances or inclinations. The "don't ask, don't tell" decree for military enlistees is symbolic of the national will to subdue nonmainstream behavior into silence.

Roots of Homophobia and Heterosexism

Social work theory explains human behavior in terms of a biopsychosocial framework. Let us apply this theory to the behavior in question—homophobia—and see if we can come to a better understanding thereby.

Biological Aspects

The fact that homophobia is seemingly unknown in some societies precludes arguments of biological determinism. Sexuality, nevertheless, is a biological drive, and the variety of sexual experience is vast if not infinite. As the Kinsey report (Kinsey, Pomeroy, & Martin, 1948) made known to the world, few people are totally heterosexual or homosexual; most of us have some sexual attraction to both men and women. Compulsory heterosexuality, however, restricts the choices. Along these lines, Kasl (1989) argues, "I suspect if it weren't for homophobia, most people would experience significant attractions to both sexes" (p. 209). And sex role researcher Daryl Bem (cited by Shea, 1996) concurs. If the culture became less strict about gender roles, he speculates, we would see a greater mix of sexuality. Evidence for this statement is put forth by Wells (1991) who discovered in an extensive survey of his students' sexual behavior an extreme avoidance by homosexuals of practices deemed gender inappropriate and/or homosexual. A wide range of sexual behavior, in fact, is characteristic throughout the animal kingdom. Many domestic and wild animals engage in sexual activity with both sexes; a small number have eyes only for their own sex (Adler, 1997). Although farmers investing in livestock may be upset at the homosexual liaisons, the animals do not seem disturbed by it: Homophobia, in other words, is distinctly human.

So what does all this have to do with homophobia? Let us try to bring this discussion one step closer by reviewing the findings of a rare experimental study conducted at the University of Georgia (Adams, Wright, & Lohr, 1996). The purpose of the study was to investigate the relationship between homophobia and latent homosexuality, to test the Freudian hypothesis that anxiety about the possibility of having homosexual tendencies may lead to an extreme overreaction and generalized hostility. Would homophobic men show more sexual arousal to homosexual cues than nonhomophobic men?

In the laboratory study, a preselected sample of straight males was divided into two groups. The first group was homophobic—defined as having an irrational fear and hatred of homosexuals and a dread of being close to them—and the other group was not. When scientists exposed both groups to heterosexual, gay, and lesbian erotic videos, over half the homophobic men elicited arousal (measured in changes in penile circumference) to videos showing gay male sex, whereas less than a quarter of the nonhomophobic group were similarly aroused. Although this experiment is limited to men and to a small sample at that, it is the first presentation of scientific evidence on the nature of homophobia. The findings of a close correlation between physiological response to homoerotic stimuli and prejudice against homosexuals is consistent with the psychoanalytical concept of reaction formation. The implications for mental health professionals in these findings are that male clients projecting anger and hostility onto gender nonconforming males and gay men would do well to sort out their own insecurities instead.

Despite the compelling evidence of psychological hang-ups, we would want to be cautious about relegating homophobia to a medical condition. This actually did happen in New Zealand while the country was embroiled in a homosexual law reform bill campaign. Homophobes were labeled as sick and diseased, and such groups as the Mental Health Foundation called for treatment for what was perceived as a morbid fear of homosexuals. Ironically, such a focus made the oppression of lesbians and gay men a personal issue while the political aspects fell to the background (Atmore, 1995). Accordingly, the reform victory that took place was less complete than it might have been otherwise.

Psychological Dimensions

Closely linked to biological urges and attractions is the psychological aspect of homophobia. Psychology is concerned with inner drives, the inner self, and how these drives manifest themselves in behavior. A psychodynamic force commonly described in the literature, and, in fact, one of the defense mechanisms originally delineated by Freud is *projection.*

Playwright Robert Anderson (1953) poignantly dramatized this paradox in his play *Tea and Sympathy.* Bill, a "man's man" and the high school coach, is inordinately concerned with the "fairy like" qualities of one of his charges. In the following climactic scene a cruel irony is revealed to the audience:

> Bill: You were more interested in mothering that fairy up there than in being my wife.
>
> Laura: But you wouldn't let me Bill. You wouldn't let me.
>
> Bill (Grabbing her by the shoulders): What do you mean I wouldn't let you?
>
> Laura (Quietly, almost afraid to say it): Did it ever occur to you that you persecute in Tom, that boy up there, you persecute in him the thing you fear in yourself? (p. 175)

In responding to presumed gay men and lesbians in this way, the homophobic individual is acting on inner conflicts over unwanted drives (Herek, 1984). These conflicts pertain to one's gender identity, sexual object choice, and/or femininity/masculinity issues. For example, unconscious conflicts about one's own sexuality or gender identity might be attributed to lesbians and gay men through a process of projection, the process of despising in others what we reject in ourselves. Contact with homosexuals threatens to make conscious those thoughts that have been repressed, thereby arousing a high degree of distress and even revulsion.

That this revulsion is far more a male than a female characteristic is borne out in the literature. There is virtually no equivocation on this point. The Western notion of masculinity that puts a premium on strength and manhood relegates the gay male to a vulnerable position in most social circles. Because insecure forms of masculinity are predicated on differentiating "real" men from women and from gay men, homophobia is a major problem among men who are unsure of their manhood (Lichtenberg, 1995). Male youths may resort to violence against gays for reasons more apparent to others than to themselves. Women, on the other hand, rarely feel compelled to beat up lesbians to prove their femininity. Characteristically, adolescent females are inclined to approach gender nonconformity in their own sex through a combination of taunting, gossip, and backstabbing.

Social Attributes

Lesbians, gays, and bisexuals who can "pass" as heterosexual seem to experience less verbal harassment and acts of discrimination and violence than those who are more visible. It is not surprising that the socialization process of gay youth involves learning to hide and that the hiding takes a serious psychological toll (Dempsey, 1994). Men and women of color experience widespread homophobia within their ethnic communities at the same time that they confront racism and ethnic prejudice in the wider society. African Americans may play dual roles, compartmentalizing their homosexuality to reduce the possibility of ostracism in the black community (Icard, 1996). Studies comparing Latinos with other ethnic groups on tolerance of homosexuality show contradictory findings (Zamora-Hernandez & Patterson, 1996). Generally less tolerant in terms of civil rights issues, Hispanics tend to be strikingly less moralistic and dogmatic concerning sexuality than European or African Americans.

The social dynamics or functions of homophobia (in a heterosexist society) are presented at length elsewhere (van Wormer, 1997). Listed among the functions are the enforcement of cultural norms for marriage and reproduction; gender role conformity, and the provision of convenient targets for scapegoating activities. Homophobia and its social counterpart heterosexism, as we have seen, serve to divert attention by individuals and the masses from the real problems of society. Just as psychologically, individuals project their personal problems onto other people, sociologically, groups and political factions can displace aggression onto those (in this case, outsiders) who are perceived as a threat to "family values." Heterosexism's pervasiveness in North American society affects us all in our everyday interactions and relationships.

Girls and boys are very directly socialized in our society to be heterosexual. Typically children are kidded by adults about "liking" boys and girls of the opposite sex. Girls are brought up on fairy tales of marriage and "living happily ever after." Boys who act like girls are called sissies and firmly derided. Tomboyishness in girls is more tolerated but only up to a point. Parents begin to squirm when same-sex friendships grow too intense or too exclusive in their eyes.

The pervasive homophobia in our culture is also demonstrated by the total exclusion of sexual minorities from mainstream history books, psychology books, or storybooks (Kasl, 1989). When a school system does attempt to introduce diversity, such as when New York City schools ordered the book *Heather Has Two Mommies* (Newman, 1989) to be used throughout the early grades, a deafening outcry by right-wing elements forced a cancellation of the project.

In a classroom assignment on homophobia, a female social work student gave the following autobiographical response (most males said they weren't affected in any way by homophobia!):

> Over the years my good friend Tom (who was on the feminine side) was the butt of many jokes and harsh pranks. During high school he suffered through verbal harassment, having his clothes soaked with water while he was attending gym class, and being socially outcast throughout our school years. At the end of our senior year he told me he was homosexual, and I told him that he was still the same person I've always known and it didn't change our friendship. I was also stigmatized by my friends' sexual orientation. During school there was very little said or done against me personally. But after graduation, and once my family realized Tom was gay, I was teased by my family and accused of being gay also. Guys who were interested in dating me were angry by my choice of friends and harassed me constantly.

This brings us a closer look at the family's role in perpetuating homophobia.

All in the Family

In the U.S. Department of Health and Human Services Report of the Secretary's Task Force on Youth Suicide (1989), it was estimated that gay and lesbian youth are several times more likely to attempt suicide than their heterosexual peers. A more recent Canadian study of male youth revealed that gay and bisexual males are nearly *fourteen* times more at risk for suicide attempts than are heterosexual males (reported by King, 1996). A new technique of having respondents answer questions via a computer lends to these data a special credence. Remafedi, Farrow, and Deisher (1991) in their study of young male suicidality found that severe family problems along with the possession of feminine gender role characteristics were significantly related to suicide attempts. Family rejection and substance abuse problems among gay youth are known to be interrelated as well (Uribe & Harbeck, 1992).

A recent analysis of the earlier suicide study clarified some points concerning gender differences (*The Advocate,* 1997). Of the 36,000 respondents, 131 teenage boys and 144 girls identified themselves as gay, lesbian, or bisexual. Twenty-eight percent of the gay boys compared to 4.2 percent of the heterosexual boys reported that they had attempted suicide. Twenty percent of the teenage lesbians compared to 14 percent of heterosexual girls reported attempted suicide. Gender nonconformity is much more an issue for males than for females, explained the author, Gary Remafedi.

The most persecuted group in the United States has to be transgenders. (The term *transgenders* refers to persons who identify with the gender of the opposite sex.) Men who dress as women are at high risk (except during Mardi Gras) of getting beaten or fired. A 1997 survey of transgenders found that 60 percent had been assaulted at one time or another (Cloud, 1998). Only Minnesota has a law protecting transgenders from job and housing discrimination, although cities all over the United States have passed similar legislation. A political movement which does extensive lobbying on behalf of transgendered persons is rapidly gaining ground. A major focus is to get greater protection from hate crimes and job discrimination.

Unlike racial and ethnic minorities, members of sexual minority groups are subject to hostility rather than support in their uniqueness. Because parents are apt to make disparaging remarks about "fags" and "queers" and to go out of their way to encourage heterosexual interest, especially if there is none shown, gay and lesbian youth become bereft of the emotional support they so badly need to withstand the daily cruelties of their peers.

In the novel, *Rat Bohemia,* Schulman (1995) traces the very devastating ways that gay people are abandoned by their families and how they form their own new families in order to fill the void. The following passage is from the point of view of David, embittered from the experience of losing a lover to AIDS:

> The boundaries of parental love are so narrow. My parents have always hated me for being gay. They've always wished I would disappear, but nothing has ever made me so nauseous and vicious as the gulf that AIDS has created between me and them. . . . This is how America treats us. . . . Now they're glad we're dying. They're uncomfortable about how they feel but really they're relieved. There's nothing on earth that could kill us more efficiently than parental indifference. (p. 89)

A study of adult gay men indicated that half of them lost friends and encountered negative responses from their parents when they disclosed their sexual orientation (Remafedi, 1987). A major gender difference revealed in a high school study by Uribe and Harbeck (1992) was that the parents of lesbians but not gay males invariably regard their daughters' homosexuality as merely a phase. For adolescents eviction from the home is not uncommon; many homeless youths are boys and girls who have ended up on the streets following arguments over their sexual orientation, dress style, and the kids they are hanging out with. Many other adolescents, however, have found that their fear of disclosure was worse than the actual reactions of family and friends (Dempsey, 1994).

A surprising number of parents become social activists on behalf of their gay and lesbian children. Chapter 11 describes the workings of PFLAG (Parents, Families, and Friends of Lesbians and Gays). There are many moving stories in the literature of once stunned, angry, and guilt-ridden parents who become strong advocates for their children through membership in the self-help group PFLAG.

Biphobia

Bisexuality makes people uncomfortable. To a social order based on monogamy and organized around dichotomous concepts such as black/white, male/female, and gay/straight, bisexuality looms as a potent threat. Once chic during the sexual revolution of the seventies, a bisexual identity became tainted in the next decade pushed by fears of AIDS and by gay identity politics. Although many bisexuals (*bis*) are monogamous for all or parts of their lives, images of promiscuity and instability prevail. Within the gay/lesbian community, bisexuality is variously construed as "sitting on the fence," "sleeping with the enemy," and betrayal of one's true identity.

The definition of *biphobia* used in this book is irrational fear of bisexuals or resistance to bisexuality. Because heterosexuals are more afraid of their latent homosexuality than of their bisexuality, this term most often refers to an antipathy toward bisexuality by lesbians and gay males. In an essay on biphobia—the counterpart to homophobia for bis—Ochs (1996) observes that bisexual women who also identify as lesbian face a greater degree of community hostility than bisexual men who also identify as gay. A lesbian who has an affair with a man is apt to be accused of betrayal and of turning one's back on one's own. When nationally prominent lesbian leader JoAnn Loulan recently found herself falling in love with a man, her followers were clearly outraged. An article in *The Advocate* entitled "Dating a Man" (Cotter, 1997) reveals the widespread disillusionment within the radical lesbian community with Loulan's personal life.

Gay male bisexuals have their own unique problems. In regard to their image as spreaders of disease transmitted to women, male bisexuals carry a special stigma. The popular tendency to see male bisexuality as the gateway through which HIV can spread from the gay to the heterosexual population does little to enhance the image of bisexuals in society. This "double discrimination" by heterosexuals and the gay and lesbian communities is seldom recognized as a force of external oppression, and yet the oppression is real and has many damaging effects, as Ochs informs us. Visible bisexuals, like visible lesbians and gay men, may be targeted for societal discrimination. Thus bisexuals are subject not only to heterosexism from the dominant society but to biphobia within the gay/lesbian social milieu as well. Additionally, the lack of social support for bisexually identified persons leaves these individuals relatively defenseless against the forces of compulsory heterosexism.

Hate Crimes Worldwide

Around the world, attacks today on homosexuals are rampant:

- A gay, Turkish seventeen-year-old, beaten and raped by the police in Istanbul, flees to the United States.
- Gay Cubans are pushed out of their country in boatloads.
- A lesbian in Costa Rica is raped by police "to show her what it is like to be a woman."
- In places as far distant as Romania and Chile, gay males are still stashed away in labor camps and prisons.
- In Colombia, hundreds of killings occur of "social undesirables," including homosexuals.
- Sodomy is punished in Iran by execution.
- In Oklahoma a gay law student detained in jail on a driving-while-intoxicated charge is repeatedly raped by inmates.
- In India a new 1995 law makes homosexual sex punishable by ten years' imprisonment.
- In Virginia a lesbian mother loses custody of her child due to her "immoral conduct" and the grandmother is awarded custody.
- An openly gay University of Wyoming student is beaten, burned, tied to a wooden ranch fence, and left for dead; he dies five days later.

A study of 151 hate crime slayings of homosexuals in the United States concluded that 60 percent involved extraordinary and gruesome violence, according to the New York City Gay and Lesbian Anti-Violence Project. Whereas guns are used in the large majority of murders in the United States, in these slayings, knives, baseball bats, clubs, and hammers were the weapons of choice (Associated Press, 1994). Why does this hostility directed against gays and lesbians seem especially pronounced at the present time?

While lesbians and gays press for equity, the resistance, anger, and hatred remind us of the depth, intensity, and ubiquity of homophobia (Hartman, 1993). For every social revolution there is backlash. Society's hostility toward gay men and lesbians is expressed today in rampant victimization. The book *Violence against Lesbians and Gay Men* (Comstock, 1991) gives statistical information on victims and their perpetrators. Physical assaults against this minority group have become quite common; this would seem to reflect a backlash accompanying publicity over gay rights. A college freshman class surveyed by Comstock reported that 16 percent of the males attacked gays. In this same sample, 30 percent of the physical violence was committed by family members—most often by fathers and stepfathers. Ninety-four percent of the perpetrators of attacks on both males and females are male. Females attack lesbians but not gay men. Eighty-five percent of lesbians who were attacked were attacked by men; sometimes the attack included rape. Black gay youth report a higher incidence of gay-related assaults than do European American and Latino gay youth; as with the others a large percentage of the violence occurs in the home (Hunter, 1990).

The increase in hate crimes against lesbians and gays, in short, reflects their increased visibility in society and the social encouragement given by the apathy of police and the courts. The upsurge in religious fundamentalism, which teaches that the so-called gay lifestyle is inherently sinful, also inspires gay bashing. The existence of antisodomy laws on the books in about half the states prevents many crime victims of "queer" bashing from even reporting the crime to the police.

From a sociological standpoint, acts of terrorism serve a normative goal by inculcating fear of violence in all persons who are members of that same category (Gibbs, 1989). In their thought-provoking analysis of hate crimes, Jenness and Broad (1997) draw a parallel between rape and antigay/lesbian assaults inasmuch as the common purpose of both forms of violence is to terrorize people who otherwise might get "out of line." Thus, violence and its corollary, fear, function to maintain the balance of patriarchal power and reinforce norms of compulsory heterosexuality.

In United States courtrooms, people accused of violent crimes often justify their actions as a reaction to sexual advances made by a gay victim, a strategy called the homosexual-panic defense. However, experts have begun raising doubts about the effectiveness of this strategy following a series of convictions (Boulard, 1995). The *Jenny Jones Show* murder case is an example. A male guest on the talk show was surprised in an encounter with a male neighbor who was secretly in love with him. Although laughing with embarrassment during the taping of the show, the surprised guest later shot and killed his admirer. His lawyers blamed the talk show for setting up a potentially volatile situation. The defense assumed that a homophobic reaction could be anticipated by the circumstances. The defendant was found guilty, nevertheless, but received a diminished sentence. Although the shooting as well as its defense underscores the virtual acceptance of antigay violence, the publicity focused almost exclusively on talk show insensitivities in exposing a heterosexual to an admirer of the same sex (*The New Republic,* 1995).

Let us turn now to the one place where lesbian and gay students have the most freedom to organize politically and come out—the college campus. Even here, harassing phone calls and physical assaults against lesbian and gay activists are reportedly gaining in intensity (Cage, 1993). At the same time, administrators at many institutions are making strides in improving the services available to gays and lesbians, and are passing antidiscrimination laws and supporting gay/lesbian studies course offerings. The much-publicized savagery against Matthew Shepard in 1998, moreover, has prompted a fierce new debate about hate and intolerance.

At a few major universities, ROTC programs have been banned due to the conflict between the military's sanctioned exclusionary practices and university human rights policies. Shilts's *Conduct Unbecoming: Gays and Lesbians in the U.S. Military* (1993) chronicles the formal and informal harassment in an organization in which 18,000 gays have been driven out over the past decade. The victimization has resulted in casualties by violence and suicide. Other countries such as Canada, the Netherlands, and Norway, in contrast, welcome gays and lesbians into the military. As Rotundo (1993) correctly states, the U.S. military's problem is *homophobia*—fear of what a tough group of heterosexuals will do to gays and how they will react to confirmation of their presence. Keep them closeted, goes the rationale, and there will be less trouble all around.

A positive legal step by the United States regarding hate crimes is the granting of political asylum to the victims of extreme antigay violence in other lands. "Quietly, U.S. Gives Asylum to Some Gays and Lesbians" declares a recent headline (Associated Press, 1996). Among case histories presented in the article:

- A gay Mexican man who was harassed and robbed by police, then raped and brutalized by soldiers.
- A gay Brazilian man who was repeatedly raped at gunpoint by police. On one occasion, he was taken to jail, where the commanding officer encouraged criminals to gang-rape and brutalize him. After fleeing to the United States, he discovered he was infected with HIV, the virus that causes AIDS.
- A feminist and lesbian activist who won asylum after arguing she could face the death penalty for homosexuality in her native Iran.
- A Russian lesbian who was arrested, expelled from school and fired from jobs, then threatened with psychiatric institutionalization to "cure" her.

Until 1990 when Congress removed sexual deviation from the list of reasons for barring someone from the United States, the Immigration and Naturalization Service kept many deserving potential immigrants out. Now an unexpected twist of fate has foreigners clamoring for political asylum on the very grounds for which they were excluded previously.

Similarly, when the Supreme Court of Canada in 1993 declared gender, ethnic background, and sexual orientation as innate or unchangeable characteristics, persecution on this basis can be claimed for political refugee status. Many of the claimants are persons with AIDS denied medical care and persecuted in their home countries. Because Europe does not accept these refugees, they come to Canada and the United States. Recent cases concern abuse in Poland, Russia, Costa Rica, and Chile.

Sexism and Homophobia

Two excerpts from the edited volume *Tomboys!* (Yamaguchi & Barber, 1995) reify the link between sexism and antilesbian activity:

> Recalling a time when she was beaten up (as a grade-schooler) by a high school boy for playing with the boys, she writes: "As I look back, this episode makes all the more chilling sense when I remember that we called that little game smear the queer. Ignorant as I was at the time of what that word really implied, I nonetheless paid the price for being queer myself. Not that I wanted to put my hands down other little girls' pants: the notion hadn't occurred to me. No, it was other parts of the male domain I had trespassed on. Sex wasn't the point: bending gender roles was." (Mullins, p. 42)

> "Are you a boy or a girl?" a friend of Alice demanded when she joined us in the backyard to play. I remember what I was wearing: jeans, cowboy boots, a red plaid flannel shirt. My short blonde hair was cut in a bowl. I wanted to sock her, because I knew the clock was ticking. We had to go to school the next year and girls wore dresses in school. (Neimann, p. 63)

In the 1950s, when Freudianism was the dominant social theory, strong women were said to be "castrating." A whole generation was effectively suppressed by the threat contained in one appellation. Today, homophobia has become the contemporary weapon for social control of women, as Pharr (1993) succinctly informs us. The feared label of many feminists is lesbian. Women who, in their attire or manner, do not conform to the cultural role expectations may be perceived as a threat to male control and dominance. Charges of lesbianism can be used to control strong and outspoken women by putting them down in a homophobic society and thus depriving them of jobs, children, and community support. Women in the military who rebuff a man's advances, for instance, risk being labeled lesbians and subject to investigation (Manning, 1995). Significantly, women today account for a disproportionate number of persons discharged for homosexuality, a number that under the military's "don't ask, don't tell" policy has risen by a striking 42 percent for both men and women since 1994 (*The Advocate Report,* 1997). Homophobia, the linchpin of patriarchy, is integral to the system of male supremacy, declare Rhue and Rhue (1997).

Within the close confines of black society, as Lorde (1984) tells us, the punishment for any female self-assertion is still to be accused of being a lesbian and, therefore, unworthy of support from the scarce black male. Compulsory heterosexuality forces women to bond with men and to distrust other women as rivals. In this lean and mean era, the politics of fear thrives on scapegoating and dividing people who might make demands. The effect on the women's movement—as women are divided from women by the male power structure—has been devastating. In Iowa, as a case in point, in 1992 the passage of the Equal Rights Amendment was halted as the right-wing elements argued that the proposed legislation would allow for same-sex marriage. The end result was that homophobia carried the day in the unexpectedly negative state referendum that followed. If a woman fears being called a dyke for being a strong person unreserved in her feelings for women and a man fears being called a faggot for being tender and sensitive, everyone loses (Kasl, 1989).

Within the movement (for gay rights) also, sexism at times rears its ugly head. Writing in *The Last Generation,* Moraga (1993) ponders discrimination within gay ranks:

> Coming to terms with [my lesbianism] meant the radical re-structuring of everything I thought I held sacred. It meant acting on my woman-centered desire and against anything that stood in its way, including my Church, my family, and my "country." It meant acting in spite of the fact that I had learned from my Mexican culture and the dominant culture that my womanhood was, if not despised, certainly deficient and hardly worth the loving of another woman in bed. But act I did, because not acting would have meant my death by despair. (p. 146)

In a society where women have relative equality and economic independence, lesbianism can blossom. Miller (1992) in his study of homosexuality around the world, concludes that for women, economic independence is the sine qua non of being able to live as a lesbian. Even where male homosexuality is tolerated, women are often constrained by traditional mores and equally by lack of the financial means to live away from one's family. There are many parts of the world, therefore, where overt lesbianism is unknown, where women dare not declare their love.

Racism and Anti-Semitism

Individuals who are in multiple marginalized categories—for example, race, ethnicity, and sexual orientation—suffer the highest levels of oppression. This pressure is maximized by internal divisiveness. For lesbians of color, for example, to fight for women's or gay rights may be seen as an attack on black or Latino males. Members of double minority groups may feel they have to choose among fighting heterosexism, sexism, or racism, sometimes failing to realize that all oppression is vested in the power structure. In this country, the dominant group consistently has been that of white male heterosexuals. Finding acceptance and support then can be especially difficult for lesbians and gay men of color who confront not only prejudice against homosexuality within their ethnic communities but also racism in the predominantly European American gay community.

A national survey of 391 black heterosexual adults indicated that negative attitudes toward homosexuality are as widespread (but not more so) among African Americans as among European Americans (Herek & Captianio, 1995). Gender differences in black heterosexual attitudes appeared to result primarily from men's as opposed to women's greater tendency to regard male homosexuality as unnatural. Respondents in this survey who believed that homosexuality is beyond an individual's control expressed significantly more favorable attitudes toward gay men and lesbians than did those who regarded homosexuality as a choice. Knowing gays and lesbians personally and lack of religious commitment were also associated with favorable attitudes.

Many African Americans of both genders, however, are very resentful when analogies are drawn between racial and sexual minority status. In a column in *USA Today,* Richardson (1997) articulates this position:

> One wonders how DeGeneres (actress who plays Ellen on the weekly sitcom show) and others could have the audacity to compare their situation to that of American blacks. Homosexuals have never been enslaved or denied the right to vote. Blacks have had to literally die for every small advancement made over 350 years; not so with homosexuals. (p. 13A)

In a similar vein, Orthodox Jewish rabbis filed a lawsuit in New York opposing a Holocaust museum because it included a group whose persecution was on the basis of "bad bedroom behaviors" along with persons persecuted because of their religion (Sidel, NPR News, 1997).

In *Zami,* Lorde (1982) refers to her dual existence: "Downtown in the gay bars I was a closet student and an invisible Black. Uptown at Hunter I was a closet dyke and a general intruder" (p. 179).

Rodriguez (1996) describes the case of the Filipino American gay male who within his own community has to deal with Filipino Americans' attitudes toward homosexuality, who are probably less tolerant, as acculturated Americans would have been in the Philippines. Within the U.S. gay community, he has to deal with attitudes of mainstream gays toward minority gays. In short, he has to deal with the anxieties of being a minority within a minority, of someone twice removed from mainstream American life. On a similar note, Sohng and Icard (1996) report that the overwhelming importance of family and kinship engenders much of gay oppression in Korean American communities. Bachelorhood is not acceptable; the kinship tradition is diligently maintained.

In the preface to her anthology *Nice Jewish Girls,* Beck (1982) writes compellingly of the feeling of exclusion of gentile lesbians from the tremendous bonding among Jewish lesbians, an exclusion that does not differ in kind from some heterosexual women's responses to lesbian bonding. But why, asks Beck, is it often difficult to see parallels between same-sex bonding and shared ethnicity? Would the recognition that it is not *either/or* (either Jew or lesbian) but *both/and* be too overwhelming? The anthology brings together lesbianism and Jewishness as a sense of coming home. Selections chronicle the intersection between Jewish and lesbian identity with special reference to the vehemence with which both groups have been and are hated; the phenomenon of passing—the deceptive attribute of merging with the mainstream, of avoiding being seen as bad, as the obvious Jew, the obvious lesbian; and the sense of belongingness even among strangers united by a common identity.

Religious Fundamentalism

A major source of strength against the throes of life is religion. And as anthropologist Walter Williams (1997) suggests, religion can be a major factor in a culture's acceptance of sexual and gender nonconformity. Both in Hindu ideology and Native American religion, androgynous beings were viewed as endowed with special spiritual powers. Their roles were formalized in a religious tradition that regarded their sexuality as a matter of destiny. For gays, lesbians, and bisexuals in modern society, however, religion can be downright hazardous. Consider the traditional Jewish imperative to marry (Weinstock, 1982): "I do know that my father has never forgiven me because I never married and never did anything to increase the tribe of Israel which is the 'duty' of every Jewish female" (p. 224).

The impact of the African American church's strict traditionalism is remembered by James Baldwin in this passage (cited in Kenan, 1994): "Owing to the way I had been raised, the abrupt discomfort that all this aroused in me and the fact that I had no idea what my voice or my mind or my body was likely to do next caused me to consider myself one of the most depraved people on earth" (p. 34).

Of the rigors of earlier convent life (Curb & Manahan, 1985), in which every effort was made to discourage "particular friendships" among the nuns, we learn: "We were told that we were sick, evil, dangerous, confused and guilt-ridden, we worked ourselves to exhaustion to purge and punish our wayward desires" (p. 158).

Children growing up as gay and lesbian in strict religious families are apt to experience dissonance between their spirituality and sexuality; sometimes the guilt feelings are overwhelming. In *Prayers for Bobby: A Mother's Coming to Terms with the Suicide of Her Gay Son* (Aarons, 1995), a woman's journey from religious fanatic—she taped Bible verses on her son's bathroom mirror—to pro-gay activist offers a strong cautionary note to parents. The mentality of the religious right is tearing families and communities apart. Since the 1980s, fundamentalist Christian extremists have come to wield political power in America. Disguised as a moral crusade to defend the traditional family, the well-endowed Christian Coalition is in reality a campaign of hate against the rights of women, gays, and lesbians. The old red menace has become the new gay menace (Berzon, 1996).

Monette (1993), who did survive a repressive childhood, comments: "You think you've put all the self-hatred behind you, the long reach of sick religions, and then some memory cuts you down, reducing you once again to the only different boy in the world" (p. 55).

In parts of the Middle East, Islamism—the fanatical branch of Islam—distorts the message of the Koran in the same way that extremist Christians distort the Bible. All forms of out-of-wedlock sexuality are suppressed with a vengeance: Feminists, adulterers, and gay males are beaten or worse.

"What the Bible Says about Homosexuality" in Box 2.1 by Penelope Duckworth and Brett Wells provides a scholarly interpretation of relevant passages of the Bible often cited by concerned Christians and Jews.

Religious oppression notwithstanding, Christian churches have become the strongest centers of gay organizations in many cities. Whether or not to perform same-sex marriage ceremonies is a burning issue among Quaker meetings. Likewise, whether or not to ordain practicing gay and lesbian pastors is a long source of controversy throughout the mainstream denominations. Even in the Bible Belt, however, lesbians and gays worship God and praise Jesus at Metropolitan Community Churches, which boast a predominantly gay and lesbian congregation. Others have found a spiritual home across the country in Buddhist groups and among liberal Unitarians and Quakers where personal freedoms are respected.

Internalized Homophobia

Jennings (1994) notes:

> I attacked anyone who suggested that gay people might be entitled to some rights, too, and I was the biggest teller of fag jokes at Radford High. But what I really hated was myself, and this I couldn't escape from, no matter how drunk or stoned I got, which I was doing on an almost daily basis by senior year. (p. 5)

BOX 2.1

What the Bible Says about Homosexuality

> We have been called to recognize that, no matter how deeply each of us may feel about homosexuality, there are other people of good faith who also take seriously the authority of Scripture and may conclude differently. We have been called to recognize that we cannot carry out our ministry if we each simply assume that we already have the whole truth and nothing at all to learn. We call on you to share our recognition of the inherent faithlessness of a closed mind, one that blocks God from illuminating old truths in a fresh way, from calling us to new understandings or from leading us into new ways of thinking.*

The concepts of homosexuality and sexual orientation are very recent. Such concepts were foreign to those who first set down the words of the Bible. Contemporary research demonstrates that the Bible is indifferent to homosexuality in and of itself. The Bible is concerned, as with heterosexual behavior, with that which violates ethical requirements. It is also important to note that few read the Bible in its original languages. Translation, by its nature, will always slightly miss the mark. St. Paul, writing in Greek to the early church at Corinth, said, "For now we see in a mirror, dimly, but then we will see face to face." All translations risk losing something of the original, but when we do not translate as the authors intended or when our words encompass more than is meant, we are risking even more, we are interpolating contemporary concepts into ancient texts.

There are instances in the Bible where sexual acts between persons of the same sex are condemned. Daniel Helminiak (1994), a roman Catholic theologian, in his book *What the Bible Really Says,*† encourages the reader of Scripture to read such passages with care, and he offers some means for clarification. He differentiates between love between two persons of the same sex, and sexual behavior between two persons of the same sex. Such a distinction is important because love and sex, both homosexual and heterosexual, are not always one and the same.

Jesus loved his disciples; this is love between members of the same sex, but a love of which sexual behavior was not a part. The Bible presents a number of examples of love between two persons of the same sex—David and Jonathan, Naomi and Ruth, Jesus and "the disciple whom Jesus loved."

In those instances in the Bible where sexual acts between persons of the same sex are condemned, these acts are not in the context of human love but clearly in the context of abuse. A key example is the "sin of Sodom," which comes from Genesis 18. In this story, Lot, a resident of Sodom, is honored to be entertaining angelic guests but the men of Sodom decide to sexually abuse, or rape the guests. Lot, in an effort to dissuade the townspeople and to show honor to his guests, offers his own virgin daughters to satisfy the men's lust.

This is a disturbing story on many counts. It bears witness to a culture in which women were of little value. When a man "lies with a male as with woman," as Leviticus 18:22 is phrased, the homosexual relationship was not what was being condemned so much as that one man would treat another "as a woman." (Homosexual behavior was also disapproved as being characteristic of Gentile culture.)‡ To many contemporary readers, the "sin of Sodom" might be Lot's willingness to sacrifice his daughters to the rapacity of a crowd. But to biblical scholars, another sin is vividly apparent; it is the gross abuse of the stranger in the town's midst and so the "sin of Sodom" is not only homosexual rape but the larger context of inhospitality to a vulnerable and trusting guest. A strong component of the Jewish ethical system was to treat the stranger with compassion because, as the Jews were told in Deuteronomy 10:19, they had been "strangers in the land of Egypt."

In the New Testament it is important to note that Jesus says nothing regarding homosexual behavior. The silence is the more significant when we consider that Jesus did have a great deal to say about human sin. The apostle Paul, writing to the early churches, did address homosexual acts. In his Epistle to the Romans he speaks of those who do not honor or give thanks to God, saying, "For this reason God gave them up to degrading passions. Their women exchanged natural intercourse for unnatural, and in the same way also the men, giving up natural

(continued)

BOX 2.1 Continued

intercourse with women, were consumed with passion for one another" (NRSV).

Contemporary scholars have studied Paul's understanding of the "natural." He did not use the word in the abstract sense of "nature" or the "laws of nature." His usage of the word in his other writing demonstrates that he understood "nature" as "a thing's particular character or kind." So, when he spoke of something as "unnatural," he meant something "out of the ordinary." That is how he viewed homosexual behavior. To him it fell among other forms of nonstandard sexual behavior (heterosexual sex during menstruation, intercourse standing up, sex with an uncircumcised man, etc.) and merited social disapproval.

While it is socially disapproved, "unnatural" intercourse is not ethically condemned. Paul saw such sexual behavior as unclean but he did not classify it as a sin. Helminiak believes that Paul made a shrewd rhetorical choice when he used homosexual behavior as an example for the fledgling church. Paul was pointing out the difference between purity issues in the Law (which have been superseded by Christ) and turning away from God, which is a sin. Helminiak believes that Paul chose the issue of homosexual behavior because, in the first century, it was a safe topic, a nonissue of sorts, whereas food taboos and circumcision were much more controversial. Paul's purpose was to bring tolerance and acceptance into the church. Twenty centuries later, biblical scholars are finding new interpretations which may enable that purpose to be realized.

*House of Bishops' Pastoral Statement on Homosexuality (The Episcopal Church), September 20, 1990.

†Helminiak, D. (1994). *What the Bible really says. Top scholars put homosexuality in perspective.* San Francisco: Alamo Square.

‡The book of Leviticus is filled with rules and regulations—Forbidden are: eating shellfish, pork, and rare meat, women entering the temple during their period, combining two kinds of fabric in one garment.

Source: Reverend Penelope Duckworth and Brett Wells, Ph.D.

The gay man who uttered these words went on to swallow a huge bottle of aspirin after his first homosexual experience. Discovered in time, his story had a happy ending: Jennings came out of the closet and, as an openly gay person, he thrived. "Those moments of desperation helped me understand why one out of every three gay teens has to commit suicide" (p. 5).

An addictions expert and acknowledged bisexual, Kasl (1989) sums up the lesbian reality: "Keeping secrets, feeling defective, not fitting in, knowing that your parents are uneasy about you at best and threatened by and afraid of you at worst create a fertile breeding ground for despair, loneliness, shame, and self hatred" (p. 212). Young women whose developmental years are marked by this kind of pain, she further states, are highly vulnerable to addictions.

The religious right not only has a harmful effect in preaching a gospel of sexual sin; "true believers" are also responsible for preventing school systems from addressing the very issue that is killing our kids. Accordingly, school-sanctioned homophobia is rampant; gay and lesbian teachers who could help dare not reveal themselves at risk of losing their jobs. As long as gay and lesbian teachers are closeted out of deference to a homophobic community, there will be a lack of positive role models for gay and lesbian children to emulate (Dempsey, 1994). A significant portion of the boys in the Uribe and Harbeck interview samples reported early same-sex experiences that parallel the "date rape" experiences of many young women. Yet because of the stigma of homosexual involvement, these students felt they could tell no one. The involvement in alcohol and other substance abuse of this sample was startlingly high.

Califia (1994) attributes the refusal of many young people to practice safe sex as a sign of self-hatred. "We're guilty about being queer," she writes. "We can't get rid of all that programming that says we are inferior, filthy, disgusting, godless, and pathological" (p. 22).

Early diagnosis and treatment of depression and substance abuse in homosexual men may prevent extreme acts of self-destruction. Psychiatrists Flavin, Franklin, and Frances (1986) report in the *American Journal of Psychiatry* of three alcohol-dependent gay men who consciously attempted to contract the acquired immunodeficiency syndrome (AIDS) virus as a means of committing suicide. One man acknowledged having intercourse with over six hundred men in the year before he received help. This patient wanted to kill himself but could not get up the nerve to do it directly.

The rate of alcoholism among gays and lesbians, although possibly exaggerated in the literature due to sampling bias, is substantial. Kus (1988) in a *Journal of Homosexuality* article cites estimates that 31 percent of gays and lesbians in a Los Angeles study and 29 percent of gay men in a Michigan sample were alcoholic. Skinner and Otis (1996), however, found high drinking rates but a relatively low rate of about 10 percent alcoholism in a southern sample of over 1,000 gays and lesbians. Marijuana and nicotine use, on the other hand, were found to be disproportionately high. More research is needed to determine the actual alcoholism rates of the lesbian, gay, and bisexual populations.

Lewis and Jordan (1989) probe the link between self-loathing due to internalized homophobia, and suicidal thoughts and alcoholism. High alcoholism rates among gays and lesbians, to the extent that they exist, would seem to be the end result of society's hostility toward gay people as reflected in low self-esteem and guilt feelings over sexuality. The act of drinking lowers inhibitions and increases risk-taking behavior. Thus, alcohol abuse may prove fatal to high-risk populations for whom safe-sex practices are essential.

Prison World

In the socially isolated prison community, sexual activity may take place under the guise of heterosexuality. Prison homophobia, ironically, is expressed through homosexual rape of weaker men by strong, heterosexual males. Victims are "made into women" and, in every sense of the word, enslaved (Irwin, 1980). In women's prisons, likewise, homophobia is expressed in a great deal of gossip about inmates who are homosexually linked. Women prisoners may, however, express their physical love for each other by forming pseudofamilies and relating to each other as mother/daughter or sister/sister. And, although this may seem contradictory, women recruited by the prison population to play butch roles may enter the families as a brother or brother-in-law as well (van Wormer, 1987). Referred to by the masculine pronoun, these inmates had become pseudomen.

Social workers doing counseling within same-sex environments, such as on a military base or in prison, need to be aware of the formidable presence of homophobia both expressed and experienced by their clients.

Implications for Social Work

Working with adolescents, working with families, working with gays, bisexuals, and lesbians —in one way or another, social workers and other mental health professionals encounter heterosexism and vestiges of homophobia every day. Furthermore, social workers may work in settings in which tolerance toward gays and lesbians is not accorded. Calling attention to the social workers' code of ethics' mandate to prevent discrimination against any person or group on the basis of sexual orientation can be instrumental in challenging practices that are contrary to the profession's moral commitment.

The autobiographical selections presented in this chapter are testimony to the wealth of suffering experienced by youth (male or female, straight, bi, gay, lesbian) due to the extreme pressures toward gender conformity. Shaming individuals into behavior consistent with the social norms can be emotionally devastating to those who sense their differentness. As the shame is internalized, self-hatred often results. Therefore, it is not surprising to find many lesbians and gay persons in treatment for depression, suicide attempts, anxiety, and substance abuse. Often the disorder is related to the stress, especially among the young of either sex of being constantly ridiculed and scorned by their peers while having no means of social support. Alienation from the traditional church's teachings, lack of access to gay-friendly counseling services, being privy to a barrage of hostile comments about "fags" and "bulldykes," feeling displeasure from one's family—all combine to close the avenues to much needed social support. Affirmation from a heterosexual or openly gay or lesbian counselor can be a powerful facilitator to self-acceptance, especially when supplemented with other affirmative experiences, such as coming-out groups and activist organizations (Matteson, 1996). Thus, the role of the social worker in his or her role of listener, advocate, and counselor can become paramount in opening the doors to new support systems and to love and self-acceptance.

Paradoxically, the 1989 report on youth suicide (U.S. Department of Health and Human Services, 1989) listed professional help as one of the risk factors to the suicidal behavior of gay youth. How could the provision of badly needed help in a time of crisis, we might ask, compound the problem? Most likely, mistakes were made in encouraging youth who were confused about their sexual identity to see their same-sex attractions as merely a passing phase and encouraging their parents in denying the client's homosexuality. Some counselors are still offering "hope" that the homosexual feeling can be changed. But when change does not occur, the suicide risk is high. Moreover, the cumulative effect of being devalued and derided in itself should be treated as a potential form of trauma that can lead to mental health problems.

Typically, closeted gay youth are referred to treatment for symptoms of their distress—anxiety, drug use, and so on; they are never asked about their sexual concerns. A suicide attempt may occur, therefore, as a cry for help, but the attempt unfortunately may be fatal. In all clients, complete sexual histories, including the matter of sexual orientation, should be taken. It is important not to assign the person to a category, such as gay, straight, or bi, until he or she is ready to self-identify with the label (Matteson, 1996). Attention needs to be devoted to unhealthy internalized scripts that have been acquired through a compulsory heterosexual upbringing. Practitioners who do not accept homosexuality or bisexuality as a natural way of life must refer gay and lesbian clients to those who do.

To help the individual victimized by society and self, social work interventions need to be geared to the societal as well as personal levels. A view of the individual in a social vacuum only contributes to the heterosexism pervasive in our society. By reframing the problem definition from individual/intrapsychic to the person in the environment, the worker begins to shift the onus of responsibility away from passive self-blaming onto activism (Brown, 1991). Implicit in this vision are specific steps toward change. Neisen (1993) approaches healing from cultural victimization in terms of three basic tasks: breaking the silence, establishing perpetrator responsibility, and reclaiming personal power. The respective self-talk is: "Mom, I'm gay," "I didn't deserve to be harassed," "I am (or *we* are) proud to be gay."

A moving poem written by an anonymous high school student (included in Singer, 1994) expresses a youth's transition from pariah to acceptance. The poem is a dialogue with God. "That is the way I made you," says God. "Nothing again will ever matter," the student concludes.

The one area of social work practice with the greatest relevance for youth suicide prevention is school social work. Adolescent persecution of so-called sexual deviants takes a tragic toll as youths flee the relentless taunting and violence in whatever way they can. School bullying can and must be stopped through effective adult intervention. School social workers can provide teacher workshops on homophobia; gay, lesbian, and bisexual speaking groups can address the student body, preferably in small groups, to respond to personal issues and concerns.

Social workers working with all male clients would do well to explore with them the role that homophobia has played in their lives, in their upbringing, and in their intimate relationships. Clients who express extreme hostility toward gays and lesbians may well benefit from an exploration of these deeply ingrained attitudes.

One of the biggest problems facing social workers, who are apt to be well versed in culturally sensitive practice, is the challenge of the bigoted client. Nothing in academic life or training prepares us for this inevitability. Clients in groups and individual settings commonly "reward" the engaging, easy-going therapist with a tirade of invectives against queers, feminists, blacks, and/or foreigners. Adopting a nonjudgmental tone and getting at the roots of the generalized anger would seem to be the most effective course of action. Developing client self-awareness is an appropriate treatment goal.

Writing in the *Encyclopedia of Homosexuality,* Herek (1990) acknowledges that thankless little research has been done on reducing individual homophobia. To the extent that individuals' motivations for their homophobia differ, multiple approaches are necessary. When expressions of homophobia are religiously based, for example, appeals to other values such as compassion and neighborliness are more likely to change attitudes than facts about gay/lesbian life. In an earlier article Herek (1984) says if bad experience is responsible for the gay antagonism, then positive contact with gays and lesbians should be encouraged. Sometimes all it takes is for a loved one to come out of the closet for attitudes to alter. If the hostile attitudes stem from insecurity over gender roles, change might occur through awareness of the basis for the hostility. Above all, the social worker needs to treat this client as any other, as one who is in pain and as one whose vulnerabilities transcend the bravado that is expressed. A helpful device for establishing rapport and empathy with an otherwise unsympathetic person is to explore his or her childhood and the messages received in childhood in considerable depth. The strengths perspective can be invaluable in uncovering survival skills in connection with powerlessness and insecurities. Together, ideally, therapist and client can discover more healthy ways of coping than through attacking other vulnerable people. Attention can be redirected toward the true or deserved source of anger.

A highly effective didactic tool for use in workshops and college classrooms is the heterosexual questionnaire presented by Martin Rochlin in Box 2.2.

BOX 2.2

Heterosexual Questionnaire

1. What do you think caused your heterosexuality?
2. When and how did you decide that you were a heterosexual?
3. Is it possible that your heterosexuality is just a phase that you may grow out of?
4. Is it possible your heterosexuality stems from neurotic fear of others of the same sex?
5. If you've never slept with a person of the same sex, is it possible that all you need is a good gay or lesbian lover?
6. To whom have you disclosed your heterosexual tendencies? How did he or she react?
7. Why do you heterosexuals feel compelled to seduce others into your life-style?
8. Why do you insist on flaunting your heterosexuality? Why can't you just be what you are and keep quiet about it?
9. Would you want your children to be heterosexual knowing the problems they'd face?
10. A disproportionate majority of child molesters are heterosexual. Do you consider it safe to expose your children to heterosexual teachers?
11. With all the societal support marriage receives, the divorce rate is spiraling. Why are there so few stable relationships among heterosexuals?
12. Why do heterosexuals place so much emphasis on sex?
13. Considering the menace of overpopulation, how could the human race survive if everyone were heterosexual like you?
14. Could you trust a heterosexual therapist to be objective? Don't you fear (s)he might be inclined to influence you in the direction of her/his own leanings?
15. How can you become a whole person if you limit yourself to compulsive, exclusive heterosexuality, and fail to develop your natural, healthy homosexual potential?
16. There seem to be very few happy heterosexuals. Techniques have been developed that might enable you to change if you really want to. Have you considered trying aversion therapy?

Reprinted with permission of Martin Rochlin, Ph.D., of Los Osos, California.

Conclusion

The scarcity of empirical research into the psychological consequences of heterosexism and rigid sex role socialization is one of the most salient facts that emerges from a review of the literature. Research on strategies for reducing homophobia is also lacking. The lack of attention to the one form of discrimination that is still widely socially acceptable is in itself a form of discrimination. Whitam (1991) takes the sociology profession to task for slighting the whole study of human rights violations of homosexuals, a marked contrast to the keen interest paid by the profession to the rights of other minority groups. To the extent that sexual minorities are studied at all it is most often in courses on social problems or deviant behavior. Some recent attention, however, is being given to the phenomenal male youth suicide rate.

That school-based homophobia is life threatening and that massive prevention efforts within all school systems are essential are evidenced in the literature and personal narratives available. That homophobia and heterosexism are not even necessary in society is apparent in anthropological studies of other cultures reviewed in this chapter. On the other hand, the fact that things can be potentially much worse is revealed in reports from parts of the globe such as places where religious extremism has prevailed. We have seen how religious extremism on the home front can be deadly as well, this in contrast to the more liberal establishments that have been great sources of spiritual healing and in some cases social activism.

The connection between sexism and heterosexism that has unfolded in this chapter is one that bears reiterating. Lesbianism as the highest form of female bonding is the ultimate threat to male supremacy. Women who are not committed to men, who do not share children with men, cannot be controlled. Or so it is thought. The accusation that feminists are lesbians or that women's rights will lead to gay rights is an effective ploy in defeating progressive legislation. Homophobia affects all women by reinforcing a tremendous fear and hatred of those who deviate from female norms. Homophobia inhibits women from expressing their masculine side and men from expressing their softer, feminine side.

At a political level, heterosexism like racism can be construed as an institutionalized form of scapegoating, as a way of diverting attention from socioeconomic problems. The extent to which heterosexism is encouraged is evidenced by the official world's initial neglect of the ravages of the disease AIDS until it was no longer defined as a strictly gay disease. The government's punishment of gays and lesbians in the military who acknowledge their homosexuality is an illustration of heterosexism in the service of homophobia, the homophobia of service men and women who might be offended by a known gay presence in their midst. Enforced invisibility, as we have seen, is one of the severest forms of oppression. The paradox of official heterosexism is revealed in the government's refusal to allow same-sex partners to marry, at the same time that family health benefits will be denied in the absence of marriage. The challenge to social work is to promote healing and empowerment by exposing the connections among psychological socially inflicted trauma, mental disorders, and the insanity inherent in forming self and identity in a heterosexist homophobic society. Using a strengths perspective, a perspective focusing on the clients' own survival skills and resources (inner and outer), the social worker helps people draw on the considerable power within themselves, their families, and their communities. This perspective is described in more detail in Chapters 8 and 11.

REFERENCES

Aarons, L. (1995). *Prayers for Bobby: A mother's coming to terms with the suicide of her gay son.* San Francisco: Harper.

Adams, H. E., Wright, L. W., & Lohr, B. A. (1996). Is homophobia associated with homosexual arousal? *Journal of Abnormal Psychology 105* (3), 440–445.

Adler, T. (1997). Animals' fancies: Why members of some species prefer their own sex. *Science News 151,* 8–9.

The Advocate. (1997, October 14). Youth at risk: Are gay youth suicide risks? New research may settle the debate, p. 15.

The Advocate Report. (1997, April 1). Could it be a witch-hunt? *The Advocate,* p. 15.

American Psychiatric Association. (1995). *Diagnostic and statistical manual of mental disorders* (4th ed.). Washington, DC: Author.

Anderson, R. (1953). *Tea and sympathy.* New York: Random House.

Associated Press. (1994, December 21). Group says study shows gay killings more brutal. *The Courier Journal,* p. A3.

Associated Press. (1996, December 8). Quietly, U.S. gives asylum to some gays and lesbians. *Des Moines Sunday Register,* p. 13A.

Atmore, C. (1995). Drawing the line: Issues of boundary and the homosexual law reform bill campaign in

New Zealand, 1985–1986. *Journal of Homosexuality 30* (1), 23–52.

Baldwin, J. (1994). Giovanni's room. In B. Singer (Ed.), *Growing up gay/growing up lesbian* (pp. 85–89). New York: New Press.

Barker, R. (Ed.). (1995). *The social work dictionary* (2nd ed.). Silver Spring, MD: NASW Press.

Beck, E. T. (1982). *Nice Jewish girls: A lesbian anthology.* Watertown, MA: Persephone Press.

Berzon, B. (1996). *Setting them straight: You can do something about bigotry and homophobia in your life.* New York: Plume.

Boulard, G. (1995, March 21). Southern justice. *The Advocate,* 22.

Brown, P. (1991). Passing: Differences in our public and private self. *Journal of Multicultural Social Work, 1* (2), 33–50.

Cage, M. C. (1993, March 1). Openly gay students face harassment and physical assaults on some campuses. *The Chronicle of Higher Education,* pp. A22–A24.

Califia, P. (1994). *The culture of radical sex.* Pittsburgh: Cleis Press.

Cloud, J. (1998, July 20). Trans across America. *Time,* 48–49.

Comstock, G. D. (1991). *Violence against lesbians and gay men.* New York: Columbia University Press.

Cotter, K. (1997). Dating a man. *The Advocate,* pp. 41–42.

Curb, R., & Manahan, N. (1985). *Lesbian nuns: Breaking the silence* [Section preface]. Tallahassee, FL: Naiad Press.

Dempsey, C. (1994). Health and social issues of gay, lesbian, and bisexual adolescents. *Families in Society 75,* 160–167.

Flavin, D., Franklin, J., & Frances, R. (1986). The acquired immune deficiency syndrome (AIDS) and suicidal behavior in alcohol-dependent homosexual men. *American Journal of Psychiatry 143* (11), 1441–1442.

Gibbs, J. (1989). Conceptualization of terrorism. *American Sociological Review 54,* 329–340.

Gramick, J. (1983). Homophobia: A new challenge. *Social Work 28* (2), 137–141.

Hartman, A. (1993). Out of the closet: Revolution and backlash. *Social Work 38,* 245–246, 360.

Herek, G. (1984). Beyond "homophobia": A social psychological perspective on attitudes toward lesbians and gay men. *Journal of Homosexuality 10* (1–2), 1–21.

Herek, G. (1990). Homophobia. In *Encyclopedia of Homosexuality* (pp. 552–555). New York: Garland.

Herek, G. M., & Captianio, J. P. (1995). Black heterosexuals' attitudes toward lesbians and gay men in the United States. *The Journal of Sex Research 32* (2), 95–105.

Hunter, J. (1990). Violence against lesbian and gay male youths. *Journal of Interpersonal Violence 5* (3), 295–300.

Icard, L. (1996). Assessing the psychosocial well-being of African American gays: A multidimensional perspective. *Journal of Gay and Lesbian Social Services 5* (2/3), 25–49.

Irwin, J. C. (1980). *Prisons in turmoil.* Boston: Little, Brown.

Jenness, V., & Broad, K. (1997). *Hate crimes: New social movements and the politics of violence.* Hawthorne, NY: Aldine de Gruyter.

Jennings, K. (1994). American dreams. In B. Singer (Ed.), *Growing up gay/growing up lesbian* (pp. 2–7). New York: New Press.

Kasl, C. (1989). *Women, sex, and addiction.* New York: Harper & Row.

Kenan, R. (1994). *Lives of notable gay men and lesbians: James Baldwin.* New York: Chelsea House.

King, M. (1996, November 12). Suicide watch. *The Advocate,* pp. 41–44.

Kinsey, A. C., Pomeroy, W. B., & Martin, C. E. (1948). *Sexual behavior in the human male.* Philadelphia: W. B. Saunders.

Kus, R. (1988). Alcoholism and non-acceptance of gay self: The critical link. *Journal of Homosexuality 15,* 24–41.

Leland, J. (1994, February 14). Homophobia. *Newsweek,* pp. 42–45.

Lewis, G., & Jordon, S. (1989). Treatment of the gay or lesbian alcoholic. In G. Lawson & A. Lawson (Eds.), *Alcoholism and Substance Abuse in Special Population* (pp. 165–203). Rockville, MD: Aspen.

Lichtenberg, P. (1995). Men, overview. In *Encyclopedia of social work* (19th ed., pp. 1691–1697). Washington, DC: NASW Press.

Longres, J. F. (1996). Preface. *Journal of Gay and Lesbian Social Services 5* (2/3), xix–xxiii.

Lorde, A. (1982). *Zami: A new spelling of my name.* Freedom, CA: Crossing Press.

Lorde, A. (1984). *Sister outsider: Essays and speeches.* Trumansburg, NY: Crossing Press.

Manning, A. (1995, January 25). A loyal soldier's painful fight for her own liberation. *USA Today,* p. 8D.

Matteson, D. (1996). Counseling and psychotherapy with bisexual and exploring clients. In B. Firestein (Ed.), *Bisexuality: The psychology and politics of an invisible minority* (pp. 185–213). Thousand Oaks, CA: Sage.

Miller, N. (1992). *Out in the world: Gay and lesbian life from Buenos Aires to Bangkok.* New York: Random House.

Monette, P. (1993). *Becoming a man: Half a life story.* San Francisco: Harper.

Moore, P. (1996). *Iowa.* New York: Hard Candy Books.

Moraga, C. (1993). Art in American con Acento. In C. Moraga (Ed.), *The last generation* (pp. 52–62). Boston: South End Press.

Morin, S. F. (1977). Heterosexual bias in psychological research on lesbianism and male homosexuality. *American Psychologist 32,* 117–128.

Mullins, H. (1995). Evolution of Tomboy. In L. Yamaguchi & K. Barber (Eds.), *Tomboys!* (pp. 40–49). Los Angeles: Alyson.

Neimann, L. (1995). Are you a boy or a girl? In L. Yamaguchi & K. Barber (Eds.), *Tomboys!* (p. 63). Los Angeles: Alyson.

Neisen, J. (1993). Healing from cultural victimization: Recovery from shame due to heterosexism. *Journal of Gay & Lesbian Psychotherapy 2* (1), 49–63.

New Republic, The. (1995, April 3). Hate crime. [Editorial]. *The New Republic 212,* 10.

Newman, L. (1989). *Heather has two mommies.* Boston: Alyson Wonderland.

Ochs, R. (1996). Biphobia. In B. A. Firestein (Ed.), *Bisexuality: The psychology and politics of an invisible minority* (pp. 217–239). Thousand Oaks, CA: Sage.

Pellegrini, A. (1992). S(h)ifting the terms of hetero/sexism. In W. Blumenfeld (Ed.), *Homophobia: How we all pay the price.* Boston: Beacon Press.

Pharr, S. (1993). Homophobia: A weapon of sexism. *SIECUS Report, Feb–March 21* (3), 1.

Random House. (1993). *Random House dictionary of the English language* (2nd ed., p. 898). New York: Random House.

Remafedi, G. (1987). Adolescent homosexuality: Psychosocial and medical implications. *Pediatrics 79,* 331–337.

Remafedi, G., Farrow, J., & Deisher, R. (1991). Risk factors for attempted suicide in gay and bisexual youth. *Pediatrics 87* (6), 869–876.

Rhue, S., & Rhue, T. (1997). Reducing homophobia in African American communities. In J. Sears & W. Williams, *Overcoming heterosexism and homophobia: Strategies that work.* (pp. 117–130). New York: Columbia University Press.

Richardson, G. D. (1997, October 17). DeGeneres' analogy of blacks, gays flawed. *USA Today,* p. 13A.

Rodriguez, F. (1996). Understanding Filipino male homosexuality: Implicators for social services. *Journal of Gay and Lesbian Social Services 5* (2/3), 93–137.

Rotundo, E. A. (March 1993). Where the military's antipathy to homosexuals came from. *The Chronicle of Higher Education,* pp. B1–B2.

Schulman, S. (1995). *Rat Bohemia.* New York: Dutton.

Shea, C. (1996, November 22). A scholar links sexual orientation to gender roles in childhood. *The Chronicle of Higher Education,* pp. A11–12.

Shilts, R. (1993). *Conduct unbecoming: Gays and lesbians in the U.S. military.* New York: St. Martin's Press.

Sidel, L. (1997, September 15). National Public Radio: Morning Edition.

Singer, B. (Ed.). (1994). *Growing up gay/growing up lesbian* (pp. 268–269). New York: New Press.

Skinner, W., & Otis, M. (1996). Drug and alcohol use among lesbian and gay people in a southern U.S. sample. *Journal of Homosexuality 30* (3), 59–117.

Sohng, S., & Icard, L. (1996). A Korean gay man in the United States: Toward a cultural context for social service practice. *Journal of Gay and Lesbian Social Services 5* (2/3), 115–137.

Tafoya, T., & Wirth, D. (1996). Native American two-spirit men. *Journal of Gay and Lesbian Social Services 5* (2/3), 51–67.

U.S. Department of Health and Human Services. (1989). Report of the secretary's task force on youth suicide (vol. 3). *Prevention and interventions in youth suicide.* Rockville, MD: Author.

Uribe, V., & Harbeck, K. (1992). Addressing the needs of lesbian, gay and bisexual youth: The origins of PROJECT 10 and school-based intervention. *Journal of Homosexuality 22,* 9–27.

van Wormer, K. (1987). Female prison families: How are they dysfunctional? *International Journal of Comparative and Applied Criminal Justice 11,* 263–272.

van Wormer, K. (1997). *Social welfare: A world view.* Chicago: Nelson-Hall.

Weinberg, G. (1972). *Society and the healthy homosexual.* Garden City, NY: Doubleday Anchor Books.

Weinstock, H. (1982). Letters from my aunt. In E. T. Beck (Ed.), *Nice Jewish girls: A lesbian anthology* (pp. 221–240). Watertown, MA: Persephone Press.

Wells, J. W. (1991). The effects of homophobia and sexism on heterosexual sexual relationships. *Journal of Sex Education and Therapy 17* (3), 185–195.

Whitam, F. (1991). From sociology: Homophobia and heterosexism in sociology. *Journal of Gay & Lesbian Psychotherapy 1* (4), 31–44.

Williams, W. (1997). Multicultural perspectives on reducing heterosexism: Looking for strategies that work. In J. Sears & W. Williams, *Overcoming heterosexism and homophobia: Strategies that work* (pp. 76–87). New York: Columbia University Press.

Yamaguchi, L., & Barber, K. (Eds.). (1995). *Tomboys!* Los Angeles: Alyson.

Zamora-Hernandez, C., & Patterson, D. (1996). Homosexually active Latino men: Issues for social work practice. *Journal of Gay and Lesbian Social Services 5* (2/3), 69–91.

CHAPTER

3 Strengths of Gay/Lesbian Culture

Gay people are born into a diaspora. . . . Our collective identity and survival depends on the ability to transmit our culture to each new generation.
—Dorothea Benz, 1997

They are the we of me.
—Carson McCullers, 1946

In a classroom exercise, a group of budding social workers, self-identified as heterosexual, are asked to role-play what they think it means to be gay and lesbian. Their account is a catalog of persecution, sex role confusion, and loneliness. Guests in the room, members of a gay/lesbian speaking panel, are silent at first. "Is this what you think being queer is all about?" asks one of the guests. "We have a lot more going for us than that." Then they all laugh. Because all the positives of gayness and lesbianism were omitted—the joy and bonding and hilarity, the insider jokes, and the pride in the culture.

Hence, the reason for this chapter is to present the side of the life that Thompson (1987) calls "the gay spirit" and, more recently, "gay soul" (1994). This latter concept is articulated by Hopcke's (1994) notion of living a life at odds with the way things seem, always being a social outsider, closeted or not. As Hopcke tells us, "We see things differently, and that's the purpose of art. There's a certain kind of creativity that gay people have that does provide for longevity and progeny and transformation, and always has, throughout Western civilization and probably beyond" (p. 219).

October 11 is the national coming-out day, a day to proclaim one's true identity to persons believed not to know. The manner of one's coming out, of course, reflects the idiosyncrasies of the group or individual. Whether one's coming out is in the manner of a "true confession" or a "celebration" probably says more about the personality of the discloser than about the process.

At the age of nineteen, the daughter of K. van Wormer, who attended Luther College (in northeastern Iowa) on the early admissions plan, revealed herself to the world, or at least to the campus community, in a letter to the student newspaper (see Box 3.1):

BOX 3.1

In Celebration of National Coming Out Day

To the Editor:

Hi! my name's Flora, and I'm a biology major, a cellist, a senior, and guess what else . . . a lesbian. I think it's important to share with people different aspects of one's personality, especially an aspect associated with prejudice and negative stereotypes.

I'm coming out because if I say nothing, people assume I'm straight, which isn't true at all. I can't even think straight! I want it to be known, because I think diversity is something to celebrate, not to shun or be afraid of. After all, why shouldn't a womyn love a womyn or a man love a man? Men and womyn are in many respects almost different species, so to me it doesn't make sense to be heterosexual, even though it's the norm.

I want to refute the myth that sexuality is a preference. If you grow up in mainstream American society, everything around you says that you're supposed to be attracted to the opposite sex, from beer ads to parents to churches . . . it's assumed at every level of society. So finding out that your attraction might be otherwise is confusing because it goes against all the propaganda you've ever learned. The feelings are new and exciting, and don't seem related to stereotypes, such as "the homely, old maid" or the tough, spikey-haired womyn. One's sexual orientation is a realization, not a choice, that can occur at any stage in life.

Since I came out to myself and friends last spring, I've been a lot happier and more self-accepting. Beginning in about January, my constant questioning, almost nagging thoughts—am I really a L . . . ?, and not even being able to think the word (no, not Lutheran), has moved to describing feelings to friends, reading lots of coming out stories, going to the march on Washington last April, and telling my brother and parents in June. It would seem appropriate to add "finally" to the last part of the previous sentence, but coming out is a continuous process . . . one is always meeting new people and discovering new aspects of what it means to be lesbian/gay/bisexual. Once the question was answered (yes, Yes, Yes!), it was simply a good feeling to know about a part of myself that had been denied and rejected for so long. Now I can have a gay old time!!

Hearing Carol West-Dallas MCC, lesbian minister, last Wednesday was really inspiring. It is amazing how much easier it is to come out today as compared to the 60's. There is certainly still harassment and discrimination, but by our being open, heterosexuals can become more educated and sensitive to the issues of bisexual/gay/lesbian persons.

Sincerely,

Flora van Wormer '94

Coming out is a defining experience for gays and lesbians, whether it is done piecemeal and situationally or whether it is done as a sort of public proclamation through cross-sex dress styles or October 11 press releases. Coming out is at once an act of moral integrity, in that it is about truth, and a commitment to community (Vaid, 1995). In fact, it is a prerequisite to active involvement in the celebrations and rituals and politicizing that characterize the gay/lesbian community.

To the person in the latent stage, wrestling with the ramifications of same-sex attraction, and perhaps seeking guidance from a role model or therapist, we can offer solace in the cultural cliché, "you are not alone."

A conscious awareness of one's culture, history, and ethos is essential for personal growth in pride in who one is. Cultural awareness connects a person spiritually and materially with all members of the tribe, with those who have gone before and those not yet born. Unlike the culture of ethnicity, imparted by parents and elders, often on the parent's lap, gay/lesbian culture is not so much absorbed as it is discovered, much later in life. The new knowledge brings with it a revelation. Discovery of a whole new way of knowing and being, increasingly known as queer culture, brings with it discovery of the self, and often a belated acceptance.

Gay/Lesbian Culture

"You are not alone," we say. "There were so many before you. . . . We can take you to the ancient past, to the magnificence of gay art, preserved forever in paintings, sculpture, and drama." An astounding amount of art—drama, music, dance—as well as distinct symbols (freedom rings, the rainbow, the pink triangle), in fact, bind the community of those who are "in the know." Lassell (1992) puts it best:

> Now, a life in the world of art has long been an option for people of our tribe, from Aristophanes to Kit Marlowe, from Tchaikovsky and Walt Whitman to Gertrude Stein and Phranc, for the very reason that the art arena—unlike that of, say, politics or business—values eccentricity and individuality of expression above all else. . . . And perhaps it is because our legacy is so palpable in the world of music, with gay forefathers to name like Aaron Copland, Samuel Barber, Virgil Thompson, and Benjamin Britten. . . . Even the AIDS quilt is art. It is credited as the largest quilt, in fact the largest piece of folk art, in history. (pp. 263, 268)

For literature that expresses gay/lesbian consciousness we can look to the South to Tennessee Williams, Truman Capote, Carson McCullers, and Dorothy Allison. Or to the North to the works of James Baldwin, Gore Vidal, or Audre Lord. As an exulting article in *MS* magazine reveals, in the post-Stonewall 1970s, marvelous publishers of lesbian books sprang up (Jay, 1993). Bidding wars have erupted for paperback rights to lesbian titles, according to this account.

The flourishing of lesbian liberation was originally an outgrowth of the public bar community (Davis & Kennedy, 1990). These bars were not only essential meeting places with distinctive cultures and mores, but they were also the central arena for the lesbian confrontation with a hostile world. From the community came the ideas and ultimately the rebellion, the riot that occurred in a Greenwich Village bar on June 27, 1969. After the gay and lesbian patrons of the Stonewall Inn were ejected by the local police, they erupted with unexpected rage and rioted for at least four nights. The world took notice. After that, gay men and lesbian women came together in a new politicized solidarity to fight for social justice. And the gay/lesbian subculture began to thrive.

Actually, preceding the unity, lesbian feminists (and feminist lesbians) developed a strong separatist subculture. This was replete with lesbian bars, literature, women's music festivals, and political groups. It was the urgency of the AIDS epidemic that got underway in the 1980s, however, that brought all the sexual minorities together as never before. Today, the brother/sister bonding, on the surface a curious development—what do men who love men have in common with women who love women and with men and women who love both?—is perhaps the greatest strength of the so-called queer network. As Vaid (1995) explains, necessity is the engine that drives people of different backgrounds to work together (p. 301). She urges, however, more coalition building across color and ethnic lines. On the bright side, Vaid further notes, "We take care of each other when we are sick, show up in a crisis, lend each other money, help each other raise children, run small businesses, and do the hundreds of things that heterosexuals rely on their families to perform" (p. 381).

Two recent developments help bring gay/lesbian essence into mainstream life. First is the recognition of lesbian and gay studies in the university course curriculum in the United States and Canada as a viable area of academic scholarship. It is as if an entire new continent for scholarship has just opened up, observes Nussbaum (1992). Conservative politicians, predictably, paint a picture of narrow political uniformity while zealots in the mass media get worked up about the sexual aspect of gay/lesbian studies course offerings. Nevertheless, the availability of such college offerings, in conjunction with active gay, lesbian, and bisexual organizations, helps initiate sexual minority college students into a supportive network. And gay/lesbian course content is vital for students preparing for the helping professions.

The second recent development with positive dividends for the gay/lesbian community is the mainstreaming of same-sex relationships in the mass media. We will now delve into the realm of contemporary television production to highlight the boom in broadcasting with gay/lesbian themes. A parallel development is taking place in the Hollywood film industry and "queer cinema."

Television Portrayals

Primed by the path-breaking *Soap* and urged on by the more formulaic *Dynasty,* gay and lesbian characters began to emerge as continuing, regular characters on series and sitcoms. Up to this period, you could count on one hand the gay/lesbian characters on television. As the decade of the nineties approached its end, however, twenty-two explicitly gay characters were appearing in recurring roles (Frutkin, 1997). Gay/lesbian weddings have appeared on numerous series, including *Friends* (with Candace Gingrich playing the lesbian minister), *Northern Exposure,* and *Roseanne.* However new and path-breaking this development, most of these weddings have forgone a kiss and presented same-sex marriage ceremonies as cuddly, desexualized mirrors of the more familiar heterosexual ritual. Notably absent are the odes to same-sex love and revisions of traditional vows that most assuredly accompany many gay and lesbian commitment ceremonies.

In three of the major "gay weddings" handled on television, interestingly enough, it is a heterosexual character who brings the nervous and fighting homosexual couple together when the nuptials are threatened. There are other problems with the mass media representation as well.

The Saint/Sinner Duality

In January 1993, NBC produced a documentary entitled *The Gay 90s: Sex, Power, and Influence* hosted by Maria Shriver. Shriver opens with a whistle-stop tour through a (heterosexual) version of gay history. The "Stonewall era" of the seventies, according to Shriver, is characterized by "an in-your-face sexuality that frightened straight America. The images of flamboyant gays and lesbians engaged in promiscuous sex—the infamous bathhouses—all this indelibly seared the consciousness and led to the severe backlash." Leaving aside for the moment her equating of "lesbian" and "gay" (women weren't exactly regulars at the bathhouses), Shriver more perniciously constructs a history that blames lesbians and gays for bringing on the backlash by their "excessive" behavior. In the context of recent attacks against gay men for "bringing AIDS on themselves," this message is particularly frightening. She then switches from the images of partying, seminude men to the emaciated body of a person with AIDS: "In the end, it was AIDS that forced them to save themselves. They changed their habits, they changed their image, they changed their tactics."

Save ourselves from what? The implication here is not that gay people rallied around each other to deal with AIDS, but rather that gays themselves needed saving as gays, and that it was the disease that made us "clean up our act." This fictional history is framed by the same "normalizing" impulse that accompanies much of popular culture:

> Gays and lesbians say they just want what most of the rest of us want—health and happiness, a good job, a loving spouse, and more and more to be moms and dads, raising kids. Going to the Little League games and the PTA. Who are these men and women? Well, they're not the stereotypes of bad movies or scare speeches. They are your neighbors, your classmates, your colleagues. You know them, but don't always know that they're gay. Tonight we are going to see what it means to be gay or lesbian. Some of it might be unsettling. Some of it might be moving. (from the broadcast, *The Gay 90s*)

Of course, there is always much truth in this normalizing discourse—and who could deny that most people want those very things? But like an earlier Bill Moyers documentary on Colorado Springs and Amendment 2, the normalizing discourse can easily slip into a kind of fracturing of the gay community into *good* gays (those who feel they are "born with it," those who are a "committed couple," those who go to church, those who have kids, those who have weddings, those who want acceptance) and *bad* gays (those who celebrate their preference as a choice, those who prefer multiple partners, those who criticize the nuclear family, those who are atheists, those who want radical social change). Moyers's earlier show offered as an answer to antigay evangelicals a pair of gay and lesbian couples who were always either attending church or gardening. A great deal of the time was spent on the religious faith of the lesbian couple and on the long-term commitment of the two men.

The narrative counterpart to these two attractive and benevolent couples was the constant reintroduction of the infamous videotape *The Gay Agenda* that the Christian right had been circulating for some time. Indeed, one of the gay men was finally pushed into a position of denouncing the images depicted on the tape (which included scenes from gay pride parades showing seminude men, dancing, phallic images, sadomasochistic gear, etc.) in order to press his case for inclusion and equality.

The price of tokenism is often isolation and assimilation. Television gays and lesbians exist in a social vacuum; they appear to have sprung fully armed from Zeus's heterosexual head: The social, political, and cultural context that "births" gay people gives way to the fiction of the fully-formed fag, parented by bravely reconstructed heterosexuals. Homophobia is rarely portrayed as just that; rather, it is usually reduced to ignorance, bewilderment, and discomfort. In the television land of gay/lesbian life, the perpetrators of homophobia (aside from the obvious gay bashers) are not offenders but are basically good-hearted souls whose liberal inclinations will out in the end. The story, in short, is usually told from the heterosexual viewpoint.

Nevertheless, although the television portrayal of gay and lesbian existence leaves something to be desired, it is a start. On March 1, 1994, an episode titled "Don't Ask, Don't Tell" that appeared on *Roseanne* is an example of a positive approach. The episode, featuring a kiss between Roseanne and another woman, caused a stir even before it aired. Prior to the episode, local television stations and networks alike ran clips from the episode, rehashing the controversy. Op-eds appeared and pundits weighed in. Like the return of the repressed, television's fascination with its own discourse produced a "Challenger" like effect whereby we saw kiss after kiss on our local stations.

The *Roseanne* episode truly represented a radical departure in its cogent and sustained attack on homophobia and its exploration of the shifting parameters of sexual desire. Although commentators predictably focused on the heretical moment of a prime-time lesbian kiss, they ignored the full substance of the episode, itself much more challenging than the brief peck on the lips. Centered around a trip to a gay bar with a regular lesbian character and her new girlfriend, the episode paraded homophobic assumptions and caused Roseanne and her husband Dan to reckon with their own homophobia.

Instead of playing the gayness itself for laughs, the object of mockery is the homophobic self. Roseanne dares to show the homophobic heart of darkness of middle America. After being kissed by Nancy's new girlfriend, Sharon, at a gay bar, Roseanne is anxious and upset, unable to articulate her discomfort (homophobia? attraction? regret?) but also eager to assert her highness. By having America's favorite working-class liberal muddle through her own reaction to sexual difference, Roseanne advanced the dialogue to a new place. When Nancy challenges Roseanne—"And we're supposed to admire you because you went to a gay bar? I'm supposed to think you're cool because you have gay friends?"—Roseanne allows the show to name the phenomenon of "lesbian chic" and critique it at the same time. She's eager to assert her hipness—"Hey. I like that Snoopy Dog Dog"—but that very eagerness exposes her own discomfort with homosexuality.

What marks *Roseanne* as different from other sitcoms is that gays are not simply token signs of cultural hipness and "diversity" but are also integrated into the life of the sitcom. *Roseanne* has done what is seemingly so simple but has proved to be close to impossible: to depict lesbians and gays as both same and different, as being part of both the dominant culture in which they emerged as well as the more marginalized culture that they inhabit by virtue of being gay. *Roseanne* set the stage for *Ellen* several years later. Although *Ellen* is now relegated to history, hopefully more multidimensional scripts of this kind will continue to hit the airwaves.

Showtime's airing of *More Tales of the City* in June 1998 generated a great deal of excitement in gay/lesbian circles. This show was gay-written, gay-produced, and pitched for a predominantly gay audience.

When Maupin's (1989) first novel, *Tales of the City,* was first televised by the Public Broadcasting System in 1994 after being produced by Britain's Channel Four, a firestorm of erotophobic controversy occurred from conservative and fundamentalist groups. Set in the

1970s in San Francisco, the first of six novels, *Tales* depicts a transgendered character who presides over a family of gays and straights, while tending her marijuana plants. The right-wing outcry intimidated PBS for a sequel, *More Tales of the City,* even though the first broadcast garnered the largest audience in PBS history. The critics praised the miniseries, which won a Peabody Award and was nominated for an Emmy. Members of Congress, however, were treated to a twelve-minute videotape of gay and straight affectional and sexual situations with nudity, courtesy of the American Family Association. What resulted was an official condemnation of the miniseries by the legislatures of Oklahoma and Georgia, the latter endangering a $20 million public television facility. At the PBS station in Chattanooga, Tennessee, a bomb threat prompted officials to pull *Tales* an hour before airtime. Other stations refused to carry the miniseries or blocked out nude scenes. Within weeks, PBS backed out of its plans to participate in funding for the follow-up adaptation from the second novel, *More Tales of the City.*

More Tales, in the end, was aired by Showtime. These autobiographical stories pick up where the first novel leaves off in 1977 when Maupin was 32. Situations are drawn from his experiences as a gay man who had not yet come out to his own parents living in North Carolina. One such situation concerned a character who wrote a coming-out letter to his parents in the book, *More Tales.* Because Maupin's parents were reading his work, this is how they found out their son was gay. Now, without the usual restriction of censorship, this raucous tragicomedy has been presented in its entirety.

Poetry as Healing

Whether because of inherent two-spirit sensibilities that is a part of their nature or because of their outsider status, gays and lesbians have expressed their love for humanity in art and literature since time immemorial. Now along comes a gay Cuban American physician who has added his story to the narrative of medicine: Campo's work (1997) politicizes medicine, violates all its boundaries, and opens up the physician and his audience to medicine's possibilities, its shortcomings, and its poetry.

Campo was originally drawn to poetry, especially closed-form, traditional poetry, because of the intense control involved in its creation; now, however, the nexus of AIDS and poetry taught him something else: "The poetry of AIDS . . . is not simply and always about assuming control. Rewritten: it is also about losing all control, about dying . . ." (p. 170). It is not too much of an exaggeration to say that poetry is Campo's "cure" for AIDS, or at least its most effective prophylactic. He offers up poetry workshops as a supplement (if not replacement) for clinical visits. His faith in poetry makes his hyperbolic assertions almost credible:

> Even if it is not a miracle cure, the brave, heartfelt poem just might be the safest and most pleasurable sex of all, providing the kind of empowerment that comes from fully occupying one's body. . . . It is felt in the heart, in the genitals, in the mouth and tongue. The poem just might contain the elusive secret formulas to life itself. (p. 194)

"Science was the perfect barrier to self-knowledge" (p. 84), ironic words coming from a physician, but Campo's life and work center on such paradoxes. In the ten essays that comprise *Poetry of Healing,* Campo (1997) explores medicine in connection with race, religion, science, public policy, professionalism, and poetry. His collection's subtitle, "A Doctor's Education in Empathy, Identity, and Desire," hints at how his work is different from what one might expect, and these differences make his work enriching and enlightening. The education Campo refers to is not the one he received at Harvard Medical School. Campo's essays describe American medicine from the inside, but Campo himself is positioned as a triple outsider—gay, Cuban American, poet—and that gives him a uniquely deconstructive perspective, one that helps him redefine what it means to be a healer.

Music

While actors act, singers, and especially those who write their own music, are presenting *themselves.* A chapter on gay/lesbian culture would be incomplete without attention to the role played by music. Music conveys a message, is associated with dance and love, and merges from underground culture to bring pleasure to the masses.

Many of the great composers of all time—from Beethoven to Tchaikovsky to Benjamin Britton to Leonard Bernstein—were gay. That this fact has been largely hidden from the general public saddened Bernstein, who declared:

> From an early age, I was aware that much of the most sublime music ever created derived from the efforts and souls of homosexuals. Our world feels free to enjoy this tireless music time and again, but not to acknowledge even the simple, mutual humanity of composers, conductors, singers, and other gay artists. (cited in Hadleigh, 1997, p. 1)

Just as homosexuality shaped music, so music shaped homosexuality. In the 1970s, new gay disco bars gave new definition to gay nightlife and demonstrated the power of the gay consumer for the first time (Miller, 1995). What disco did for gay male community, "women's music" did for lesbians. Miller describes the role of "women's music" in terms of a major glue that held the lesbian-feminist culture together in the 1970s. Starting off as folk music, women's music encompassed a variety of styles; lyrics were sometimes overtly lesbian. In *Sing Out!*, Hadleigh (1997) presented the success stories of out-of-the-closet recording artists such as Melissa Etheridge, k.d. lang, and the Indigo Girls. The music of such artists provides common ground to lesbians of all ages all over the world. When lesbians are coming out or getting acquainted, shared interest in music, including listening to CDs, romanticizes the relationship and promotes closeness. And as Miller (1995) suggests, it is not just the music but the philosophy and publicized lives of such performers that make them important role models to young lesbians.

Recommendations from Film and Literature

From Hollywood, *Making Love,* produced in 1982, sensitively portrays the suffering of a devoted wife coping with the inevitable "betrayal" of a gay husband, and *Philadelphia,* produced in 1993, handles AIDS from a moving personal and political angle. From British cinema,

Priest, recently available on video, is an emotionally powerful presentation of a gay Irish priest wrestling with issues of guilt and public humiliation. More recent recommendations are the Canadian gay morality tale, *The Hanging Garden,* for its frank exploration of family relationships; *Straight Man,* for retelling the well-known story of Oscar Wilde's persecution and for the outstanding cast and quality of the acting; *The Object of My Affection* because of its unique depiction of a star-crossed love affair between a straight woman and gay man; and *In and Out* because of its humorous qualities in portraying a catastrophic outing of a gay teacher.

From the world of lesbian literature, we recommend *Zami: A New Spelling of My Name,* the classic coming-of-age memoir of Audre Lorde (1982) who recaptures her Harlem girlhood unpretentiously and poetically. More recently, Dorothy Allison's (1992) *Bastard Out of Carolina* chronicles the pains of growing up lesbian in a violent, poor white trash household. Similarly, *A Stone Gone Mad* by Jacquelyn Park (1991) deals with an adolescent's pain coming to terms with her sexuality. On the wild, humorous side, *Confessions of a Failed Southern Lady* (King, 1985) provides a delightful series of lesbian liaisons in the Deep South. Academics of all persuasions would undoubtedly enjoy a perusal of *No Previous Experience: A Memoir of Love and Change* (Elspeth, 1997) about an affair between two Canadian female professors.

For gay males and their allies, E. M. Forster's (1971) posthumously published *Maurice* provides a sensitive account of an upper-class schoolboy who has a crush on an older schoolmate. The high-quality movie of the same name is available on video. One of the most celebrated of gay male novels is the *Dancer from the Dance,* in which Andrew Holleran (1978) has created a world of mythic glamours and a lifestyle centering around music and dance. The memoirs of Tennessee Williams (1975) provide a fascinating portrait of a gay genius's initiation into adulthood.

Conclusion

Gays, lesbians, and transgendered people have turned marginality into a creative art form—life form really—as this chapter has shown. This art form has been expressed at the level of art, music, theater, film, and dress. From the institutionalized gay teacher/learner relationships of ancient Greece to the exalted role of two-spirited Native Americans who were keepers of the culture, to the queer cinema and lesbian novelists of today, there are many avenues of pride for gay or lesbian youth seeking affirmation of who they are. Social workers and other therapists counseling this population (and who does not?) would do well to further engender this pride first by familiarizing themselves with some of the vast resources at hand and with the local organizations, events, and newsletters.

In northeastern Iowa, for example, the newsletter *Accessline* provides listings of gay/lesbian-friendly churches, self-help groups, upcoming pride celebrations, film festivals, and reviews of recent drag queen beauty contests. Central to a strengths approach is an awareness of community support systems and resources. The self-help group saying, "I can't do it alone but together we can," is remarkably applicable here.

Gearing isolated gays and lesbians toward the richness of gay/lesbian heritage and of contemporary cultural and festive events can empower them in ways that all the therapy in the world cannot. In the European-North American part of the world where gay/lesbian identity is a force for identity and solidarity, there is a life of fulfillment to be had, a strength in likeness, a fortification against the daily cruelties and insults. And above all, there is fun and merriment to be enjoyed. Queer humor is like any other but more so—raucous, ribald, cynical, and singularly outrageous. Such humor is replete with insider jokes and stories, many pertaining to shocked homophobic reactions at some of their antics. The tragedy of AIDS, certainly, has put a damper on things. Still, the strength of the human spirit and of the gay/lesbian spirit lives on. Indomitably.

REFERENCES

Allison, D. (1992). *Bastard out of Carolina.* New York: Dutton.

Benz, D. (1997). Myths and facts. In L. Witt, S. Thomas, & E. Marcus, *Out in all directions: The almanac of gay and lesbian America.* New York: Warner Books, p. 374.

Campo, R. (1997). *Poetry of healing: A doctor's education in empathy, identity, and desire.* Scranton, PA: Norton.

Davis, M., & Kennedy, E. L. (1990). *Hidden from history: Reclaiming the gay and lesbian past.* New York: Penguin.

Elspeth, C. (1997). *No previous experience: A memoir of love and change.* Toronto: Viking.

Feinberg, L. (1993). *Stone butch blues: A novel.* Ithaca, NY: Firebrand Books.

Forster, E. M. (1971). *Maurice: A novel.* New York: Norton.

Frutkin, A. (1997, February 18). Television's 23 gay characters. *The Advocate,* pp. 30–31.

Hadleigh, B. (1997). *Sing out! Gays and lesbians in the music world.* New York: Barricade Books.

Holleran, A. (1978). *Dancer from the dance: A novel.* New York: Morrow.

Hopke, R. (1994). The union of sames. In M. Thompson (Ed.), *Gay soul: Finding the heart of gay spirit and nature with sixteen writers, healers, teachers and visionaries.* (211–228). San Francisco: Harper.

Jay, K. (1993, July/August). Is lesbian literature going mainstream? *MS,* pp. 71–73.

King, F. (1985). *Confessions of a failed southern lady.* New York: St. Martin's Press.

Lassell, M. (1992). An explosion of creativity. In B. Berzon (Ed.), *Positively gay: New approaches to gay and lesbian life.* Berkeley: Celestial Arts.

Lorde, A. (1982). *Zami: A new spelling of my name.* Trumansburg, NY: Crossing Press.

Maupin, A. (1989). *Tales of the city.* New York: Harper & Row.

McCullers, C. (1946). *The member of the wedding.* New York: Bantam Books.

Miller, N. (1995). *Out in the past: Gay and lesbian history from 1869 to the present.* New York: Vintage Books, 422–438.

Nussbaum, M. (1992, July 13 & 20). The softness of reason. *The New Republic,* pp. 26–35.

Park, J. (1991). *A stone gone mad.* Los Angeles: Alyson.

Thompson, M. (Ed.). (1987). *Gay spirit: Myth and meaning.* New York: St. Martin's Press.

Thompson, M. (Ed.). (1994). *Gay soul: Finding the heart of gay spirit and nature.* San Francisco: Harper.

Vaid, V. (1995). *Virtual equality: The mainstreaming of gay and lesbian liberation.* New York: Anchor Books.

Williams, T. (1975). *Memoirs.* Garden City, NY: Doubleday.

CHAPTER

4 Growing Up Lesbian, Gay, or Bisexual

For everyone who believes telling the truth will make a difference.
—Linnea Due, 1995, dedication for *Joining the Tribe*

If you were to yell "nigger," teachers would come out of the classroom, people in the hallways would object. But "faggot" is just public access, anybody can say it and it doesn't matter.
—Linnea Due, 1995

The social and behavioral science literature is replete with conjectures that homosexuality in youth is only a phase. "Normal" heterosexuality will prevail in adulthood. Therefore, homosexuality in our preadolescents and preadults is discounted. The result is a primarily invisible group of individuals who are most often fearful and consequently secretive about disclosing their homosexuality. The reprisals of coming out are too great to bear for most. Confusion, self-hatred, and a greater failure than heterosexuals to complete the developmental task of identity formation involving delayed socialization for intimate relationships, threatened loss of family, and limited career, vocational, and leisure choices create life difficulties that are more likely to result in runaways, attempted suicides, completed suicides, drug and alcohol abuse, and missed school because of feeling unsafe. Our cultural perspective ignorantly focuses only on adulthood homosexuality, which is often perceived as a choice individuals make when their heterosexual experiences have proven disastrous.

Identity Formation

As early as four or five, children in school or at home will call another agemate "fag" or "queer." Although children are not cognizant of the meaning of these words, they do know that they have powerful and hurtful implications. Children have usually heard homophobic as well as other prejudicial words used by parents, older siblings, classmates, or through media early in their development.

No child wants to be called or known as a "fag." Hence, children actively try to take on characters that the culture values, often covering up or denying who they are. In Wells's files is the following account:

> As a very young child of about five, I couldn't reconcile the differences that I felt between my ranging gender proclivities and attractions to good-looking same-sex individuals with what my parents, teachers, and peers were telling me. I remember sitting with my mother and some of her friends when they were talking about the upcoming marriage of my older sister. I said that I wanted to marry a person like David. My embarrassed mother said that that was sick. I remember feeling shamed and humiliated. It was a few years later that I realized she was talking about fags.

Identity formation refers to the development of personal identity, as core individual characteristics, and social identity, one's self in relation to others. Although unstated, a fundamental and underlying assumption of the bulk of the research literature on childhood adolescence and identity formation is that "normative" development is presumptively heterosexual. The successful transition from childhood to adulthood involves developing an attraction for and attachment to individuals of the other sex. Although many theorists in the social and behavioral sciences acknowledge that same-sex feelings and attractions are typical among children and adolescents, developmental theorists such as Erikson (1968) assert that this typical phase of development gives way to mature relationships that develop between individuals of the "opposite" sex. This standard assumption is problematic because it omits a significant segment of the population and assumes that youthful gays and lesbians either do not exist or are so marginal that it is not worth dealing with them. What if, because of society's negative views about your sexual identity, you do not feel good about yourself at home, in school, or with peers? How does this affect and frame your identity? What if the basic messages you receive do not acknowledge or support you as someone who self-identifies as being a lesbian, gay, or bisexual young person? These questions illustrate the need for reframing social development theory to encompass lesbian, gay, and bisexual identity formation, an identity that occurs in a hostile, rather than nurturing, environment.

What makes research in this area difficult is the fact that despite attempts to eradicate heterosexism and homophobia, myths and stereotypes about people who are lesbian, gay, and bisexual abound. Although the American Psychiatric Association declassified homosexuality as an illness in 1973, the perception that homosexuality is "abnormal" is still prevalent within this society and, more specifically, within the societies of the social sciences. Sedgwick (1993) determined that in 1980 the new *DSM-III* (*Diagnostic and Statistical Manual of Mental Disorders*) did not include, for the first time, an entry on homosexuality as a dysfunction. Yet it did, nevertheless, have a new category of dysfunction: gender identity disorder of childhood. Sedgwick responded to this recent dysfunction by stating:

> Nominally gender-neutral, this diagnosis is actually highly differential between boys and girls: a girl gets this pathologizing label only in the rare case of asserting that she actually is anatomically male (e.g., "that she has, or will grow, a penis"); while a boy can be treated for Gender Identity Disorder of Childhood if he merely asserts "that it would be better not to

> have a penis"—or alternatively, if he displays a "preoccupation" with female stereotypical activities as manifested by a preference for either cross-dressing or simulating female attire, or by a compelling desire to participate in the games and pastimes of girls. (pp. 156–157)

Sedgwick further suggested that although gay activists were influential in depathologizing homosexuality as a category within the *DSM-III,* they have been less zealous in their efforts to remove the stigma attached to effeminate boys and others who do not conform to gender-congruent behaviors and roles. Unfortunately, the same categorization of gender identity disorder appears in the *DSM-IV,* which was published in 1995. Sedgwick illustrates how gender-appropriate behaviors are institutionalized and defined as essential and natural categories of masculinity and femininity. Given that societal norms and mores about gender roles and sexual identity are ingrained in children as young as three years of age, those who profess alternate gender roles and sexual identity are at risk for ridicule, rejection, and often violent reactions. Gender incongruency is a violation of one of our most basic and cherished cultural norms—that "good" girls are inherently feminine, that "good" boys are inherently masculine, and that when they reach adulthood they will be "good" heterosexuals.

Living in a Heterosexist and Homophobic Culture

Of the 30 million children and adolescents between the ages of ten and twenty in the United States today, Deisher (1989) estimates that 10 percent or 3 million are lesbian, gay, or bisexual or are questioning their sexual identity. Yet, researchers across disciplines either ignore this population as an authentic category of youth or they continue to perpetuate misinformation about lesbian, gay, and bisexual youth.

Whereas gay and lesbian youth are confronted with typical issues of adolescence such as sexuality, independence from parents, and peer pressure, their concerns are magnified by emotions, feelings, and attractions that run contrary to the pervasive messages and norms of a dominant heterosexual society. In short, lesbian, gay, and bisexual youth must also deal with these facts: They are lesbian, gay, or bisexual or question their sexuality; they are isolated; they are victims of homophobic attacks; and they are two to three times more likely to attempt and commit suicide than other youth (Gibson, 1989).

Remafedi, Farrow, and Deisher (1991) found that 41 of the 137 gay and bisexual males aged fourteen to twenty-one had reported suicide attempts, with almost half describing multiple attempts. These authors further explained that a third of all suicide attempts in their sample population were attributed to personal or interpersonal turmoil over homosexuality. One third of first attempts occurred in the same year that respondents identified their homosexuality or bisexuality. Yet, despite these stresses and high rate of suicide among this group of our adolescent population, professionals, volunteers, and community members at local, state, and national levels appear ill-equipped and/or unwilling to deal with lesbian, gay, and bisexual youth.

Indeed, this was exemplified at the national level when the Bush administration attempted to exclude Gibson's (1989) study on gay, lesbian, and bisexual teen suicide from a comprehensive national study on adolescent suicide. The reason given for the exclusion was that the contents of the report ran contrary to traditional family values (Geh, 1989). In rejecting Gibson's study, Louis Sullivan, the former secretary of the Department of Health and Human Services (cited in Geh, 1989), commented that,

> Federal policies must be crafted with great care so as to strengthen rather than undermine the institution of the family. In my opinion, the views expressed in the paper ran contrary to that aim. . . . "Gay Male and Lesbian Suicide" does not in any way represent my personal beliefs or the policy of this Department. (p. 1)

That such a high-ranking official of a recent administration denounced this study, a document that is perhaps the most comprehensive analysis of gay and lesbian adolescent suicide to date, certainly indicates the extent to which homophobia pervades our society. In a review of the literature on gay, lesbian, and bisexual adolescents, many researchers (Gibson, 1989; Hunter & Schaecher, 1987; Remafedi, Farrow, & Deischer, 1991) agree that the prevalence of homophobia is by far the single most damaging influence on lesbian, gay, and bisexual youth. All young people who identify as gay or lesbian, and even young people who may not necessarily identify as lesbian or gay but who may be perceived as such, are potential victims of verbal or physical assaults. Gay and lesbian youth are also at greater risk because of a compulsory obligation to attend school. Dennis and Harlow (1986) claimed that lesbian and gay adolescents quickly learn that ". . . public high school often means ridicule from teachers, violent harassment from fellow students, and refusals from administrators to punish verbal and physical attacks upon these youth" (p. 446). Hetrick and Martin (1987) also commented that "violence against the homosexually oriented is endemic, particularly for the homosexual adolescent. These acts of violence range from the slap in the school hallway to rape" (p. 29). The reluctance of school officials to protect gay students and to punish perpetrators of harassment shows, at the very least, their tacit acceptance of homophobia as acceptable behavior (Hetrick & Martin, 1987). High levels of personal prejudice, ignorance, and fear result in negligible intervention by teachers, counselors, administrators, and school board members when homophobic attacks occur (Uribe & Harbeck, 1991).

Additionally, the continued perception that homosexuality is abnormal contributes to a sanctioned culture of intolerance and hatred toward people who are lesbian and gay, and one of the manifestations of this intolerance and hatred is violence (e.g., Matthew Shepard). Young people who are gay and lesbian, and even those who are not gay, but who might be perceived as such, are targeted for harassment and violence. Nowhere are these manifestations of intolerance and hatred more apparent than within the primary contexts of adolescent development—schools, families, and peers. Teachers often remain silent when students taunt other students with antigay remarks (Dennis & Harlow, 1986) or support antigay sentiment; parents respond to their gay and lesbian children with verbal harassment and physical violence (Hunter & Schaecher, 1987); nongay youth will sever ties with lesbian and gay peers out of fear that others might discover that they are associated with someone who is gay or lesbian (Hunter & Schaecher, 1987); and, within the context of leisure, play, and sports, when a male or a female does not conform to gender-appropriate behavior, he or she is taunted with antigay slurs: "fag," "dyke," "lezzie," "queer," or "sissy."

Many lesbian, gay, and bisexual adolescents (and adults) do not believe that they can count on traditional sources of support, such as their families, friends, peers, teachers, coworkers, neighbors, clergy, and physicians, if they come out. This perceived limitation on significant others' willingness to be supportive creates hurt and pain resulting in increased stress, which in turn is exacerbated by a lack of human resources to help cope with that stress (Jones & Gabriel, 1998).

Sexuality Education

If homosexuality is mentioned in the school setting, it is most often in the context of derision and contempt. Indeed, a survey of college senior family life educators revealed that homosexuality would be the most difficult topic to teach about in human sexuality and family relationships classes. As one teacher said, "If you portray gay/lesbian relationships unbiasedly, students will label you as one of them." Labeling someone as lesbian or gay, whether or not they are, impacts on a person's life more than any other characteristic. Let's say I have a guest speaker in my class and I introduce that person as a social worker, churchgoer, community volunteer, parent, and as gay or lesbian. What characteristic becomes most prominent as class members identify my guest speaker? What might you assume my guest speaker's topic would be?

Teachers who have grown up in a homophobic society often reflect those views out of ignorance, fear, and prejudice. From Wells's files:

> In my senior high school English composition class, a teacher whom I very much liked and respected revealed a prejudicial and an ignorant side of herself that I must have assumed wasn't there. She had asked our class to write about social changes occurring at the end of the twentieth century which we were to read aloud in class. I chose to write about gay/lesbian parenting, since my mom is a person who is lesbian. As I read my paper aloud to the class, a student interrupted with, "Yuk. That's gross." Two others chimed in with negative comments before our teacher said that they should let me finish my paper before commenting; and, then, my teacher said that she also thought lesbian/gay parenting was not appropriate before I could proceed. I was so upset and furious at her that I ran out of the classroom crying. I went to the office and called my mom to tell her what had happened. She set up an appointment with my teacher when she was able to reach her several days later. My mom said she was glad for the time interval so she could calm down. When she spoke to my teacher she tried to provide her with information about gay/lesbian parenting, hoping my teacher wouldn't assume that all families are only made up of heterosexuals.

When formal instruction about sexuality occurs in school classrooms, homosexuality often is omitted or mentioned in a negative context. Because government funding is directed toward abstinence-only programs, teachers and speakers on sexuality education present a very heterosexist view of sexuality, by addressing intercourse prevention. The assumption is that there are no gay, lesbian, and bisexual students in class or that they do not count.

Feeling Different

Many adolescent lesbians and gays report feeling "different" from their peers since earliest childhood. The differences these youths describe include mixed or variable gender identity and roles; romantic attractions toward and fantasies about sexually mature, good-looking, same-sex individuals; and the sense or awareness that these interests, feelings, and attractions are different from what is prescribed. From Wells's files:

> I always knew that I was different than others my age; that I saw the world and people in it differently. I can recall a response from my mother that told me that someday I could talk with her about those differences, but as yet I hadn't defined. We were watching a ballet on television and I said to my mother, "I'd like to dance like that when I grow up." She said, "Honey, you can if you want to."
>
> My mother died shortly thereafter. But her words of approval carry me through to this day!

The sense that one is different in gender and sexual interests most often is kept secret by gays and lesbians. Those who come out as adults and participate in research studies dealing with sexual orientation offer only a beginning toward understanding their perspectives of childhood and adolescence. It is estimated that approximately 10 percent of the American population is sex role incongruent; that is, they do not conform to traditional and conventional roles of masculinity or femininity. Individuals who do not conform to gender stereotypes are probably more likely to come out. They are often labeled as gay or lesbian anyway, so by coming out they are more likely to develop a support system. However, they also perpetuate the stereotypes that gays are effeminate and lesbians are masculine. Not all effeminate males and masculine females are gay or lesbian. Perhaps 10 percent? If 10 percent of the population is estimated to be gay or lesbian and 10 percent is sex role incongruent, we would expect that a similar percentage of both gays and lesbians and heterosexuals might be gender-role incongruent. Tentative data are showing that there may be a greater likelihood of effeminate boys to define themselves as gay or bisexual than masculine boys. Research on "tomboy" girls is underway to determine the likelihood of a lesbian or bisexual identity. However, what about masculine boys and feminine girls? Perhaps they have an easier time passing, which may make it more difficult to come out to family and friends. Only sexual contacts and confidants would be permitted to know. After masturbation and heterosexual coitus, same-sex relations is the most common sexual experience for American men and women. Research on married males who engage in homosexual encounters and affairs unbeknownst to their wives is a fairly common occurrence.

The Washington Star's report by Lynn Rosellini in November 1975 on gay athletes caused a stir following Washington Redskin football running back David Kopay's admission that he was gay. Kopay commented that gay males in the ranks of professional football are more common than people believe, reflecting the stereotype that masculine sports figures could not be gay; that gays are effeminate males who do not engage in athletics. Kopay was caught in a lie between the masculine myth he so beautifully personified in public and the private reality of his life.

In Kopay and Young (1977), Kopay wrote, "People think of homosexuality as some kind of curse. I knew it was a natural part of me—and always had been, even when I was dating Miss Washington and the Rose Bowl Queen" (p. 14). He continued, . . . "When I looked at what people told me were homosexuals, I thought I'd be sick to my stomach. None of the guys I know are like that" (p. 18). Finally, Kopay observed, . . . "Why I played football is a question as difficult for me to answer as why I am homosexual" (p. 47).

Garner and Smith (1976) reported that 8 percent of eighty-two college sportsmen from age twenty to twenty-five reported exclusively same-sex activity, including fellatio and anal intercourse, and between 14 percent and 35 percent of college athletes ranging over five universities had engaged in at least two same-sex acts of fellatio and/or anal intercourse to a point of orgasm over the past two years. These authors commented that fear of discovery and reprisal likely reduced the number of respondents who admitted having engaged in same-sex sexual behavior.

The implication that gender roles and sexual orientation are somehow related has been perpetuated as a bias in theory and the research literature as well as through stereotypes. As a result, the range of people over diverse interests, abilities, and backgrounds fails to accurately assess how many people might be included. The purpose here is not to provide categories and labels for people but to suggest that where people range regarding sexual orientation, there is more like a bell-shaped curve than a skewed one with heterosexuality being overrepresented and lesbian, gay, and bisexual orientation underrepresented.

To Come Out or to Try to Be Invisible

The Academy Award–winning documentary film about Harvey Milk, the former San Francisco supervisor, showed that he clearly understood the pain and the stress that lesbian and gay youth experience. His words, although spoken twenty years ago, still apply today (Schmiechen & Epstein, 1986):

> Somewhere in Des Moines or San Antonio there's a young gay person who all of a sudden realizes that he or she is gay and knows that if their parents find out, they will be tossed out of the house; the classmates will taunt the child; and the Anita Bryants and John Briggs [will] continue doing their bit on T.V. That child has several options: staying in the closet or suicide. Then one day that child might open a paper that says homosexual elected in San Francisco and now there are two new options—one is to go to California and the other is to stay in San Antonio and fight.

Milk, who was the first openly gay person to be elected to public office, was assassinated in 1978 as was Mayor George Moscone, who supported Milk, by Dan White, a former city council member and firefighter from San Francisco who failed to be reelected. Milk's assassination serves as a constant reminder to gay and lesbian people of the most extreme and violent manifestation of homophobia—murder.

Whereas the bulk of research about lesbian and gay youth has narrowly focused on coming-out issues (Hetrick & Martin, 1987; Martin & Hetrick, 1988; Zera, 1992); on pathological issues such as drug and alcohol abuse, suicide, truancy, and unsafe sex (Gibson, 1989; Kourany, 1987; Remafedi, Farrow, & Deischer, 1991); and on identity formation (Cass, 1979; Froiden, 1989; Sophie, 1985); very little attention has been paid to the contexts of identity formation within schools, family, peers, work, and leisure (Kivel, 1996). In their study about a gay/lesbian youth group in Chicago, Herdt and Boxer (1993) have begun to address the contexts of identity development by discussing some of the developmental, clinical, and life-stage issues affecting lesbian and gay youth. However, they add that more research needs to focus on how gay and lesbian adolescents formulate and institute their life course around their social environment and what it means for them to be marginalized and, perhaps, ostracized.

Unfortunately, it would appear that for lesbian and gay adolescents to experience leadership through social interaction, they would have to be perceived as heterosexual. Otherwise they might refrain from participating in certain activities such as organized sports, clubs, choruses, drama, elected offices, and as active learners in the classroom. O'Conor (1994) has suggested that in order to survive in school, many gay and lesbian teens have to construct a false, heterosexual self. Some teenagers have sex with opposite sex members in an attempt to prove that they are straight to avoid being called "queer," "fag," or "dyke." Lesbian and gay people may also engage in antigay violence as a shield to hide their own homosexuality (O'Conor, 1994).

Minority Adolescents

Research on minority adolescents who are gay, lesbian, or bisexual has typically focused on pathological behaviors (i.e., drug and alcohol use, prostitution, unsafe sex, and suicide). For minority youth, marginalization in the United States may be greater than for white teens because family, church, and community emphasize a group allegiance over personal independence. Also, a gay/lesbian orientation may be viewed as a deviant white influence preventing marriage and/or reproduction. Adherence to religious beliefs, family expectations for heterosexual union and offspring, and community mores and obligations would affect black Americans, where church and community are usually inseparable. Affected also are Hispanic Americans, including Mexican, Cuban, and Puerto Rican Americans, as well as others originally from primarily Catholic nations that embrace the Catholic Church's hierarchical beliefs. Others similarly affected are Asian Americans, including those from China, Japan, Korea, Vietnam, Thailand, Cambodia, and the Philippines, who place greater importance on family tradition and community mores than do either second or third generations of these peoples, who have more often adopted the individualism valued culturally by white Americans. Although there is greater racial tolerance in the gay/lesbian community, those minorities who are more removed from their immigrant generation and who are individualistic still face prejudice and discrimination as they try to fit into white gay/lesbian America or remain separate from it and who may be seen by white gays as separatists. More often race or ethnicity may add to greater ostracism if a particular individual does not conform to what is considered physically appealing. Minority adolescents are even less likely than white Americans to get family support if or when they come out.

Native Americans have traditionally been the most tolerant and welcoming to gay, lesbian, and bisexual youth, referring to them as "two spirits," representing the complete masculine/feminine person. Western influence has eroded that acceptance within Native American people, but as tribes embrace their ancestry and tradition, acceptance may prevail.

The Role of the Social Worker

Although the majority of well-trained social workers do not invest in reparative, ex-gay therapy, too many question a young person's unequivocal declaration that he or she is lesbian, gay, or bisexual by considering the adolescent too young to know his or her orientation or by considering it a phase. Too often the social worker who counsels young people trivializes orientation declarations from adolescents, often speaking to their own discomfort and ignorance about gay, lesbian, and bisexual youth. Wells's files hold the following account:

> It was hard enough to disclose the fact that I was gay to the first psychiatric social worker that I saw, but when he passed over what I'd said without dealing with it, I felt unacknowledged. Since he didn't seem to want to deal with what I'd said, I had nothing else to say. The second psychiatric social worker I saw told me I was depressed and that depressed teens often think that they're gay. It was a stage in my depressive state. I was misdiagnosed until I went to college. I am gay; and, I'm also obsessive compulsive. I'm still angry at these two so-called professionals for making it more difficult for me to deal with my orientation. I trusted them with my core and they violated me. I'll never seek professional care from another straight male psychiatric social worker.

It is paramount that social workers recognize that gay, lesbian, and bisexual youth see their sexual orientation as natural and as an essential part of their identity. Although their sexual identity, like other aspects of identity, is socially constructed and socially produced within the contexts of cultural values and norms, the social worker needs to be an advocate for gay, lesbian, and bisexual teens because supportive others may not be readily available.

On a cautionary note, because many parents may believe that their daughter or son is confused about her or his sexual identity and that affirming a gay, lesbian, or bisexual identity more often sways youth, education for parents and guardians of lesbian, gay, and bisexual youth is essential. The lesbian, gay, or bisexual social worker may stand in double jeopardy in this regard: pushing toward gay, lesbian, or bisexual identity formation as well as accused of behaving seductively. In selecting a lesbian, gay, or bisexual social worker for an adolescent who has already come out but is dealing with related issues, the accusation that gay, lesbian, and bisexual social workers are proselytizing is not as likely to become an issue. The social worker, whether gay, bisexual, lesbian, or heterosexual, needs to be comfortable with her or his own sexual identity and feel comfortable with, as well as informed about, gay, lesbian, and bisexual youth and the issues they present. Parents, Families, and Friends of Lesbians and Gays (PFLAG) may be a recommendation to parents and teens as a supportive group of others who care for and love gay, lesbian, and bisexual adolescents.

Conclusion

The unwillingness to acknowledge the existence and specific problems of lesbian, gay, and bisexual youth, such as verbal and physical harassment, ostracism and isolation, brought on by an antigay/lesbian society adds stressors and barriers for gay, lesbian, and bisexual adolescents to make the transition from childhood to adulthood successfully. Moreover, the issues associated with adolescent identity formation—cognitive, social, emotional, biological and moral—are further exacerbated by cultural narratives that tell young people, either directly or indirectly, that to be lesbian or gay is bad and that you must conform to compulsory heterosexuality.

Perhaps the most important coping strategy for young gays and lesbians is learning to present a heterosexual front or to remain invisible as a lesbian or gay person. The fear that someone might discover their lesbian, gay, or bisexual identity is so pervasive in self-reporting interviews that concealing their orientation takes great psychological and physical energy. Withdrawing from family and peers, investing in gender-appropriate activities and mannerisms when possible, or finding a reason other than being gay or lesbian to avoid the most uncomfortable and interesting activities that outwardly demonstrate straightness are part of the charade. Leisure and work activities that might be enjoyable are sacrificed so others might not pick up on a sense of differentness. It is unclear what the long-term effects of these constraints might be in terms of identity development, but the more immediate impact would be a lack of skill development in areas in which one's identity might be discovered, resulting in missed social and leadership opportunities. From a wellness and health perspective, anger, both self-directed and other directed, can and often does lead to depression, alcohol and drug use, risk-taking sexuality, runaways, and suicide.

Social workers need to believe that lesbian, gay, and bisexual youth are "normal" and that youth of color, including gay, lesbian, and bisexual youth, are not viewed primarily as engaging in problem behaviors. Then perhaps social workers as well as researchers and theorists would not conceptualize lesbian, gay, and bisexual youth as representing a deficit model but, rather, employ the perspective that within every group of young people, there will be diversity based on race, ethnicity, gender, and sexual identity.

REFERENCES

Cass, V. (1979). Homosexual identity formation: A theoretical model. *Journal of Homosexuality 4* (3), 219–235.

Deisher, R. (1989). Adolescent homosexuality: Preface. *Journal of Homosexuality 17* (1/2), xiii–xv.

Dennis, D. L., & Harlow, R. E. (1986). Gay youth and the right to education. *Yale Law Journal & Policy Review 4* (2), 447–478.

Due, L. (1995). *Joining the tribe.* New York: Anchor Books.

Erikson, E. (1968). *Identity: Youth and crisis.* New York: W. W. Norton & Company.

Froiden, R. (1989). The formation of homosexual identities. In G. Herdt (Ed.), *Gay and lesbian youth.* London: Harrington Park Press.

Garner, B., & Smith, R. W. (1976, June). Are there really any gay male athletes? An empirical survey. Paper presented at Society for the Scientific Study of Sex Conference, San Diego, CA.

Geh, J. (1989, November 2). Sullivan tosses suicide report. *The Sentinel,* p. 1.

Gibson, P. (1989). Gay male and lesbian youth suicide. Alcohol, Drug Abuse, and Mental Health Administration, *Report of the Secretary's Task Force on Youth Suicide.* Volume 3: *Prevention and Interventions in Youth Suicide.* DHHS Pub. No. (ADM) 89–1623. Washington, DC: Superintendent of Documents, U.S. Government Printing Office.

Herdt, G., & Boxer, A. (1993). *Children of horizons: How gay and lesbian teens are leading a new way out of the closet.* Boston: Beacon Press.

Hetrick, E. S., & Martin, A. D. (1987). Development issues and their resolution for gay and lesbian adolescents. *Journal of Homosexuality 14* (1/2), 25–43.

Hunter, J., & Schaecher, R. (1987). Stresses on lesbian and gay adolescents in schools. *Social Work in Education 9* (3), 180–186.

Jones, M. A., & Gabriel, M. A. (1998). *The utilization of psychotherapy by lesbians and gay men: Findings from a nationwide study.* Unpublished paper. New York: 1 Washington Square N, #G2, 10003–6654.

Kivel, B. (1996). In on the outside, out on the inside: Lesbian/gay/bisexual youth, identity and leisure. Unpublished dissertation. Athens, GA: University of Georgia.

Kopay, D., & Young, P. D. (1977). *The David Kopay story.* New York: Arbor House.

Kourany, R. F. C. (1987). Suicide among homosexual adolescents. *Journal of Homosexuality 13* (4), 111–117.

Martin, A. D., & Hetrick, E. S. (1988). The stigmatization of the gay and lesbian adolescent. *Journal of Homosexuality 15* (1/2), 163–183.

O'Conor, A. (1994). Who gets called queer in school? Lesbian, gay and bisexual teenagers, homophobia and high school. *The High School Journal 77* (1/2), 7–13.

Remafedi, G., Farrow, J. A., & Deisher, R. W. (1991). Risk factors for attempted suicide in gay and bisexual youth. *Pediatrics 87* (6), 869–875.

Rosellini, L. (1975, November). Gays in professional sports. *The Washington Star.* p. 1.

Schmiechen, R. (Producer), & Epslein, R. (Director and Co-Producer). (1986). *The times of Harvey Milk.* [Film]. Beverly Hills, CA: Pacific Arts Video.

Sedgwick, E. K. (1993). *Tendencies.* Durham, NC: Duke University Press.

Sophie, J. (1985). A critical examination of stage theories of lesbian identity development. *Journal of Homosexuality 12* (2), 39–51.

Uribe, V., & Harbeck, K. (1991). Addressing the needs of lesbian, gay, and bisexual youth: The origins of PROJECT 10 and school-based intervention. *Journal of Homosexuality 22* (3/4), 9–28.

Zera, D. (1992). Coming of age in a heterosexist world: The development of gay/lesbian adolescents. *Adolescence 27* (108), 849–854.

CHAPTER

5 Sexuality and Homosexuality

The opposite of death is desire.

—Tennessee Williams, *A Streetcar Named Desire*

Whether they admit it or not, what really bothers people about gays and lesbians is their sexuality. What is called homophobia, therefore, is really *erotophobia,* a revulsion, fear, or dread of sexuality. A student in one of Wells's human sexuality classes exemplifies well how this is manifested. After viewing explicit videos of same-sex sexual relationships in order to ascertain that they are human sexual behaviors, rather than gay, lesbian, or heterosexual behaviors, the student announced in front of eighty peers, "I wasn't homophobic until I saw those videos!" Not true. To see and recognize sexual behaviors as part of human experience, aware that what people enjoy and want is a very personal choice and may differ from someone else's choice regardless of the makeup of the sex of the individuals involved in the sexual relationship, is to begin to free ourselves from our erotophobic socialization.

The Language of Sexuality

We live in a culture, a world generally, in which we are strongly socialized to hold very negative attitudes and beliefs about sexuality. In our own predominant cultural socialization, one of the most significant determinants of our negative responses comes out of slang language usage for sexual behavior, sexual anatomy, and sexual orientation. Referring to sexual behaviors as *fucking* or *screwing* and sexual anatomy as *meat, cock,* or *cunt* and gays and lesbians as *fags* or *dykes,* we learn very early, often by age five, that these words are powerful, hurtful, and negative. When we refer to sexual relations as *the dirty deed* and to educationally explicit videos as *dirty movies,* we're repeating the erotophobic responses about sexuality that we've been taught since early childhood. It bears mentioning that slang terminology about sexuality may take on different meanings other than profanity as we mature and give varied meanings to sexuality. Slang language may come to be used and viewed as erotic, as well as denoting power, control, and domination.

Gays and lesbians are not immune to the effects of language regarding their sexual orientation and sexual expression. Words used to refer to lesbians and gays and their sexuality are overwhelmingly negative, primarily stereotyping them as sex role incongruent and sexually deviant. Reactions to hurtful language have fostered a movement by repressed minority groups in our culture to reclaim slang language or words formerly used to hurt, discredit, humiliate, discriminate, and put another person down. By incorporating words as *fag, queer,* and *dyke* into positive self-definitions, gays and lesbians are showing a history of survival and taking power away from those who are prejudicial and discriminatory. The use of slang language by outsiders, heterosexuals, to refer to gays and lesbians may escalate to gay bashing, resulting in personal injury or death for the victim.

However, the overall effects for most people is to relate slang references to sexuality as vulgar, obscene, bad, and dirty, coloring our adult perceptions of sexuality in general. Interestingly, slang sexual terms in the Western world are used as formal terminology in Nigeria. So on Nigerian television, *cock, cunt,* and *fuck* are used as proper words whereas *penis, vagina,* and *coitus* would be considered Nigerian slang and inappropriate for an audience. This occurred because the oppressors used *penis, vagina,* and *coitus;* the common soldier used *cock, cunt,* and *fuck.* The oppressed population identified with those who were among them. No culture has a sexual language, per se, that is, a language for sexuality that can be used in all social contexts yet is erotic. Instead, we draw from slang, formal or medical terms, euphemisms, and baby talk. If we use inappropriate words in a certain social context we may be censored or rejected. Thus, choosing words to talk about sexuality may be a risk to our status within a group or by another person. This may be why many people do not use erotic words or any other words to talk about sexuality. If you have ever wondered why it is so difficult to talk about sexuality, you have to choose the "right" words for the "appropriate" social context. Because of our varying socialization and comfort with sexuality, men and women, gays and straights view what is erotic language differently.

The Effects of Erotophobia

For heterosexuals, erotophobia interferes with developing comfortable and pleasurable sexual relations. It is one thing to recognize that there are sexual behaviors that are not appealing to you and to refuse to participate in those. It is quite another thing to find certain sexual behaviors appealing but to eliminate them from your sexual repertoire because of homophobic, or more appropriately, erotophobic reactions.

Research findings (Wells, 1992) suggest that virtually all heterosexual males and females classify sexual behaviors as predominantly heterosexual or predominantly homosexual rather than not orientation specific. Except for vagina-penis coitus, all sexual behaviors occur across orientation categories. Those human sexual behaviors most frequently designated as homosexual are the use of vibrators (misinterpreted) as penis substitutes for lesbian vaginal penetration; stimulating one's own genitals with a sexual partner; and kissing a partner after the partner had performed fellatio or cunnilingus. College women and men are similar in their reluctance to participate in sexual behaviors that they think are homosexual or that they think a partner would label as such. As a result, both sexes limit themselves in the sexual behaviors that are available to them. Couples may find themselves locked into rigidly defined sexual behaviors out of fear of rejection by a partner. This often leads to routine sexual interaction. Consequently, sexual practices become predictable, affecting sexual frequency and overall sexual enjoyment. Interestingly, the vast majority of people who engage in same-sex relations do not define themselves as gay or lesbian.

Discrimination under the Sodomy Laws and the Defense of Marriage Act

As of May 1995, twenty-two states and Puerto Rico had laws banning sodomy, oral and anal sex, or nonprocreative sex, between consenting adults. In only eleven states, the sodomy laws apply to heterosexuals as well as gay and lesbian couples. Although many heterosexuals could be prosecuted for breaking sodomy laws, gay men have usually been singled out for prosecution. Slowly states have been decriminalizing sodomy. In 1986 the U.S. Supreme Court upheld the rights of states to maintain their sodomy laws after hearing the *Hardwick v. Bowers* case.

Michael Hardwick was arrested on August 3, 1982. A police officer entered his apartment to collect unpaid parking tickets with the permission of his roommate and without a search warrant. The officer went to Michael Hardwick's bedroom and found him engaged in oral sex with a male partner. Hardwick was arrested and charged with sodomy. This case reached the Georgia Supreme Court and was prosecuted by Georgia attorney general Michael Bowers. The Georgia Supreme Court upheld that state's sodomy law, which is punishable by up to twenty years imprisonment. Hardwick appealed to the U.S. Supreme Court for a hearing claiming unconstitutional arrest and the Court agreed to hear his case. In a vote of 5–4, the Supreme Court said that the Constitution does not protect homosexual relations between consenting adults in the privacy of their own homes. Thus, each state had the right to outlaw same-sex sexual acts. Supreme Court Justice Lewis Powell, who retired from the Court following that decision, regretted his swing vote to constitute a majority for maintaining sodomy laws. Michael Hardwick served time in prison and died of AIDS after his release.

In 1991, Michael Bowers had offered employment to Robin Shahar. When he discovered that she was planning a same-sex union, he withdrew his offer for a position in his office. She sued and lost. In his court argument, Bowers said that "he could not separate the way someone does their job from the way they respect the law" (Trotman, 1997, p. 13). During the Hardwick and Shahar trials, Bowers was carrying on an adulterous affair dating from 1986 to 1997. Adultery in Georgia is also a crime just as is sodomy, but Bowers was never prosecuted. He did drop out of the Republican race for governor yet has retained his position as state attorney of Georgia (Trotman, 1997, p. 13).

Hawaii circuit court judge Kevin Chang ruled in *Baehr v. Muike* (1996) that Hawaii's refusal to grant marriage licenses to same-sex couples violated the state's constitution. Judge Chang based his ruling on the state's failure to show that the well-being of children and families would be adversely affected by same-sex marriages. This decision made Hawaii the first U.S. state to recognize same-sex marriages and led to a mass rush in other states to prevent recognition of such marriages. A public referendum in Hawaii in 1998, however, seems to have precluded this possibility.

Advocates of same-sex marriage believe that banning it is a form of sex discrimination and is a violation of the U.S. Constitution, which states that by law every person is entitled to equal protection. Banning same-sex marriages that may be recognized in other states denies gay and lesbian couples legal and financial benefits that are granted to heterosexual couples, for example, to inherit from a spouse who dies without a will to avoid inheritance taxes between spouses, to make medical decisions in the event of a partner's critical injury or illness, to receive social security survivor's benefits, to bring a wrongful death suit, to live in a neighborhood zoned as "single family only," to seek child custody, and to secure employee insurance benefits for a spouse. There are numerous other benefits, which by law only heterosexuals enjoy, referred to as heterosexual privilege.

Both the sodomy laws and the Defense of Marriage Act are based upon what people who are gay and lesbian do sexually. Commonly, sexual behavior between monogamously committed, consenting same-sex adults is labeled promiscuous by our elected government officials as well as by the general public. The double standard is clear.

Etiology of Sexual Orientation

All too often the biased question asked is, "What causes homosexuality?" This question is biased in addressing only one end of the sexuality continuum. The one-sided causality question, furthermore, implies deviance. For example, what causes crime? What causes disease? With few exceptions, college textbooks in psychology and human sexuality with their one mandatory chapter on sexual orientation present homosexuality as a condition to be explained. Missing, of course, are any theoretical perspectives on how individuals might become heterosexual. The only reference to heterosexuality under the generic heading of sexual orientation is as a mere dimension on the Kinsey rating scale. Typically, homosexuality is explained in terms of psychoanalytic theory, social learning theory, hormone imbalance, and biological predisposition. Significantly, in every other chapter of these texts, the focus is on heterosexuality.

Scientifically, the question asked should be, "What causes sexual orientation?" In other words, "Why are individuals found to identify with a variety of sexual orientations along a continuum?"

To date, research evidence, often flawed, can be used to support a range of reasons why people fall along a continuum of sexual orientation. Included is speculation about socialization, prenatal hormones from mother and/or embryo/fetus, biological predisposition and genetics, transgenderism that fuses sexual orientation to feminine or masculine traits, as well as a combination of biology and life events that are varied for each individual. The key seems to be who each of us can be in love with combined with sexual desire. Our romantic and sexual fantasies tell more about us than do our sexual behaviors.

Sex Role Incongruity

Feminists may argue that masculine and feminine traits are socially constructed stereotypes about acceptable and unacceptable male and female behavior within a rigid cultural context. Transgenderists will argue that sexual orientation is bilateral so that people are gay, bisexual, or straight and are also more or less feminine, masculine, and/or androgynous. Currently research findings report that about 10 to 15 percent of the population are sex role incongruent. That is, as males or females, peoples' behaviors are more feminine than masculine or more masculine than feminine, respectively. Gay males and lesbians are no more or less likely to be sex role incongruent or sex role congruent than are heterosexual males or females. Stereotypes of gay males behaving as limp-wristed, lisping effeminates and lesbians behaving as masculine, combat-ready foot soldiers permeate our imaginations, often because that reflects the narrow range of our experience. When the gay male who is effeminate and the lesbian who is masculine come out, although a small percentage of the gay and lesbian population, they are more likely to become visible representations because they are labeled as stereotypes anyway. Such individuals acknowledge their obvious nonnormative bearing in order to be who they feel they are and to develop a support system of friends and/or family members.

Research Findings

Evidence is mounting to support a genetic component or biological predisposition for sexual orientation. The concordance rate for homosexuality is significantly higher for identical twins than it is for all other siblings. The likelihood of finding other gay or lesbian relatives in a family increases when a family member comes out. The National Gay Task Force ran a poster campaign a number of years ago to try to bring homosexuality into family awareness, making it easier for people to acknowledge their sexual orientation by stating, "Who in your family is gay?"

This does not mean that sexual orientation is fixed or inflexible, but no research record exists of an individual jumping from one end of the continuum to the other end no matter how motivated he or she is to change his or her sexual orientation. Actually sexual orientation appears to be a relatively stable characteristic over the life course. Individuals identify attractions and feelings toward others as they go through life. We are indoctrinated into expected sex roles through gender socialization and, even more profoundly, heterosexual sexuality. As a result, people may not consciously understand the implications of their romantic and sexual attractions until a later time in their lives because of strong societal taboos against same-sex affectional and sexual relationships. So an individual who marries heterosexually only later to leave that relationship for a same-sex partner might be assumed to have changed his or her sexual orientation. Actually, this individual would have had the flexibility or lack thereof in partner relationships. Those who might be less concerned with the sex of a partner would more often be bisexual or in the middle of the continuum. As people move in either direction from the middle of the continuum, there is usually less flexibility in relating romantically and sexually to both sexes. However, a person may not necessarily follow his or her sexual orientation in partner selection. Individuals who unconsciously or consciously marry heterosexually, but who have a predominantly homosexual orientation, or individuals who live with a same-sex person in a sexual partner relationship, but who are predominantly heterosexual, find other bonds may supersede sexual interest. In this regard same-sex sexual and affectional partners may be a choice. Yet, for the vast majority of people who identify themselves as gay, lesbian, or bisexual, no choice is involved; it is who they are. Simply ask those individuals who are lesbian, gay, or bisexual. The majority will tell you it is their nature. In a nonbigoted world, it should not matter whether choice is involved in matters of sexual orientation. Parenthetically, it does matter. People are less likely to oppose gay rights if those who are lesbian, gay, or bisexual are "born that way." Fear is also expressed by gays and lesbians who state that if genetics is found to be conclusive in the etiology of sexual orientation and those genes can be detected during pregnancy, a couple who learns that they are going to have a lesbian or gay child may more likely abort that fetus. The 1997 movie *Twilight of the Gods,* adapted from a play by Jonathan Tolius introduced on Broadway in 1993, hauntingly deals with that premise.

Establishing Sexual Orientation

The importance of one's homosexuality in her or his life may vary greatly. For some it is secretive or revealed to very few. For others it is their most influential trait. Friendships, political ideologies, consumerism, religiosity, definitions of family, and decision making revolve around being lesbian or gay. Individuals who are members of racial or ethnic minorities in the United States may respond in various ways to their multiminority status. That is, for some, race and ethnicity will be more influential than their sexual orientation, whereas for others sexual orientation will predominate. Members of racial and ethnic minorities may oscillate between these two variables at various times of their lives based on which characteristic others use to express prejudice and/or discrimination.

Gay and Lesbian Children and Adolescents

Erotophobia may be particularly difficult for youngsters who come to recognize a same-sex romantic and sexual attraction. Denial and self-hatred resulting in internalized homophobia stem from negative parental or family views, peer reactions, and societal condemnations of homosexuality, often based on religious interpretations leading to difficulty in developing a positive self-worth. Romantic and sexual interactions that most adolescents experience as a part of developing decision-making skills necessary to prepare them for adult romantic and sexual roles are delayed, making gay and lesbian adolescents more vulnerable to suicide attempts as well as successful suicide. At least half of all adolescent runaways are gay or lesbian, many thrown out by parents or family members when their homosexuality is discovered. Children learn early, often on the playground in kindergarten, that to be called a "fag" is a powerfully negative label even though very few understand the full implications of the term.

Many adolescents have sexual fantasies involving people of their own sex. Some engage in sex play with same-sex individuals. The meaningfulness of these fantasies and behaviors varies widely depending on the romantic and sexual interpretation these have in each person's life at that point and beyond. For approximately 4 percent to 10 percent of the population, the significance of early romantic and sexual attraction to members of their own sex becomes stronger and more obvious. Some gay men and lesbians report awareness of being "different" in early (age five) to middle (age ten) childhood.

The research literature reports stereotypical feminine interests and behavior for some gay men when boys. These include a preference for girls' games, playing with dolls, imagining themselves as dancers or models, or being called a sissy during their youth; or a lack of stereotypical masculine behaviors, such as a preference for boys' games including rough-and-tumble play, a desire to emulate one's father, or imagining themselves as a sports figure. However, the literature conversely finds a higher percentage of college athletes, up to 20 percent, than college nonathletes who have engaged in homosexual activities. Most of these athletes also report sexual activities with females as well. Perhaps there is a higher percentage of the population that is capable of responding to both sexes erotically than self-reports indicate and that athletic, in-shape men and women blur the rigid ends of the dichotomy to label themselves as gay or straight.

Gay and lesbian adolescents usually have some heterosexual dating experiences but report ambivalent feelings about them, saying they preferred not to kiss or be sexually involved with such a date. Rather, they preferred a friendship basis for any type of heterosexual relationship.

Society has difficulty accepting adolescents as sexual beings. In fact the majority of parents do not want their children to have positive attitudes toward masturbation! When young people express a gay, lesbian, or bisexual orientation, those closest to them report being uncomfortable. This reaction results in a secretive and an invisible population due to the dire consequences wrought by homophobic reactions of significant others in their lives. Very few of these adolescents feel they can talk to their parents about their sexual and affectional attractions.

Much unnecessary suffering could be prevented were parents to have no expectations for their childrens' sexual orientation, to tell their children, it is okay to bring home a same-sex or an other-sex romantic partner, to tell them it is okay to express their sexuality.

Establishing Intimacy

In late adolescence and young adulthood, men and women are confronted with a vitally important developmental task, that of establishing intimate relationships in sexual unions. A relatively small minority of people define themselves as bisexual, or having sexual involvement and romantic attraction to both men and women. For those who are heterosexual, the task of developing and solidifying sexual orientation is simplified because of societal expectations and support. But for those who are lesbian, gay, or doubt their sexual orientation, the task of coming to grips with who they are sexually and intimately is acutely more difficult because they are violating fundamental societal norms in attempting to solidify their sexual orientation. Thus, for gay, lesbian, and bisexual individuals, confirming their sexual and affectional orientation may take considerably longer, and in too many cases may never be fulfilled as full-functioning sexual beings. This is not to assume that because someone is nongay they achieve full-functioning sexual status. Because of erotophobia, most people do not realize their sexual potential whether straight or gay or lesbian.

The percentage of people who are bisexual does not appear to be changing within the population. However, more people are embracing that label as they recognize sexual attractions to females and males. Formerly, unless people were in the middle of the sexual orientation continuum, they identified as either heterosexual or homosexual. When gay, lesbian, and bisexual panel members come into classes to address students regarding sexual orientation, it is common to hear bisexual panel members state that although they recognize other-sex attractions, they lean more toward the homosexual end of the continuum or vice versa. What is changing is the definition of bisexuality, which is expanding to include a wider range of the continuum than was formerly recognized.

Identifying oneself as gay, lesbian, or bisexual may take considerable time and occur in a number of stages, referred to as the coming-out process. From a sexuality and intimacy perspective this first involves a recognition that one can be erotically attracted to same-sex individuals through fantasy, behavior, or both. People vary greatly as to how they might respond to this conscious awareness of homoeroticism, with some seeking sexual intimacies in the company of others so predisposed whereas some may suppress any overt sexual contact with others and fantasize or use erotic material while masturbating. Usually recognition of homoerotic interests precedes homosexual activities with others by several years. A milestone in gay or lesbian sexual and affectional identity is a person's first love affair that unifies romantic erotic love. Finally, lesbians or gay men may embrace identification and affiliation with the gay subculture. This may mean living in a world of gay friends and supportive family members and patronizing gay-owned establishments.

Lesbians, Gay Men, and Bisexuals in Heterosexual Marriages

There are no reliable numbers regarding gay men, lesbians, and bisexuals who are participting in or have participated in a heterosexual marriage. Estimates run into the millions. Gays and lesbians who marry heterosexually span a wide range of awareness at the time they marry; however, those who are cognizant of their sexual orientation at the time of marriage may be in denial about who they are or feel pressure to marry heterosexually. Most love their spouse at the time of marriage and want children. Some believe that having a marriage partner will help them overcome their same-sex feelings or that they can channel their energies into their marriages and families so as to obliterate same-sex sexual desires. Rarely does this seem to work in maintaining the heterosexual relationship as an intimate, sexual union. Both members of the dyad report loneliness, alienation, and depression as the gay or lesbian spouse pulls away physically and psychologically from the relationship.

When heterosexual partners discover a spouse's homosexuality, they usually feel deceived and ashamed of themselves and their choice in a marriage partner. Conversely, the lesbian or gay spouse often expresses remorse, sadness, and guilt for having hurt loved ones. If they have children, the gay or lesbian parent may fear rejection and loss.

Disclosure of homosexuality usually results in separation and divorce. Many lesbians and gays are parents at the time their marriages end. It is important for them to affirm their lesbian or gay identities by seeking bonds within the gay community as well as to maintain their parenting role. Because negative stereotypes portray gays and lesbians as self-centered and antifamily, fusing their identities and their parenting role becomes crucial.

For the heterosexual spouse whose marriage has dissolved or been based on what may be seen as deception, the task of reclaiming self-affirmation may best be established through counseling and supportive others. In larger metropolitan areas support groups for heterosexual ex-spouses of gays, lesbians, and bisexuals are available. Issues that may be pertinent to these ex-spouses are their choices of a partner, their attractiveness, and sexuality.

When a gay man selects a heterosexual marriage partner, he often seeks out someone who he perceives as less threatening or demanding sexually. The female partner describes him as someone who behaved as a gentleman during courtship. Within the marriage relationship, she is likely to be the sexual initiator. Because females are not taught to be sexual initiators in most cultures, sexual relations occur infrequently or not at all. Lesbians are less likely than gay men to be aware of their sexual orientation at the time of marriage. They may also have traditionally assigned roles as wife and mother. They may indeed love their husbands and participate in sexual relations. Their choice in partners is usually the sensitive, gentle, caring male.

Often the marriage dissolves when heterosexually married gay men or lesbians fall in love with someone of the same sex, realizing their unfilled intimacy, affectional, and sexual needs in their heterosexual union.

For an understanding of how bisexuality is experienced by a married bisexual female, see Box 5.1.

BOX 5.1

On Bisexuality, Choices, and Miss America: Award Winning Scholarship Essay

I like to label people. I think we all do. It is so nice when people fit into categories and groups, when we can look at someone and say, "Oh, he's gay," and feel like we know all about him. I think society encourages us to think this way. Our political candidates are either liberal or conservative, people are either white or black, and even contestants on the Miss America Pageant are organized like Barbie dolls. There is Literacy Barbie, and Domestic Abuse Barbie, and AIDS Awareness Barbie. Each woman has her own separate platform which defines her, and she is judged on that one aspect alone, not her feelings on any other issues.

The problem with this is that although we like to label others, we find that we despise being labeled ourselves. Our lives are multifaceted, and it would be as wrong to judge someone on his or her political views according to his or her religious affiliation, party, or skin color as it is to judge someone's ability to serve in the military because of his or her sexual orientation.

But we all do this, every day, every time we meet someone, and we are known to others by our religion, our job, and our family status, even though these aspects of our lives may have little to do with the person we feel ourselves to be. Obviously, this kind of thinking can lead to dangerous generalizations, from everything from "Feminists are man-haters" to "Politicians are all corrupt" to "Gay men always abuse little boys." None of these statements is true, and yet we often judge people based on these kinds of things. Often, we can be somewhat correct, but too often we are way off-base. For example, why do people assume that since Prince Charles was a bad husband he is a bad father? Why do we assume that all gay people want the right to marry?

The point of this essay is to bring to light our tendency to make generalizations about people based on one aspect of their lives. Having done that (I hope), I now want to bring to your attention several myths about bisexual people which I want to dispel. Of course, what you are about to read is only my experience as a bisexual woman, and will not hold true for all bisexual people. These are my opinions. But I think that they are mostly true.

1. Bisexual people cannot make up their minds. They are really gay or straight, and are just confused.

It is true that I don't know if I should call myself gay or straight, or both or neither. Bisexuality has traditionally been grouped with homosexuality because it is not heterosexuality. But if a bisexual person is not straight, then he or she is also not gay.

We are not confused or indecisive. Bisexuality is not a middle ground. It is an orientation all in itself, and does not involve "choosing" any more than any other orientation.

2. Bisexuals are straight people who want to be accepted by the gay community, or vice versa.

Pretending to be bisexual is just as wrong and unhealthy as pretending to be straight (or gay). I'm sure that people do this, but it is not the sign of a sane or truthful person. True bisexuals may want to belong to one group or the other, and they may feel more comfortable with friends of a certain orientation. This is not choosing. Remember, you can't change your orientation.

3. Bisexuals cannot ever be satisfied with one person. Falling in love with someone is not dependent on anything except your compatibility with that person. Yes, it is possible to be bisexual and monogamous, to only want to be with one person. I do it every day and have for the past two years. I can't tell you if it is any harder than if you are gay or straight because I have never experienced it any other way. For me, it is easy.

4. Bisexuals who have opposite-sex partners are choosing the easy way—passing—and are doing so because they have been pressured by society. Yes, it is nice to pass. Being in a heterosexual relationship is a lot more acceptable, and no one need know that I am bi. But many people do know, because I have

(continued)

BOX 5.1 Continued

chosen to be out, and this effectively cancels my "passing" to anyone except strangers.

I am sure that some bisexuals, if not many, choose to be with an opposite-sex partner because it is easier. I did not. My falling in love had nothing to do with my husband's gender. I think that the bisexuals who do pass because of their "straight" relationships may be mostly those who consider themselves straight, and are afraid to identify as bi. However, for those who do, the gay community can be as unfriendly to those who have opposite-sex partners as the straight community can be to those who have same-sex partners. If straight society influences bisexuals, then gay society does too, and those bisexuals who choose to "pass" as gay to fit in with the "family" are just as wrong. We are pretty much damned either way, so we would appreciate it if we were not judged by which gender we "chose" for our partners.

5. Bisexuals are nymphomaniacs.

Oh, please. Someone did once tell me this, claiming that people who call themselves bisexual only do it to get away with cheating on their partners or spouses.

First of all, we know (I hope) that bisexuals can be satisfied with one person, and second of all, if I am a nymphomaniac, then so is Santa Claus.

6. Bisexuals belong in one world—either gay or straight—and they have to choose.

I have struggled with this idea before, and I shall try to explain to you my views. Bisexuals are truly neither gay nor straight, nor are we completely separated from those two orientations. I think that a lot of bisexuals do feel they have to choose, and I am sad for them. I would hope that by marrying a man I have not cut myself off from my gay family, and that by being bi, I have not become "not straight." Bisexuality is a hard road to walk, and I did not "choose" to be bi because I pass, or because I can't make a commitment to either side, or because I want to be both gay and straight, choosing one here and one there like choosing heels or flats, depending on the occasion. (I'm sorry if I lost all you butch lesbians with that analogy.) I was born bi, like thousands of other men and women, and we shall all spend our lives trying to figure out exactly what that means.

Source: by D. M. Seager; printed with permission of D. M. Seager, Iowa State University.

Affectional and Sexual Expression

What same-sex couples do affectionately and sexually usually provokes strong negative emotions in our erotophobic society. Aversion may be based on fear of one's own arousal, learned disgust, breaking what one sees as moral or religious codes of conduct, and ignorance.

Recall that Adams, Wright, and Lohr (1996) studied arousal in self-reported heterosexual college males by measuring penile blood engorgement during a gay homoerotic film after dividing respondents into high and low homophobic groups. Less than a quarter of the low homophobic group showed penile engorgement whereas over half of the high homophobic group had penile engorgement. These findings do not mean desire for erotic interchanges with other males but, rather, that responding to two attractive people engaging in sexual behavior can be stimulating regardless of the actors' sex. It might also be suggested that those individuals who claim exclusive heterosexuality and fear any response to same-sex activity form the strongest negative reactions to such presentations. These same individuals are more likely to harbor hatred against gays and lesbians, possibly with violent reactions to people perceived to be lesbians or gays.

Our culture actively teaches its members that sexual organs, sexual fluids, sexual expression, sexual desire, and the naked human body are dirty, pornographic (particularly gay expressions of affection and sexuality), vile, and disgusting. It's one thing to say a particular sexual behavior, expression, or body part is not appealing; it's quite another to respond with "gross," "yuk," and censorship of erotic but not pornographic displays of sexuality. Our taboos taught through embarrassment, shame, punishment, and violence yield angry, calloused individuals who are more likely to victimize and hurt others or who cannot fully take responsibility for and enjoy their own sexuality.

Characteristics of Erotophobes

Individuals who support extrinsic fundamentalist religious doctrines (in other words, those who think everyone should believe the way they do) are the most erotophobic, sexually rigid people. They do not think in abstract terms but simplify gender roles and sexuality into "right" and "wrong." Their belief system views gays as the degradation and downfall of humankind. They do not believe lesbians and gays are moral people but are out to corrupt and convert others to their way of life. Often homophobes refer to the "gay lifestyle." C. A. Tripp (1975) said that gays and lesbians may have no more in common with each other than the coffee drinkers of the world; that is, people are unique. Representatives of the Catholic Church state that it's not sinful to be homosexual; however, it is sinful to act on it. Mainstream religious denominations are struggling with their acceptance of lesbian and gay members and clergy. Most world religions take a dim view of homosexuality. Only the Unitarian Universalists, Quakers, and Church of Christ members openly welcome and ordain gay and lesbian clergy. The Metropolitan Community Church founded by Troy Perry in 1968 in Los Angeles for Christian lesbians and gays welcome all members.

People who have a good friend or close family member who is lesbian or gay are more accepting of gays and lesbians. Indeed, those who classify themselves as anything but exclusively heterosexual along a heterosexual–homosexual continuum are less erotophobic. Characteristically, these individuals have invested time and energy into building and maintaining friendships and family relationships as well as engaged in greater self-awareness than many other people. During their self-discovery through self-psychoanalysis, they are more likely to have read accurate information about lesbians and gays that dispells stereotypes and misconceptions. Accurate information reduces homophobia.

Affectional and sexual behavior is still the most difficult aspect of homosexuality (as well as heterosexuality) for Americans to deal with. Viewing an explicit video is not a prescription to engage in what is being depicted, but to show that the range of human sexual behaviors covers a broad spectrum of the population. Behavior does not necessarily indicate what is going on in people's heads, which is the greatest part of our sexuality.

Similarities in Lesbian, Gay, and Heterosexual Sexuality

Every culture teaches its members, overtly or covertly, the sexual scripts that correspond to normative sexual behavior within that culture. This includes the sequence of sexual acts deemed appropriate for the level of intimacy within a relationship. Many people in the United States either do not believe that homosexuals, particularly males, can achieve the same feelings of intimacy as heterosexuals or discount the sexual intimacy of gays and lesbians as lustful and sinful.

Actually, the physical and personality characteristics that people find sexually attractive in one another are similar across the sexual orientation continuum. Although each of us may hold varying sexual scripts for what we deem appropriate and comfortable in forming a sexual relationship, we are influenced by our cultural norms, perhaps most similarly in the sequence of sexual behaviors we engage in to achieve sexual gratification. Most of us begin our sexual intimacies by holding, hugging, rubbing, caressing, and kissing. We move into deep kissing and fondling with and without clothing, including genital touching, masturbation, and oral-genital contact. At this point, heterosexual couples most often engage in coitus whereas gay males and lesbians use mutual masturbation and fellatio and cunnilingus to achieve orgasm. Only about half of all heterosexual women experience orgasm with any regularity through coitus with a male partner. Anal intercourse is incorporated into sexual intimacy with some regularity among some gay male couples, most often in mutually exclusive relationships. Some heterosexual couples occasionally to frequently use anal intercourse in their sexual repertoire. The sexual scripts of most couples are predictable and often settle into patterns and routines over time. Keeping sexual intimacy interesting and exciting proves to be a challenge for most romantic couples, regardless of their sexual orientation.

Differences in Lesbian, Gay, and Heterosexual Sexuality

Regardless of sexual orientation, people engage in similar behaviors stemming from learned sexual scripts or socialization. The vast majority of Westerners begin a sexual encounter in a loving relationship by holding and kissing. Most sexual communication is through touch, so caressing, rubbing, and stimulation of body parts designated as erogenous zones are the primary focus. Kissing and caressing become more intense and erotic when unclothed skin to skin contact occurs. When naked, couples may continue holding, kissing, and manually stimulating each other, often moving directly to their partner's genitals. Mutual masturbation and oral-genital contact may or may not be a prelude to coitus for heterosexual couples, whereas for gay and lesbian couples these behaviors are more likely to be used to achieve orgasm. Anal intercourse is practiced by more gay men than by heterosexuals. Lesbians may manually stimulate their partner's anus but do not penetrate the rectum as a common sexual technique. Nor is it the predominant means of achieving orgasm for most gay men. When anal intercourse is a part of a gay couple's repertoire, most often it is reciprocal. Because unprotected anal intercourse with a penis or a shared vibrator is the riskiest behavior for HIV transmission, male condoms should always be used for gay, lesbian, and heterosexual couples. If any couple is inserting vibrators or dildos into their vaginas or rectum that have been used on a partner, each insertion should require a new unused condom.

People are not spontaneous about their sexual activities but are usually predictable. Generally, research reports that sexual behaviors for most people follow sexual scripts. These scripts designate which criteria need to be present before someone engages in sexual activity as well as what they will do during sexual activity.

Lesbians and gay males give more erotic pleasure to their partners, are less goal oriented, are less likely to allow interruptions to ruin the mood of their sexual interactions (Masters & Johnson, 1979), and are more likely to talk with their partners about what they want sexually as well as use more erotic language (Wells, 1990) than heterosexuals.

Specifically, differences in dyadic sexual relationships for sexual orientation and gender show up when examining breast stimulation and oral-genital contact (Masters & Johnson, 1979). Lesbians are the most likely of couples to include breast stimulation both orally and manually in their sexual behavior, spending equal time on each breast, as well as ask for their partner's reaction. Gay males pay less attention to breast stimulation than lesbians but perform such stimulation more often than heterosexuals. Whereas lesbians and gay males state that they always enjoy breast stimulation, heterosexual females experience less enjoyment and communication than lesbians and consider their partner's pleasure in giving stimulation as more important than their own level of enjoyment. Masters and Johnson (1979) report that only 3 percent of heterosexual females very briefly stimulated their male partner's nipples either manually or orally. Heterosexual males pay less attention to breast stimulation than lesbians and gay males and do not ask their female partners for their reactions. Unlike gay males, heterosexual males usually do not consider their nipples sensitive to erotic stimulation. Masters and Johnson (1979) continue by stating that lesbian couples show the most positive response to giving and receiving cunnilingus. Similarly, gays enjoy giving and receiving fellatio. Heterosexual males are as positive about being fellated as are gays, but they are relatively less enthusiastic and skillful in performing cunnilingus than are lesbians. Heterosexual females regard fellatio as a challenge to becoming sexually effective and experience some arousal themselves. However, they complained about their male partner's forcefulness in performing cunnilingus, yet they do not communicate this to their partner. Heterosexual males view cunnilingus as a means of leading up to coitus.

By observing gay male couples taking their time in their sexual interaction, Masters and Johnson (1979) found that these partners knew how each one wants to be stimulated and provided that stimulation. Partners use a slow, teasing approach and do not rush orgasm, often bringing their partner to a point of ejaculation, backing off, beginning again, intensifying orgasm, when it occurs. In contrast, heterosexuals strive for orgasm without sustaining pleasure but as a goal to obtain more quickly. Both gay males and lesbians experience greater genital vasocongestion than do heterosexuals because of sustaining sexual pleasure for a longer time. As well, lesbians reported higher sexual frequency and are more orgasmic than heterosexual females (Coleman, Hoon, & Hoon, 1983).

Gender divisions are sometimes made in the sexual roles gays and lesbians engage in with a sexual partner. Although most often sex between gay men or lesbians is sex between equals, sexual roles can be differentiated along stereotypic masculine and feminine lines based on body build and appearance. For gay males, according to Bell and Weinberg (1978), frequency of sexual behaviors were as follows: (1) fellatio; (2) mutual masturbation; (3) anal intercourse; and, (4) body rubbing or interfemoral intercourse—rubbing the penis between the partner's legs until orgasm (Weinrich, 1994). Post AIDS/HIV does not find a significant change in sexual priorities for gay men. Gay men are significantly more likely to use condoms for safer sex than had occurred pre–HIV/AIDS.

For lesbians, the most common sexual activities are hugging, snuggling, kissing, cunnilingus, mutual masturbation, and tribadism—one woman lying on top of the other, making rhythmic thrusting movements to stimulate their clitorises (Weinrich, 1994). The use of dildos and analingus, mouthing the anus, appear to be uncommon behaviors for lesbians.

Gay males and lesbians have more in common with each other regarding their open-ended definitions of sexuality than with heterosexuals. Lesbians and gay males more often name pleasure, emotional response, and intimacy in their sexual relationships, whereas heterosexuals focused on gender issues and sexual intercourse. Masters and Johnson (1979) state that heterosexuals have a great deal to learn about communication and sexual pleasuring from lesbians and gay males. Previous research by Wells (1990) regarding the use of erotic language in gay and lesbian relationships versus heterosexual relationships shows that gay males and lesbians use more erotic language within a sexual relationship than heterosexual females and heterosexual males.

Lesbians and gay males appear to have charted their own sexual interaction and communication styles, outside conventional sexual roles, that allow for a greater range of sexual expression within their relationships than is generally found in heterosexual relationships. Although the potential for expanding definitions would be similar for heterosexuals, erotophobia (Ficarrotto, 1990) and the fear of being labeled as gay or lesbian seem to restrict heterosexuals to traditional modes of sexual expression and communication (Wells, 1990). Heterosexuals are more consistently found to be constrained by tradition and conventional gender roles (Blumstein & Schwartz, 1990; Symons, 1979; Tripp, 1975; Wells, 1991).

However, females show greater similarities in their definitions of sexuality than males with gays and heterosexual males showing the greatest differences. Expanding personal and interpersonal definitions of sexuality for heterosexual males and heterosexual females may yield greater potential for more pleasurable and expressive sexual relationships.

Safer-Sex Decision Making

Gay males were the first identified to be infected with HIV in the United States. They still make up significant proportions of North Americans who have been infected with HIV as well as those diagnosed with AIDS, although other populations are being infected at a greater rate currently than are gay males.

Gay communities nationally have responded to the AIDS crisis by effectively organizing service and educational programs to stop the spread of HIV and support infected individuals. Significant reductions of risky sexual behaviors have occurred within the gay community. However, changes have not been uniform, particularly among younger gay males. Too many people, including young gay males, engage in sexual practices that are known to transmit HIV. The riskiest of these practices is unprotected anal intercourse.

Rectal walls have little elasticity, tear easily, and absorb liquid. The viral load in HIV is greatest for those body fluids that contain high concentrations of white helper-T cells. These include blood and semen.

Each person needs to develop a sexual policy in adult, consenting sexual relationships that considers risk factors for sexually transmitted infections, including HIV. Unfortunately, our erotophobic society has made accurate and accessible information difficult to get. Educational and media presentations on HIV transmission are vague and inconsistent. Precautionary terms such as *sexual contact* along with pushing abstinence, which is unrealistic for most people, cover up and ignore pertinent information and behavior contributing to infection rates.

The equation for sexual behavior would include a partner's sexual history, mutual feelings of love and desire, and condom use. Fear of contracting HIV or giving it to loved ones is also part of the decision-making process.

The need for continued public intervention programs in the male gay community is recognized. To date the lesbian population has been virtually neglected even though transmission rates in this group of people are lower than in others. Programs need to focus on the details and context of sexual decision making (Ames, Atchinson, & Rose, 1995).

Building a relationship between two individuals can be an intricate and complicated affair. In a society that stigmatizes gayness and lesbianism and same-sex sexuality, developing and maintaining a solid, loving coupleship can be extremely difficult. The risk of HIV infection adds significantly to the concerns individuals face.

Conclusion

In an erotophobic society sexual expression is often perceived as dirty, disgusting, and lustful, particularly same-sex sexuality. Although sexual behaviors are similar across sexual orientations, the assumptions are that gay males and lesbians engage in homosexual behaviors that differ vastly from heterosexual behaviors when, in fact, sexual behaviors that people engage in are more appropriately deemed as human sexual behaviors.

Gay men and lesbians do differ sexually from their heterosexual counterparts in that they are less goal oriented, communicate more, use more erotic words, do not let interruptions ruin the mood, and bring their partners to greater vasocongestion before orgasm. Gays and lesbians more often include pleasure, intimacy, and emotions into their definitions of sexuality than do heterosexuals. An interesting response by heterosexual college students regarding who has the most and least inhibited sex found that heterosexual males thought that they were most inhibited and that they thought gay males were least inhibited whereas heterosexual females reversed their responses. The implications this may have for heterosexual relationships are profound, perhaps leading to heterosexual male anger and frustration at female partners as well as envy and anger for the lack of sexual inhibitions heterosexual males believe gay males have. It is what people do sexually that raises erotophobic responses and this is a more potent reaction when lesbian and particularly gay sexuality is considered. Social, religious, and legal institutions support homophobia, devaluing gay and lesbian relationships in youth and adulthood and making them more vulnerable to attacks. Through their practices, social workers can take leadership roles in providing a safe haven for gays and lesbians through support for their relationships as well as speaking out against ignorant myths and institutionalized homophobia. Comprehensive human sexuality courses are often not included in college programs for those who will be counseling youths and adults about sexuality in their professional lives.

REFERENCES

Adams, H. E., Wright, L. W., & Lohr, B. A. (1996). Is homophobia associated with homosexual arousal? *Journal of Abnormal Psychology 105* (3), 440–445.

Ames, L. J., Atchinson, A. B., & Rose, D. T. (1995). Love, lust, and fear: Safer sex decision making among gay men. *Journal of Homosexuality 30,* 53–73.

Bell, A. P., & Weinberg, M. S. (1978). *Homosexualities.* New York: Simon & Schuster.

Blumstein, P., & Schwartz, P. (1990). Intimate relationships and the creation of sexuality. In D. P. McWhirter, S. A. Sanders, & J. M. Reinisck (Eds.), *Homosexuality/heterosexuality: Concepts of sexual orientation* (pp. 307–320). New York: Oxford University Press.

Coleman, E., Hoon, P., & Hoon, E. (1983). Arousability and sexual satisfaction in lesbian and heterosexual women. *Journal of Sex Research, 19,* 58–73.

Ficarrotto, T. J. (1990). Racism, sexism, and erotophobia: Attitudes of heterosexuals toward homosexuals. *Journal of Homosexuality 19* (1), 111–116.

Marcus, E. (1982). *Making history: The struggle for gay and lesbian equal rights, 1945–1990.* New York: HarperCollins.

Masters, W. H., & Johnson, V. E. (1979). *Homosexuality in perspective.* Boston: Little, Brown.

Symons, D. (1979). *The evolution of human sexuality.* New York: Oxford University Press.

Tripp, C. A. (1975). *The homosexual matrix.* New York: McGraw-Hill.

Trotman, A. (1997, July 8). A famous defender of sodomy laws confesses to adultery. *The Advocate,* Issue 737, p. 13.

Weinrich, J. D. (1994). Homosexuality. In V. L. Bullough & B. Bullough (Eds.), *Human sexuality: An encyclopedia* (pp. 277–283). New York: Garland.

Wells, J. W. (1990). The sexual vocabularies of heterosexual and homosexual males and females for communicating erotically with a sexual partner. *Archives of Sexual Behavior 19,* 139–147.

Wells, J. W. (1991). The effects of homophobia and sexism on heterosexual sexual relationships. *Journal of Sex Education and Therapy 17* (3), 185–195.

Wells, J. W. (1992). Heterosexual university students' perceptions of homosexual behavior. *Annals of Sex Research, 5,* 171–179.

Williams, T. (1980/1947). *A streetcar named desire.* New York: New Directions.

CHAPTER

6 Gays, Lesbians, and Bisexuals in the Workplace

Understanding and addressing the issues raised by gay, lesbian, and bisexual employees requires a commitment like that made by corporations to understand and address the needs of African Americans, Latinos, women, Jews, the disabled, and others who face obstacles in their efforts to be fully productive members of the workplace.

—Brian McNaught, 1993, *Gay Issues in the Workplace*

In Canada, provincial legislation protects the rights of gays, lesbians, bisexuals, and transgendered persons to access to services, housing, and employment; Alberta's well-publicized resistance was squelched in a recent Supreme Court decision requiring legal protection against discrimination (De Mont, 1998). In the United States, however, in forty states an employee can be fired for being gay or lesbian. Yet surveys in the United States reveal that 80 percent favor equal rights in housing and job opportunities for gays and lesbians; similar attitudes prevail in Britain (Burr, 1998). Until the law catches up to the public sentiment, however, the sexual minority worker faces an ongoing dilemma of whether to take a risk and come out on the job or to live a double life, keeping home and work forever separate. And whatever the law says, openness in certain professions such as teaching, the ministry, and correctional work will probably always be problematic.

So how do people negotiate having a stigmatized "private" self within the public context of paid employment? What is the psychological toll of pretending, of not being who you are, for most of your waking life? What is the psychological toll of wondering who knows and who doesn't and if questions about one's personal life are an attempt to pry or merely be friendly? From the worker's perspective, to what extent do stereotypes about lesbian, gay, and bisexual people affect their attitudes and behaviors? And finally, why should social workers be concerned about issues that affect lesbian, gay, and bisexual people in the workplace? The purpose of this chapter is twofold: to identify and explore issues that affect lesbian, gay, and bisexual people at work, and to examine the role that social workers can play in affecting workplace attitudes and behavior toward sexual minorities.

Lesbians, Gays, and Bisexuals in the Workplace

Given the fact that approximately 20 million people in the United States are lesbian, gay, and bisexual, a very high percentage of whom work for a living, it seems likely that virtually all workers in this country interact with lesbian, gay, and bisexual people as colleagues, bosses, clients, and/or customers (Kivel & Wells, 1998). The reality, which is parallel to the situation of lesbians and gays in the U.S. armed forces, is that lesbian, gay, and bisexual people have always been and will continue to be employed outside of the home in the public context of work. A 1992 survey of lesbians and gay men indicated that 47 percent of gay men and 40 percent of lesbians are employed in professional and managerial jobs (Overlooked Opinions, 1992). Yet, despite the fact that lesbian, gay, and bisexual people are such an integral part of the public workplace, they are, at the very least, rendered invisible by the absence of policies that include them individually and/or as part of a familial relationship. At worst, they are harassed verbally and, in some extreme instances, they are the targets of physical violence.

Employment Issues

Perhaps the most troublesome of the many issues that lesbian, gay, and bisexual people face in the workplace is invisibility (Kivel & Wells, 1998). Herek (1996) refers to this lack of recognition of gays and lesbians as "psychological heterosexism"—an attitude, belief, or assumption that people are heterosexual, and that heterosexuality is preferable to homosexuality. Often heterosexism and homophobia are intertwined. Relevant to the workplace environment, Winfield and Spielman (1995) identify four types of homophobia—personal, interpersonal, institutional, and cultural. Institutional homophobia manifests itself in terms of the absence of relevant nondiscrimination policies and/or the lack of domestic partner benefits when spousal benefits are provided. Cultural homophobia or heterosexism is at the root of resistance to progressive pro-gay and pro-lesbian policies in the organization.

Heterosexism, as we have seen in Chapter 2, is tied to culturally accepted and culturally sanctioned gender roles and sexual orientation. Regardless of whether or not one's sexual orientation is made public, even the perception that one is different is enough to incite and provoke a variety of negative behaviors ranging from derogatory comments to murder. The workplace is often an arena for all four forms of homophobia. Crude and derogatory references to lesbians and gays are made as "jokes" in public and private gatherings, the assumption being that all those present are heterosexual. Moreover, within the hierarchy of paid civilian employment, negative attitudes toward gays and lesbians have consistently been found to be more prevalent in the business world than any other workplace environment. In their groundbreaking book, *Straight Jobs, Gay Lives: Gay and Lesbian Professionals, the Harvard Business School and the American Workplace,* Friskopp and Silverstein (1995) interviewed more than 100 graduates from the Harvard Business School, their partners, and other family members between the years 1991 and 1994. Their book provides hundreds of firsthand, descriptive, narrative accounts of the kinds of comments, jokes, and behaviors that lesbian, gay, and bisexual people have experienced in the workplace. Friskopp and Silverstein (1995) note that

> The most commonly reported form of discrimination by far that gay professionals reported took the form of a hostile atmosphere created by antigay jokes or comments. Dorothy, who is highly closeted at work, said, "You know, being antigay is the last prejudice that it's OK to have. It's politically incorrect to do all sorts of things, but it's OK to bash gays . . ." (p. 116)

The attitude that "it's okay to bash gays" takes many forms—antigay/lesbian remarks made by teachers to their students in elementary and secondary school classrooms; antigay remarks heard on the playground as children call each other "queer" and "fag"; antigay rhetoric used to humiliate new recruits at armed services boot camps; and antigay remarks heard in locker rooms, remarks used to shore up one's masculinity. Such homophobic attitudes not only negatively affect lesbian, gay, and bisexual employees in the workplace but may also contribute to a hostile work environment that negatively affects every employee (Winfield & Spielman, 1995).

Within the context of paid employment, satisfaction with one's work and one's workplace is an important predictor of success on the job. Perhaps even more salient to job satisfaction and success are the perceptions that one develops and brings to the workplace —perceptions about the workplace environment in terms of social interaction and support from colleagues as well as those in authority. This includes self-acceptance. Satisfaction in the workplace affects other areas of one's life, and one's life affects one's satisfaction with work. If acceptance at one's workplace is conditional, that is, based on socially acceptable norms of sexual orientation, then people who are lesbian, gay, or bisexual may feel the need to conceal part of their identity because of the very real fear that they may lose their jobs, that they may not be promoted, and/or that their co-workers will either blatantly or subtly reject them. If people who are lesbian, gay, or bisexual do not feel "safe" (either emotionally or physically) in the workplace, if they have to be concerned about others' perceptions and the possibility that they may be harassed, how can they be expected to be "themselves," to be honest about who they are, and to be honest in their interactions with co-workers? There are two ramifications of concealing one's identity. First, because psychological adjustment and feelings of well-being for people who are lesbian, gay, or bisexual are associated with being able to be honest about their sexual orientation, having to hide can be psychologically damaging and can, in turn, affect their performance on the job. Second, the ability to be honest about their sexual identity is often related to greater job satisfaction and, ultimately, greater individual and perhaps even collective productivity. Ellis and Riggle (1995) found that gays and lesbians working for companies with nondiscrimination policies that include sexual orientation were more satisfied with their jobs than were their counterparts in companies without such policies.

The advantages of being openly gay or lesbian are many. First and foremost is friendship. Sharing one's joys and sorrows is one of the aspects of work that prevents burnout and provides a source of emotional release. Openly gay males and lesbians often find each other anyway; sometimes, as among heterosexuals, intense friendships and even office romances develop. Another aspect of openness is that fellow workers will go to greater lengths to avoid offensive bantering and curb their insensitivities. Workers who are out of the closet can advocate for their gay and lesbian customers, clients, and/or students, as the case may be.

Organizational culture is important because it sets up the context for what is valued and rewarded within an organization and clarifies behavioral norms and expectations (Van Den Bergh, 1994). Workplace environments are typically divided along formal and informal lines. The formal environment of the workplace is dictated by policies that explicitly identify behaviors (i.e., no sexual harassment, nondiscrimination based on sex, race, etc., the length of the workday, overtime, etc.) that are acceptable and unacceptable in the workplace. The informal environment is governed by a set of culturally sanctioned norms, which is implicitly conveyed through interactions with co-workers (i.e., what people choose to share about themselves, their relationships, and their families), through comments about items in the news (e.g., gays in the military, etc.), and through the signs and symbols that are conveyed (i.e., pictures, postcards, cartoons) in their private and/or public space. (How many of us growing up stopped to think that the pictures we display on our desks at work and the items we choose to display on our cork boards would be sites for personal and political comment? How many people who are heterosexual appreciate the difficulty of deciding whom to bring to work-related social events?)

Heterosexism at work can be exacerbated by other identity issues such as gender, race, HIV status, disability, and/or ethnicity. In other words, women, people of color, people with disabilities, and so on, may experience multiple layers of discrimination regarding their sexual identities. Although the Americans with Disabilities Act precludes any adverse employment action toward individuals who have AIDS, individuals with this disease as with any other characteristic can be eliminated based on some other pretext.

Employer Response

In 1998 an attempt to pass legislation in the United States Senate to protect lesbian, gay, and bisexual individuals from discrimination in the workplace failed by a vote of 49 to 50. Despite that fact, ten states have passed antidiscrimination laws and more than 350 employers extend fringe benefits such as health insurance coverage to the partners of gays and lesbians (Mathis, 1998).

The Employment Non-Discrimination Act (ENDA), a bipartisan piece of legislation, would have made it illegal for employers with more than fifteen employees to discriminate against people who are lesbian, gay, or bisexual in hiring, firing, promotion, and compensation policies and practices. Detractors of the bill, such as Robert Knight of the Family Research Council, have argued that "under this bill, a man could come to work one day in a dress and high heels and say that his transvestism is an integral part of his sexual orientation" (Reynolds, 1994, p. 8). Such comments further illustrate the blurred boundaries between gender identity and sexual orientation and the very real sanctions that are imposed against those who violate gender expectations, for example, in this instance, that women wear dresses and men wear pants.

Contrary to the opposition's main argument that such a bill would provide lesbian, gay, and bisexual people with "special rights," the bill, in the minds of many, "is the right thing to do; it is the sensible thing to do; and it's the business-like thing to do" (Reynolds, 1994, p. 8). Although legislation has failed to pass at the federal level, many states are passing nondiscrimination laws to protect lesbian, gay, and bisexual people in employment, and approximately 25 percent of Fortune 1000 corporations have some type of official personnel policy that prohibits discrimination against gay and lesbian workers. In addition to the personal costs associated with discrimination, employers must also be aware of the economic costs. Kovach (1995) suggests that

> As businesses face greater competition, both domestically and globally, companies will have to ensure that they're recruiting the most qualified candidates available . . . it's self defeating for a company to deliberately cut itself off from a particular talent pool just because of misgivings about that group's lifestyle . . . [another argument against discrimination] is based on the costs of discrimination on taxpayers, consumers and corporations. Taxpayers and corporations bear the cost for discrimination in that an estimated 42,000 gay workers are dismissed each year due to sexual orientation. This translates into a $47 million loss in terms of training expenditures and unemployment benefits. (p. 49)

Varied companies and organizations—Adolph Coors Co., Walt Disney Co., Sun Microsystems, IBM, Lotus, Microsoft, Times-Mirror, Knight Ridder, and many universities (e.g., University of Iowa, University of Minnesota, Stanford, Harvard, Brown, etc.)—have implemented nondiscrimination policies based on sexual orientation and, to take it one step further, many of these organizations also provide benefits for domestic partners (Kivel & Wells, 1998). In some instances, the lesbian, gay, and bisexual domestic partners must sign affidavits that attest to the fact that they are in a primary relationship, that they jointly own a house or other property, and that they have been together in a monogamous relationship for at least one year. In the United States, heterosexual couples who are at least eighteen years of age (and in some states even younger) and who have known each other for only a day (or even less) can get married and they will automatically be entitled to their spouse's health benefits, death benefits, and social security benefits, and they typically do not have to provide proof of their marriage when they complete benefits paperwork. Yet, couples who are lesbian, gay, or bisexual must provide documentation to substantiate the authenticity of their relationships. This type of discrepancy is just one of many that lesbian, gay, and bisexual people experience in the workplace. Despite attempts to develop inclusive policies and legal protections against discrimination, fundamental attitudes about people who are lesbian, gay, or bisexual are more difficult to influence and, ultimately, to change. Some employers, recognizing that policies are not enough, have begun offering diversity training to their employees. Knight-Ridder "is running 'sexual orientation in the workplace' seminars at all its newspapers. There are no exceptions. . . ." (Fitzgerald, 1996, p. 12). Sun Microsystems provides in-house training programs on diversity and the company sponsors focus groups for African Americans, Hispanics, disabled persons, women, and sexual minorities. According to Major (1993),

> The focus groups, working with their friends and support organizations outside the company, take a proactive role in bringing minority applicants to hiring managers who, at this point, are no longer exclusively white males. The focus groups are proactive on issues within the company once the minorities are hired. (p. 13)

An entire issue of *The Advocate* (Meers, 1998) called "Gay Cops: Out in the Precincts and on the Streets" is devoted to recent developments in shattering the "blue wall of silence." According to the cover story, the work environment faced by gay and lesbian officers in this "most macho of professions" is complex: "Most gay cops will say that they expect—and don't mind—a little good spirited sexual banter on the job. But when teasing becomes persecution, gay officers who can be forceful when necessary . . . increasingly won't tolerate it" (p. 28).

Generally, as Meers suggests, lesbian officers, due to their tough image, seem to have less difficulty being out than gay men. As one lesbian sheriff quoted in the article puts it, "The occupation is dominated by heterosexual males. There's this bizarre idea that a woman who's a lesbian is somehow one of the guys. A gay officer is more of a threat to the whole macho mystique" (p. 28). In a British survey of gay, lesbian, and bisexual police officers, half of whom led "double lives" on the job, similar sentiments were expressed concerning gender differences (Burke, 1994). Many lesbian officers in both countries, however, face obstacles because of their sex rather than their sexual orientation.

Perhaps the most blatant workplace venue where lesbian and gay civil rights are abrogated is the U.S. military (Van Den Bergh, 1997). Although cases involving gay men have dominated the media, servicewide, as Van Den Bergh indicates, women are three times more likely to be investigated and discharged for homosexuality. Women who resist male attentions or who bring sexual harassment complaints are vulnerable to having their own sexual practices investigated. The combination of sexism and heterosexism is strident. Britton and Williams (1995) explain the intractibility of the U.S. military policies in terms of an institutional and cultural privileging of a heterosexual masculine ideal. The kind of bonding and solidarity encouraged by military leaders to create a strong fighting force must be above all suspicion of homoeroticism. Presently, the bonding would become suspect if openly gay and lesbian soldiers were included in the equation. Interestingly, in the less puritanical countries of Australia and Canada, exclusive policies have fallen in the fight for sexual equality.

These are but a few of the examples of companies and organizations that are and are not taking a proactive role in changing the workplace environment and workplace attitudes toward people who are lesbian, gay, or bisexual.* For a positive story concerning rare acceptance of transsexualism in an Iowa professor, see Box 6.1.

*Yet, as one human resources manager at Xerox Corporation noted, "no matter how the company as a whole treats you, it's the idiot in the cube next to you who will make your life hell" (Swisher, 1996, p. 53).

BOX 6.1

Iowans Accepted Sex Change, Professor Tells Audience

Iowa has accepted her as woman, Deirdre McCloskey, a University of Iowa professor who was a man until two years ago, told a standing-room-only crowd at Iowa State University Friday.

"Fortunately, I got to continue my career and stay in heaven—that's Iowa," she said during a Women's Week speech punctuated by laughter and applause at the ISU Memorial Union. "I thank God that I've been able to come out here."

McCloskey, who was Donald McCloskey until the fall of 1995, said her friends on the coasts think wrongly that Iowa is hateful.

"In fact, it's the sweetest state I know," said McCloskey. "I've received no hate mail, none zilch.

"Compared to some other times and places, Iowa and academic life and the 1990s . . . are good places to come out. And coming out is an incredible relief, isn't it?" McCloskey asked the largely student audience of more than 400, many of whom were gay, lesbian, bisexual, or transsexual.

She added: "When we've all come out at last, when the closets are used for keeping clothes instead of people, when all the hatred based on fear is dissipated, we will all have gotten our prayer answered, the prayer of identity: 'Let us be who we are, dear Lord. Please, God, let me be the person you made.' "

Good Will

The transition from man to woman was "the most interesting thing I've ever done," said McCloskey. It also was the most terrifying, she said, because she had to depend on the good will and good sense of others.

"The students have been wonderful," she reported. "It turns out that they care about how you teach, not how you look."

McCloskey, 55, a Harvard-trained educator who teaches both economics and history at the U of I, had this advice for the students: "Live your life in a loving but courageous way, combining the feminine and masculine virtues."

McCloskey said she will have another coming out Sunday when she is baptized as "Deirdre" at Trinity Episcopal Church in Iowa City. "They've been tremendously supportive," she reported. "They treat me like one of the ladies of the church."

McCloskey said becoming a woman was not a career move. She said she would not have advanced as far as she did as a man if she had been a woman. But, she said, times are changing. "The opportunities for young women are opening up at a wonderful rate," said McCloskey, "and I want to contribute to that."

Students Benefit

McCloskey said her students are benefiting from her transformation. "My style has changed," she said. "I'm sympathetic, but I'm more insightful, I think."

McCloskey, who graduated from Harvard in 1964 when it still was an all-male university, has asked that her degree be changed to Radcliffe, Harvard's sister school for women. "They won't change that," she said, "but I'm now an official member of the Radcliffe alumni association, and my 35th is in 1999 and it will be fun."

From *Des Moines Register,* October 11, 1997, p. 2A. Reprinted by permission of the *Des Moines Register.*

Roles for Social Workers and School Guidance Counselors

Social Workers

Social workers can make significant contributions in terms of influencing knowledge, attitudes, and behaviors about and toward people of diverse orientations. Social workers can assume a variety of roles—direct service provider, educator, administrator, advocate, colleague, friend, and ally—all of which can either directly or indirectly influence how people perceive and interact with people who are lesbian, gay, or bisexual.

The direct service most closely related to work are Employee Assistance Programs (EAPs). The EAP practitioner who provides confidential services, usually in a neutral location, will likely encounter gays and lesbians in connection with the usual counseling issues: substance dependence, relationship problems, workplace stress, and depression. It is essential that the EAP worker make clear his or her openness to concerns of sexuality and sexual orientation. EAP practioners are in an ideal position to help reduce heterosexism in the work environment by conducting workshops on homophobia and sexual harassment.

In the role of a direct service provider, social workers can provide support, counseling, and referrals for a variety of issues. Some of these issues include coming out to oneself, coming out to family members and friends, dealing with harassment on the street and in the workplace, dealing with homophobia in the workplace, managing a dual identity, and finding or enhancing one's voice to be able to ask for nondiscrimination policies and domestic partner benefits in the workplace. In addition to counseling and referrals, making oneself available as an ally or providing a "safe" space for lesbian, gay, and bisexual people is also important. One way to convey this is through displaying signs or symbols at the office (e.g., a rainbow sticker or flag, a lambda symbol, a pink triangle, and information about organizations, including lesbian, gay, and bisexual organizations, etc.) that indicate that this is a safe space.

One major difference between social work and some other helping professions is the strong ethical stance that the profession has taken in support of gay and lesbian rights (Appleby & Anastas, 1998). Social workers' commonly enunciated public advocacy in conjunction with proclamations of lesbian leaders in the field helps create a climate at social work agencies conducive to self-disclosure for gay and lesbian staff.

In the most extensive Canadian study of its kind, Health Canada funded a four-year study that looked at the health care and social service needs of 1,233 lesbians, gays, bisexuals, and transgendered people (Coalition for Lesbian and Gay Rights in Ontario, 1997). Of those who had seen a social worker, 17 percent reported that they were not understood or dealt with respectfully. The lack of recognition and acknowledgment of transgendered people was more profound. A sample of Canadian curriculum content revealed minimal attention to issues of sexual orientation. Eighty-nine percent of respondents stated that mental health professionals need training to better deal with lesbians, gays, and bisexuals. Interestingly, of service providers, medical doctors and social workers were seen as the least problematic. Next came psychologists and religious leaders. Psychiatrists were seen as the most problematic. Hopefully, now that the Canadian Association of Schools of Social Work requires the inclusion of content on oppression in the social work curriculum, Canadian social workers will be even more attentive than at present to the needs of gays, lesbians, and bisexuals.

Bragg (1997), an openly gay practitioner in Iowa, presents four case histories of gay and lesbian social workers, all of whom are open to colleagues and clients to various degrees. One of the subjects, Rich, states that he typically does not come out to his clients unless they are gay or lesbian and there is a good reason to do so. He does, however, have a picture of his lover on his desk and openly identifies him if asked.

Social workers who are in administrative positions can take a proactive role in changing the work environment by developing and lobbying for inclusive workplace policies.

They also are in a key position to develop policies that lead to an environment free of anti-gay/lesbian jokes and slurs. In-service diversity training can address such topics as coming out, parenting (foster, adoptive, biological), issues affecting elderly lesbian, gay, and bisexual people, working with lesbian, gay, and bisexual youth, issues relevant to people of color who are lesbian, gay, or bisexual, and HIV and AIDS (prevention and intervention strategies). As educators, social workers can draw their employees' attention to such resources as Parents, Families, and Friends of Lesbians and Gays (PFLAG), Human Rights Campaign Fund (HRCF), National Gay/Lesbian Task Force (NGLTF), Lambda Legal Defense and Education Fund, the National Center for Lesbian Rights, and state and local organizations.

Social workers are unique because they can play so many different roles—advocate, educator, counselor, and so on—and they can provide support in a variety of ways. For people who are lesbian, gay, or bisexual, these different roles allow for the possibility that a lesbian, gay, or bisexual employee will be able to respond to harassment in the workplace, that a lesbian, gay, or bisexual parent will retain custody of a child, that a lesbian, gay, or bisexual thirteen-year-old can find a support group, and that a gay or lesbian senior will be able to find housing without fear of being harassed and evicted because of issues surrounding sexual identity.

School Guidance Counselors

Schools can play a key role in adolescent development by providing an environment free of harassment and offering services and curriculum that reflect the life experience and sexual orientation of students. Although school social workers can help when a child is in trouble, school guidance counselors are generally in a more central position to reach out to individual students, teachers, and the school community. Many counselors, unfortunately, stress the academic and career aspects of counseling to the neglect of students' social needs. For all adults who are actively working with children, courses on sexuality and sexual diversity are essential. Such courses need to include strong elements of self-awareness work. Students training to be guidance counselors would want to consider such questions as the following: What are your thoughts and feelings about working with people who are lesbian, gay, or bisexual? What are your thoughts and feelings about seeing lesbian, gay, and bisexual people being affectionate with one another? What are your thoughts about lesbian, gay, and bisexual people and issues of morality? What are your thoughts and feelings about teachers in elementary and junior high school who are openly lesbian, gay, or bisexual? Gays and lesbians as parents, adoptive parents, foster parents? Working with thirteen- and fourteen-year-olds who self-identify as being lesbian, gay, or bisexual or who are questioning their sexual orientation? Working with bullies who persecute "queers"?

As we saw in Chapter 2, the individuals in the highest-risk group for adolescent suicide, especially among males, are those dealing with uncertainty over issues related to sexual orientation. And the biggest danger is to students wrestling with these issues alone without same-sex friendships. Substance abuse is common and increases the chances for suicide. Youths who do declare their homosexuality are at high risk for being kicked out of their homes; more than a third of runaway teens are gay and lesbian. School guidance counselors and social workers attached to schools are in an ideal position to engage in suicide prevention work with all youth. Central to this work is to "be there" for young persons wrestling with sexual identity issues.

School counselors can use their local PFLAG organization as a resource. In some high schools, PFLAG posters are placed on display in hallways with numbers for students to call with questions concerning sexual orientation.

Some helpful guidelines for gay/lesbian-supportive counselors or teachers are:

- Help institute programs in the school to prevent bullying and verbal abuse of students who are deemed different.
- Organize workshops on sexual orientation for student leaders, faculty, and administrators.
- Provide school-based support for gay/lesbian youth and their families.
- Encourage an atmosphere in which gay and lesbian teachers feel free to be role models to students.
- Encourage classroom gay, lesbian, and bisexual panels from a nearby college or university.
- Organize informal rap sessions for interested parties.
- Make sure the school library contains helpful information about homosexuality.
- Link students and their families with helpful community resources.
- Maintain strict confidentiality in all services provided.
- Support education geared to safer sex and to prevention of high-risk behaviors including substance abuse, which is closely associated with unsafe sex.

Buoyed by surveys that consistently show wide public support for legislation banning discrimination in the workplace, gays and lesbians and their allies can be expected to continue to push for protective legislation. In key positions to be respectable role models to gay and lesbian youth and ambassadors to the straight community, teachers, unfortunately, have borne the brunt of a right-wing offensive against gays and lesbians who work with children. It is much easier, however, for college professors to self-disclose their sexual orientation. Martin (1995) makes the case for the importance of gay and lesbian social work students to have self-identified lesbian and gay professors who can model leadership and political advocacy.

Conclusion

Various issues have been identified in this chapter, issues of concern for lesbian, gay, and bisexual people. We have seen how social workers, through the different roles that they can assume, can make a difference in the lives of people who are lesbian, gay, or bisexual. EAP practitioners and school counselors have roles to fulfill. The context of work, for most of us, is such an integral part of our lives, it seems critically important that social workers take a proactive role in changing the workplace environment and in changing attitudes about and behaviors toward people who are lesbian, gay, or bisexual. Persons of all sexual identities should be able to take for granted that they work in an environment that is free of harassment and discrimination, that they can talk freely about their partner and what they did over the weekend, that they can display photos on their desk without fear of retribution, and that they can be assured that benefits will be extended to their partner without requiring "proof" of their relationship. Social workers can and should work toward making this vision a reality.

REFERENCES

Appleby, G., & Anastas, J. (1998). *Not just a passing phase: Social work with gay, lesbian, and bisexual people.* New York: Columbia University Press.

Bem, D. J. (1996). Exotic becomes erotic: A developmental theory of sexual orientation. *Psychological Review 103* (2), 320–335.

Bragg, K. (1997). Being a gay or lesbian professional in a psychiatric hospital for adolescents. *Journal of Gay and Lesbian Social Services 6* (4), 25–38.

Britton, D., & Williams, C. (1995). "Don't ask, don't tell, don't pursue": Military policy and the construction of heterosexual masculinity. *Journal of Homosexuality 30* (1), 1–26.

Burke, M. (1994, Spring). Homosexuality as deviance: The case of the gay police officer. *British Journal of Criminology 34* (2), 192–203.

Burr, C. (1998, June 15). Tony Blair pushes gay rights in Britain. *U.S. News & World Report,* p. 36.

De Mont, J. (1998, April 13). Mission accomplished: A seven-year battle gains recognition for gays in Alberta. *Maclean's,* p. 56.

Dennis, D. L., & Harlow, R. E. (1986). Gay youth and the right to education. *Yale Law & Policy Review 4* (2), 447–478.

Ellis, A. L., & Riggle, E. D. B. (1995). The relation of job satisfaction and degree of openness about one's sexual orientation for lesbians and gay men. *Journal of Homosexuality 30* (2), 75–85.

Fitzgerald, M. (1996, October 12). Workplace 'out'-reach. *Editor and Publisher,* pp. 12–13, 52.

Friskopp, A., & Silverstein, S. (1995). *Straight jobs, gay lives: Gay and lesbian professionals, the Harvard Business School and the American workplace.* New York: Scribner.

Herdt, G., & Boxer, A. (1993). *Children of horizons: How gay and lesbian teens are leading a new way out of the closet.* Boston: Beacon Press.

Herek, G. (1996). Psychological heterosexism in the United States. In A. D'Augelli & C. Patterson, (Eds.), *Lesbian, gay and bisexual identities over the life span.* London: Oxford University Press.

Kivel, B. D. (1996). In on the outside, out on the inside: Lesbian/gay/bisexual youth, identity and leisure. Unpublished doctoral dissertation, The University of Georgia.

Kivel, B. D., & Wells, J. W. (1998). Working it out: What managers should know about gay men, lesbians, and bisexual people and their employment issues. In A. Daly, *Workplace Diversity* (pp. 103–115). Washington, DC: NASW Press.

Kovach, K. A. (1995, August). ENDA promises to ban employment discrimination for gays. *Personnel Journal 74,* 42–55.

LeVay, S. (1993). *The sexual brain.* Cambridge, MA: MIT Press.

Major, M. J. (1993). Sun sets pace in work force diversity. *Public Relations Journal 49* (6), 12, 13, 32.

Martin, J. I. (1995). Gay and lesbian faculty in social work: Roles and responsibilities. *Journal of Gay and Lesbian Social Services 3* (4), 1–12.

Mathis, D. (1998, June 28). America grapples over rights for gays. *Des Moines Register,* p. AA1.

McNaught, B. (1993). *Gay issues in the workplace.* New York: St. Martin's Press.

Meers, E. (1998, March 3). Good cop gay cop. *The Advocate,* pp. 26–34.

Overlooked Opinions. (1992). *Gay Market Report, 3.* Chicago: Author.

Reynolds, L. (1994). Proposed bill would ban workplace discrimination based on sexual orientation. *HR Focus 71* (10), 1, 8.

Sedgewick, E. K. (1990). *Epistemology of the closet.* Berkeley: University of California Press.

Stein, A., & Plummer, K. (1994). "I can't even think straight": Queer theory and the missing sexual revolution in sociology. *Sociological Theory 12* (2), 178–187.

Swisher, K. (1996, July/August). Coming out in corporate America. *Working Woman,* pp. 50–53, 78–80.

Van Den Bergh, N. (1997, March 6–9). Getting a piece of the pie: Protection, inclusion and equity for lesbians and gay men at the workplace. Paper presented at the Council on Social Work Education, Chicago, Illinois.

Walters, A. S. (1995). Bring homophobia out of the closet. *Journal of Sex Education & Therapy 21,* 231–237.

Winfield, L., & Spielman, S. (1995). *Straight talk about gays in the workplace: Creating an inclusive, productive environment for everyone in your organization.* New York: American Management Association.

CHAPTER

7 Aging Gays and Lesbians

To the extent that each of us is a survivor of life, we are all aging.
—Raymond M. Berger, 1982

Contrary to the myths accepted by many in Western society, the elderly are highly sexual beings with sexual thoughts and desires that persist into advanced age for most older people. Unfortunately, sexuality of the aged is a neglected topic; hence, the sexual needs of the elderly are often ignored by family members, medical professionals, caregivers, and society in general. Moreover, it is the health care personnel and the caregivers to the elderly as well as families of the elderly and the general public who are often uninformed and misinformed about the sexual attitudes and behaviors of the elderly. Such a lack of accurate information and the reliance on myths result in less effective care and reduced opportunities for sexual expression by the elderly.

Society expects all other biological systems to function throughout life except the sexual one. In sexually repressive American society, there is such a widespread underestimation of the sexual potential of the elderly that younger people often fail to realize that elders, if given the opportunity, can continue to expand their sexual repertoires and are much more sexual than younger people believe. In addition, sex in our society is clearly associated with power. Because elderly people, in particular elderly women, have relatively little power, as compared to their younger cohorts, it stands to reason that the elderly are perceived as being asexual.

American society is still influenced by the philosophy that equates sexuality with procreation. For elderly women whose prospects for having babies are either nonexistent or unrealistic, this viewpoint offers little beyond self-denial. Moreover, American society focuses on youth. Sex is reserved for the young, the beautiful, and the fully able-bodied who reserve sex for heterosexual expression. Because our society does not consider the elderly to be beautiful or to be physically capable of engaging in sexual practices, we do not typically view them as sexual beings. In examining the myth of sexlessness of age, the double standard of aging views women as losing sexual desirability earlier than men. Women are viewed as aging sooner and as being less attractive than older men, which may result from the equation of women with biology. If sexuality and youth are equated with reproduction, particularly for women, then the postmenopausal woman becomes "old" often twenty years before a comparably aged man. There are several dimensions of this double standard of aging: (1) Women are viewed as sexually ineligible earlier than men; (2) a man, even an unattractive man, can remain eligible well into old age; (3) a relationship between an older man and a younger woman is seen as "normal" whereas one between an older woman and a younger man is seen as questionable or obscene; and (4) there are two standards of attractiveness for men (the adolescent youth and the distinguished older man), whereas there is only one standard of attractiveness for women (the adolescent, young woman).

The double standard of aging may also result from the Judeo-Christian tradition, which is based on the concept of men resembling God (Wolf, 1991). According to Wolf, the Judeo-Christian creation story teaches women to believe that their bodies are inferior to men's, as "second-rate matter that ages faster" (p. 93). God made Adam from clay, in his own image; Eve is an expendable rib. ". . . God breathed life directly into Adam's nostrils, inspiring his body with divinity; but Eve's body is twice removed from the Maker's hand, imperfect matter born of matter" (p. 93).

A man's wrinkles will not define him as sexually unattractive until he reaches his late fifties. For men, sexual value is defined more in terms of personality, intelligence, and earning power than physical appearance. Of course, men do not age any better physically than women. Men age better only in terms of social status.

We are trained to see time as a flaw on women's faces whereas it is a mark of character on men's faces. Women are culturally defined by their physical appearance.

Although older women may express feelings of uselessness and incompetence when their reproductive capacities cease, they may also feel a sense of freedom associated with old age because they are no longer obligated to conform to society's standards of beauty. In other words, older women may be relatively immune to the negative self-image implied by the double standard. Aging, in fact, may represent a liberation from rigid gender role expectations for both women and men. Strict adherence to socially prescribed gender roles is largely a pattern of youth.

To be considered sexually desirable in most of the world's cultures you have to be young, firm, and attractive. People across the earth regardless of race, ethnicity, or cultural perspectives ascribe to similar characteristics for someone seen as good-looking or, perhaps, beautiful: generally, a tall, shapely physique; muscularity for males; firm, rounded breasts and buttocks for females; full lips, large eyes, straight nose, and a long neck for both men and women. Sex appeal includes symmetry in body form and facial features as well as straight, white teeth, signifying good health. Individuals must display reproductive potential through healthy skin tone and energetic vitality.

The aging population is commonly viewed as having lost what may have once been physical beauty and, consequently, their sex appeal. Romance and sexuality are for the young. Older North Americans are stereotyped as asexual and physically unappealing. Their sexuality is discounted by such remarks as "dirty old man" and "ridiculous old woman." For older gay males, the words used to stereotype them, such as "old queens" and "trolls," are particularly biting because they embody a triple stereotype. The implication is that they are old and lecherous as well as unmasculine. Older lesbians may be referred to as "old dykes," but because they are largely invisible, they are not ridiculed to the degree as are old gay men. A 1998 unpublished thesis by Karen Cunningham found that aging lesbians are less likely to be seen as sexual beings than are young lesbians, owing to their unrecognized status as old lesbians as well as old women.

Lesbians and Aging

Older lesbians are thought to be nonexistent, not only by society, but often also by the lesbian community. In the feminist academic press there is little or no mention of lesbian elders, and the gerontological world seems oblivious to the sexuality of old people in general, let alone that of old lesbians. When articles on sexuality do appear in noted journals like *The Gerontologist,* they are about heterosexual practices or in rare instances about homosexual men (Auger, 1990). Lesbians who are old are thus in triple jeopardy, as they are old, female, and lesbian—three oppressed groups in North American culture. Society hates women who love women, and so the lesbian, who escapes male domination in her private home, receives it doubly at the hands of male society; she is harassed, outcast, and shuttled to the bottom.

However, a number of features of lifelong lesbian orientation may contribute to the more optimistic approach to aging of lesbians that suggests just the opposite. Although women often have lower incomes than men, and lesbians have not shared in a husband's income, surveys usually find lesbians are better educated and in higher-paid jobs than heterosexual women. If they have no children, their time and energy have been directed toward building careers, and the money they have made has been used to enhance their own lives. Furthermore, it is more often expected in lesbian relationships that each partner works.

Lesbians tend to have close networks of friends that may substitute for estranged family members. Also, like their heterosexual counterparts, most older lesbian women have a partner and expect to grow old together. Heterosexual women are often younger than their husbands, with a longer life expectancy than their mates. Thus, heterosexual women may be widows for a considerable period of their lives. On the other hand, lesbian couples are on the same life-expectancy curve and if a partner is lost, the pool of same-age mates remains. Because the greatest motivator for many men to begin a new relationship is the physical appearance of the woman, older women face the future with a fear of losing the ability to attract (or maintain) a heterosexual partnership. Lesbians, like other women, place less emphasis on youth and/or beauty in their partners; thus, they are generally less threatened by the changes age brings in their own appearance. Lesbians may have an easier time dealing with aging for this very reason. An older lesbian woman whose lifestyle has departed from society's standards may be better prepared to cope with the accompanying stigma of not only being a lesbian but also of being old. The older lesbian woman knows the stigma of nonconformity and, therefore, understands that being a lesbian, which is less valued and less powerful than being a heterosexual woman, may help her to prepare for the experience of old age.

The invisibility of lesbians and aging lesbians in particular works in contradictory ways both to conceal a lesbian's experiences with aging and to reinforce prevalent stereotypes about lesbians. Nothing is known about whether lesbian aging experiences differ from those of heterosexuals. Stereotypical beliefs about aging lesbians and aging can prevail in the absence of evidence to the contrary. Heterosexist bias and homophobia work together to instill in lesbians the fear of discovery and subsequent persecution. The silence that results from their fear helps to reinforce the stereotypes about lesbians and seals the double standard. Lesbians are absent from public institutions of the gay culture, such as bars, nightclubs, and bathhouses, and, therefore, are unavailable for sociological analysis. This is like stating that heterosexual women cannot be studied because they are not found in strip joints, sports bars, and locker rooms. Older lesbians are overlooked not only because they do not participate in the gay subculture that attracts sociologists of variant behavior, but also because they are subsumed by gerontologists under the category of aging women in general in which lesbian experiences tend to be reduced to the level of simple friendships or confidante relationships. Even the concept of the lesbian community tends to ghettoize lesbian experience and isolate it further from that of other women.

The notion that lesbians might have better experiences with aging than heterosexual women, although not without possibilities, poses further questions. This idea rests on the premise that lesbians in their younger years have learned to cope with being society's outsiders and, in essence, have achieved a level of crisis management that could serve them well as they age. This view is rather like a new version of the puritanical notion that suffering is good for you in the long run. There is no empirical support to suggest that crisis management is cumulative.

In a culture in which people are used to denying their age, aging individuals regardless of their sexual orientation may feel unattractive and frightened about the aging process. The Old Lesbian Organizing Committee (OLOC) is a national organization of lesbians over sixty years of age that helps old lesbians gain a more positive perspective of aging by giving up an attempt to pass as younger and as heterosexual (Healy, 1993).

Gay Men and Aging

Gay males place greater emphasis on youth than do lesbians, much as heterosexual men emphasize youthfulness in their female partners. Yet, there is speculation that older gay men often learn to deal with their stigmatized status and, therefore, are better prepared to deal with aging than are heterosexual males. A converse view states that these same gay men may find that ageism doubles the effects of stereotyping, making the aging process as difficult for gays as for heterosexuals. A prevalent belief about aging and gay males is that young gay men find older gay men repulsive as potential sexual partners. Younger gays are also said to shun older gays because of a nagging reminder that they will someday be old and, hence, unattractive. Older gay men may also be perceived as becoming eccentric effeminates, repulsing others, as they age. Perhaps the most damaging stereotype is that older gay men are unfulfilled sexually, becoming desperate letches preying on young men. Most older gay men socialize and partner with peers near their own age rather than predominantly with younger gay men. Feelings that younger gay men may not identify with and understand the older gay male may underlie a preference for agemates. It is not uncommon for older gays to avoid younger gays because the elder believes that younger gays hold contempt and derision toward older gays. Most younger gays see older gays as unexciting and dull. What is known about older gay men does not bear that out. Like any other segment of society, gay men are varied in their interests, activities, social adjustments, and sexual behaviors. Most are sexually active, many in loving, long-term relationships, some with partners outside their primary union; others are celibate, and still others masturbate.

Living Arrangements

The popular stereotype that older gay men and lesbians lead their lives alone in social isolation is a myth. The vast majority of older gays and lesbians live with a partner, roommate(s), friends, or family members. For most lesbians and gay men there is a steady source of companionship and support. Sharing a home with another person or other people provides a haven from the often hostile outside world. Older gays and lesbians frequently sustain meaningful relationships throughout their lives. Berger (1982) states that many gay couples considered themselves to be lovers and as such shared a deep emotional commitment to one another; however, the sexual relationship had diminished. For some of these couples, sexual liaisons occurred outside of the relationship, although all other aspects of their lives were integrated.

Social and Psychological Adjustment

Because we are raised in a culture that views same-sex romantic love as dirty and disgusting, the majority of gay men have reported shame over their sexual feelings at some point in their lives, often during adolescence. Most gay men overcome their initial feelings of shame and guilt as they reach adulthood. In fact, older gay men are less anxious about their same-sex sexual relations than are their younger counterparts. To the heterosexual observer, gays are seen as sexually uninhibited or more commonly as promiscuous.

As gay men age, they no longer conform to the common mental image of the sexually active gay male in his twenties or thirties. The older gay man does not fit this stereotype, so aging may insulate him from a sexual orientation label. There may be both benefits and penalties for the aging gay man; his sexual nonconformity is less threatening to a homophobic society and he is stereotyped as asexual. Growing older is a concern for the majority of people in a youth-oriented culture and aging for gay men is no more an issue than it is for others. Supportive special relationships and psychological adjustment are related to how integrated the gay man is in his community.

Variations between Gays and Lesbians

Although there is a paucity of research regarding older lesbians and gays, a few recognized variations are known. Lesbians express greater fluidity in their sexual orientation and are more likely to have been or be heterosexually married. They are more likely to have children than gay men. Lesbians are more likely to be living in a long-term relationship than are gays, in part because of life span differences. These variations may affect family support available to lesbians and gays.

Gay men are more likely to be financially secure than are lesbians, as males compared to females are generally. Lesbians and gay men of color who are older are also likely to have less financial stability.

Long-Term Care for Older Gay Men and Lesbians

Society stereotypes older gay men and lesbians as lonely individuals, devoid of social support, and estranged from their families of origin. However, this characterization is as far from the norm as are generalizations about the elderly in general.

Many older gays and lesbians are an integral part of their families of origin, whereas others have been rejected by all or some of their family members. Although significant numbers of lesbians and gay men acknowledge and come to terms with their sexual orientation in adolescence or early adulthood, others agonize over heterosexist expectations, perhaps never coming out or only doing so later in life. This may be a time of liberation following retirement to avoid jeopardizing employment. Or coming out may come after the death of a spouse.

Yet, if older lesbians and gays have given up on developing pair-bonded same-sex relationships as they age or deem coming out as too costly to their welfare, the facade will likely continue. No longer living under the protection of heterosexual privilege as an elder or having given that up early in one's life, trust in family, religious and legal institutions, and the medical and psychiatric professions for today's older population does not come easily. Experience for virtually all is distrust of a system that stereotyped, rejected, condemned, incarcerated, or institutionalized them because of their sexual orientation.

Fear of disclosure causes many gays and lesbians to conceal their sexual orientation. This often invisible aging population seeks anonymity to avoid prejudice and discrimination. Self-reports by older lesbians and gays reveal blatant discrimination when they seek health and long-term care services.

Connolly (1996) provides an excellent case study that chronicles special needs of gays and lesbians in long-term care and the legal system. Connolly focuses on the discrimination and lack of legal support lesbians and gays face when a partner dies.

Conclusion

The age of forty is a benchmark in the aging process. Although forty is not considered by most to be the beginning of old age, it marks one as no longer young. During the forties there are physical signs of aging such as gray hair and facial wrinkles. College texts on aging gay or lesbian families as well as research on older gays and lesbians generally provide little material for guiding professionals in their understanding and ability to guide or advise lesbians, gay men, and those who love them. Popular perceptions are that gay men age prematurely and are "over-the-hill" at age thirty. Without youthfulness, one loses sex appeal. Gay men who are no longer sexually appealing because they have lost their youth and who are considered unattractive to boot are called "trolls," "toads," "aunties," and "waxworks." Wrinkle bars/rooms are social gathering places for older gay men. The physical standard of attractiveness gay men apply to a sexually appealing partner is no different than what heterosexual men use to rate sex appeal for females. Males, regardless of their sexual orientation, generally are looking for younger-looking, fit, sexually attractive partners.

Older lesbians may cope very well as a result of their own isolation from the heterosexual culture. The benefits of growing old as a lesbian, without the societal expectations and pressures that are placed on heterosexual women, are yet unknown. Lesbians who are old are hidden or invisible partly because of the lack of research on them. Past investigations, along with feminist scholars, have ignored the issues of the aging woman and, in doing so, have kept the fastest-growing segment of our population invisible; yet for the aging lesbian this invisibility may prove to be advantageous. In general, older lesbians are thought to be nonexistent, not only by the media but often also by the lesbian community. Older lesbians do not enjoy the privilege of patriarchal masculinity, but, in the eyes of the American population, they are not perceived as lesbian either; therefore, older lesbians may not suffer the burden of being labeled homosexual.

REFERENCES

Auger, J. (1990). Lesbians and aging: Triple trouble or tremendous thrill. In S. D. Stone (Ed.), *Lesbians in Canada* (pp. 29–34). Toronto: Between the Lines.

Berger, R. M. (1982). *Gay and gray: The older homosexual man.* Urbana, IL: University of Illinois Press.

Connolly, L. (1996). Long-term care and hospice: The special needs of older gay men and lesbians. *Journal of Gay and Lesbian Social Services 5* (1), 77–91.

Cunningham, K. E. (1998). Attitudes toward lesbians: An exploratory study. Unpublished thesis, University of Northern Iowa, Cedar Falls, Iowa.

Healy, S. (1993). Confronting ageism: A MUST for mental health. *Women and Aging 5* (1), 41–54.

Wolf, N. (1991). *The beauty myth: How images of beauty are used against women.* New York: William Morrow and Company.

CHAPTER

8 Counseling with Gay, Lesbian, and Bisexual Clients

I would never consider a patient healthy unless he had overcome his prejudice against homosexuality.

—George Weinberg, 1972, *Society and the Healthy Homosexual*

In any successful therapeutic setting, the client and therapist have to "click" or establish a rapport. Acceptable intervention strategies directed toward problem solving for those concerns and issues the client brings to the therapist are also vital. Individuals who may be struggling with aspects of their sexual orientation most often deal with self-identification and coming out, as well as internalized homophobia resulting in self-acceptance, sexual, and intimacy difficulties.

Compared to the 10 percent to 12 percent of the general public who seek mental health services, a whopping 42 percent of gays and lesbians do so, according to a recent survey reported in *The Advocate* (1997).

Self-Identification

Coming to grips with one's sexual and romantic attractions to same-sex individuals in a hostile societal environment often results in scrutinizing the meaning of these desires in order to determine the strength or extent of one's drive for a gay or lesbian union. During this process, people frequently try to enforce heterosexuality to avoid becoming and perhaps identifying with a sexual minority. Such persons may act out sexually, withdraw, immerse themselves in a fundamentally conservative religion or bargain with God, invest in denial, attempt or commit suicide, or attempt to change their sexual orientation.

Dealing with homosexual desires by trying to change one's sexual orientation has never been successfully documented. This does not mean that individuals are inflexible in their sexual orientation. Perhaps recognizing feelings, attractions, or desires that become conscious after exposure to information and experiences may bring about greater awareness. However, people do not move from exclusively homosexual in desire or behavior to exclusively heterosexual. Outcomes for such so-called therapeutic interventions result in attempts to suppress desires and alter an individual's natural proclivity with seriously negative repercussions. Individuals usually become severely depressed and suicidal. If they have undertaken heterosexual marriages or relationships, these typically are sexually deprived of interest and passion regarding intimate and desirable relations. Sexual interaction usually results in homosexual fantasies in order to function. As time passes, sexual relations most often deteriorate and if the relationship continues, there is no sexual contact. Meanwhile, the gay or lesbian partner may seek sexual and romantic relationships outside the heterosexual union or masturbate to satisfy sexual anxieties.

A lesbian panel member who spoke to one of Wells's classes on a regular basis described her sexual desire for an intimate female partner as natural for her. She often said that to have engaged in heterosexual sex would be unnatural for her. She likened her example to being left-handed and having adults push her as a child to use her right hand to hold a spoon or a pen. The attempt opposes a person's natural inclination and interferes with mastery in developing skillful writing and handling utensils. The same can be said for developing a comfortable and fulfilling sexual and affectional relationship.

Conversion or Ex-Gay Therapy

In 1997 the American Psychological Association (APA), the world's largest association of professional psychologists, passed a resolution that portrays therapeutic approaches to so-called change of sexual orientation, referred to as ex-gay or conversion therapy, as unnecessary and ethically questionable. The APA now affirms four basic principles related to psychological counseling for lesbians, gay men, and bisexuals. Those principles are (1) that homosexuality is not a mental disorder and that treatment to change one's sexual orientation is unwarranted; (2) that psychologists do not condone or participate in discriminatory practices with lesbian, gay, and bisexual clients; (3) that psychologists respect the rights of individuals, including lesbian, gay, and bisexual clients, to privacy, confidentiality, self-determination, and autonomy; and (4) that psychologists obtain appropriate consent to do therapy in their work with lesbian, gay, and bisexual clients.

The APA undertook an investigation into so-called reparative therapies or pastoral counseling for gays after such conservative right-wing religious groups as Exodus and Transformation Ex-Gay Ministry purportedly damaged clients by setting up false expectations through what has been called psychological terrorism. Those practitioners who invest in ex-gay therapy are usually associated with extremist religious groups that promote the illusion that sexual orientation can be changed to further their own political aims. Their tactics are described as psychological terrorism performed by practitioners who harbor intense biases against people who are gay or lesbian.

The APA resolution does not prevent practitioners from using conversion therapies but, rather, requires that clients be apprised of peer-reviewed research that cites the limitations and difficulties of such ex-gay therapy before consenting to undergo treatment. To date, there is no evidence to support a successful change in sexual orientation from exclusively homosexual to exclusively heterosexual. Research suggests that people may have some flexibility in their orientation, recognizing sexual attraction to females and/or males at various periods in their lives. As individuals identify feelings, fantasies, and attractions, they may become more aware of their own sexual orientation. Because the erotophobic culture in which we live teaches us to abhor, ridicule, and devalue homosexuality, any accurate understanding of where people might fall on a heterosexual–homosexual continuum is a guesstimate at best. The long-term outcome for those who have undergone conversion therapy is chronic depression, preoccupation with suicide, and loss of sexual desire.

Counseling from a strengths approach helps clients to experience self-validation including their sexual orientation. Emphasis is on living a full, happy life as a fully functioning person. Ex-gay therapy, in contrast, is decidedly negative. It is an outgrowth of attempts by clients to bear up under an antigay society and family rejection. Although some clients may give their consent to conversion therapy, many are coerced into doing so. Those most vulnerable are young people at the mercy of confused, ignorant parents or adult guardians seeking to erase their own shame or guilt over their child's homosexual orientation. Allowing ex-gay therapy to remain a therapeutic option ensures that many will endure potentially costly, painful, and traumatic procedures that could increase rather than relieve suffering.

Exodus is a nationwide network of "ex-gay" ministries that claim to be able to help gays and lesbians become heterosexual. "Freedom from homosexuality is possible through repentance and faith in Jesus Christ as Savior and Lord," the group's literature says. Such repentance begins "the process whereby the sin's power is broken, and the individual is freed to know and experience true identity as discovered in Christ and His Church. That process entails the freedom to grow into heterosexuality" (Mirken, 1998, p. 5).

Survivors of these organizations are coming forward in growing numbers to call the ex-gay movement a dangerous fraud. They paint a disturbing picture of groups filled with paranoia, and controlled through indoctrination and fear, often using techniques that are eerily reminiscent of Jim Jones's People's Temple, or, more recently, Heaven's Gate.

Bruce Mirken tells the story of Christian singer Jallen Rix. Rix, who grew up in a family of "very staunch fundamentalists," says he can remember feeling same-sex attractions as early as age six or seven, though he didn't quite understand what they meant. But by the time he was a senior in high school he understood, "and I began to get petrified." In the mid-80s, while attending Westmount College, a Christian school in Santa Barbara, he went to an ex-gay support group called Desert Stream in search of help.

The group met weekly, and new members were quickly instructed on the supposed causes of sexual orientation—dominant mother and passive father, the Freudian view. The notion seemed too plausible to Rix since it somewhat paralleled his own family experience. Still, why wasn't his brother, who grew up in the same environment, gay as well? And what of the many members whose backgrounds didn't match the theory at all? Group leaders insisted the answer was to try harder to understand what had gone wrong in their childhoods, leading to session after session where people were digging the dirt trying to figure out what was wrong with their upbringing.

Ultimately, Rix says, no one really changed. There were people who could follow the behavior and the structure, but when you sat them down they still had these feelings.

Rix ended up riddled with fear and guilt. Eventually he left the cult-like group and has since reconciled his sexuality and his faith, and says he is far happier now than when he was trying to stifle his gayness.

Stages of Coming Out

The process of coming out refers to individual acknowledgment of his or her homosexuality and others with whom that information is shared. This process occurs over a lifetime because people usually assume in our culture that people are heterosexual unless they are told otherwise. There are recognizable stages that a person goes through in the coming-out process. Coming out entails risk because doing so may jeopardize relationships with family and friends as well as employers and co-workers. Yet, coming out is a crucial means of obtaining self-validation. By acknowledging one's gay or lesbian orientation, an individual begins to reject the stigma and condemnation associated with it. Coming out to family members often results in a crisis, but the family usually adjusts by accepting the lesbian or gay member. Ignorance and misinformation about gay and lesbian sexuality, religious beliefs, prejudice, and discrimination often interfere with an initially positive response by family members, straining family relationships. Following disclosure to family and friends, lesbian and gay individuals usually report a sense of relief that their secret is out and that they can now be themselves without trying to cover their true nature. Along with feelings of relief comes a strengthened resolve to develop supportive relationships, enabling the gay or lesbian person to reduce feelings of isolation, loneliness, depression, and alienation.

Lesbians and gay males are out to varying degrees depending on their personal comfort level with who they are as well as the perceived risk involved in self-disclosure. Some may not be out to anyone, not even to themselves. Some are out only to themselves or their partners; others are out to close friends but not to their families or employers. Still others may be out to everyone. Yet, due to fear of reprisal, dismissal, or public reaction, gay and lesbian teachers, clerics, police officers, military personnel, and politicians, as well as members of other professions in which loss of work would be a risk if one's sexual orientation were revealed do not acknowledge the truth about themselves to employers, co-workers, and the public.

When an individual comes out to those recognized as heterosexual, the process usually occurs in stages. In the initial or pre-coming-out stage, an individual may not consciously recognize same-sex attractions but may experience discomfort with oneself because of fears or anxiety dealing with homosexuality. A person may defend himself or herself against any feelings associated with same-sex attractions and embrace heterosexuality. Reaction formation and rationalization may be used in denial.

The second stage involves a beginning awareness of an understanding of same-sex romantic and sexual attraction. Individuals begin to examine heterosexist beliefs, that is, assuming that everyone is heterosexual, and that heterosexuality is preferred. People may choose to talk to someone else about their feelings or come out to others.

In the exploration stage, individuals develop gay friendships, perhaps a romantic/sexual partner relationship, and socialize within the gay and lesbian community. Through contacts in the lesbian and gay community, individuals develop a social support network within the context of their emerging identity.

Integration is the acceptance of one's gay or lesbian identity, which ranges in significance for different people over their lives. At this point in the coming-out process a gay or lesbian identity is incorporated into other aspects of one's life (i.e., personal, social, and political). People in this stage describe their sexual orientation as who they are and integrate other developmental tasks into their lesbian or gay identity.

Social Worker's Role in the Coming-Out Process

Because coming out is a continual life process involving disclosure to new acquaintances in changing situations, people may ebb and flow with those who can know. In counseling settings, coming out is one of the crucial issues presented in therapy by lesbian and gay clients. It is, therefore, vital for professional social work therapists to provide support and validation for their clients' disclosures of what they believe to be their sexual orientation.

When a client suggests that there are problems in dating relationships, the therapist seeks clarification by openly asking, for example, "Are your dating relationships with women and/or men?" The message is that all responses are okay. The therapist might continue to ask what is troubling about the relationships, for example, "What is uncomfortable about your dating relationships?" Questions that are considerate, yet directly supportive, will aid in diagnosing the presenting issues of concern, particularly if sexual orientation is an issue. The client might probe the therapist as well to determine the therapist's willingness to be understanding and supportive. Clients may hedge on giving information or camouflage information that might label them negatively. The therapist needs to recognize that possibility as well as the validation of gay and lesbian relationships by taking an affirmation stance. Validation of lesbian and gay relationships should be given the same caliber as heterosexual relationships. It is important to identify for the client who has expressed concerns over same-sex attractions the degree to which feelings and fantasies are directed toward same- or other-sex individuals. If it is determined that a client has been heterosexually dating, yet expresses dishonesty in that dating role because she or he is romantically and sexually attracted to same-sex individuals, but has not revealed that to anyone because of fear of rejection, identifying cultural bases of homophobic beliefs others hold is imperative. Hypothesis testing by having the client evaluate his or her own homophobic beliefs in light of personal experiences often reveals a discrepancy; for example, people whom the client knows to be gay or lesbian are fine individuals contrary to homophobic beliefs. The therapist shows the relativity of beliefs and the characteristics of someone known to the client to be gay or lesbian in order to increase flexibility in thinking. In addition, the therapist summarizes the link between beliefs the client may hold and the emotional reactions those beliefs may elicit.

As therapy progresses, reducing internalized homophobia is key. Diagramming coming-out growth gains on a continuum from 0 percent to 100 percent as therapy continues may determine the client's readiness to reveal himself or herself to a range of others.

Sex Therapy

The model for sexual functioning until very recently has been to treat disorders and dysfunctions for orgasmic heterosexual coitus. There was no mention of gay and lesbian sexual concerns until this decade.

For lesbians and gays, sexual issues differ from those of heterosexuals in a number of ways. Although gays and lesbians may deal with desire, erectile, or orgasmic difficulties, the context in which they occur varies significantly from that of heterosexuals. Lesbians and gays focus on sexual concerns other than coitus whereas this remains the key issue for heterosexuals. In sex therapy gays most often experience aversion to anal eroticism and lesbians report aversion to cunnilingus. Anorgasmia or lack of orgasm is not usually a concern for lesbians, whereas for heterosexual women anorgasmia is a frequent complaint. Lesbians are socialized as adhering to the female role in the United States, which may make initiation of sexuality more difficult, affecting sexual frequency. Sexuality also is defined for women by men to mean penetration. What counts in sexuality surveys is the frequency of coitus. Thus, a masculine heterosexist model of sexual encounters is not applicable for lesbians because erotic touch without any vaginal penetration may be defined personally as a complete sexual experience. Gays more often deal with lack of ejaculation rather than premature ejaculation or erectile dysfunction due to societal and internalized homophobia.

Indeed, gays and lesbians must deal with rampant erotophobia regarding their sexuality. Fear of violence makes it difficult for gays and lesbians to openly express affection the same way heterosexuals can and often do. Holding hands, hugging, or kissing in the view of others brings charges of flaunting homosexual behavior whereas the identical affectional behavior by heterosexuals may go unnoticed or is considered as standard fare. Consequently, lesbians and gays learn to repress their public expression of feelings, which frequently carries over into their private affectional and sexual expression. The result may adversely affect sexual desire, create sexual aversion, guilt, and negative feelings about sexual activity.

Gays must deal with the public association between their sexual expression and HIV. Although HIV infects women and men regardless of their sexual orientation, the first infection of HIV in the United States struck gay men. The disproportionately high number of gay males who have died of AIDS increases the feelings of vulnerability, risk, and fear gay men may have surrounding sexual activity. Grieving the loss of friends, lovers, and partnerships leaves many depressed and anxious over establishing affectional and sexual relationships. More are worried about contracting HIV even if they practice safer sex. For HIV-positive gay men, fear frequently centers around infecting loved ones. Gay men who are HIV positive are more likely to experience sexual dysfunctions out of concern for a partner than are noninfected gay men.

The sexual concerns of lesbians and gays require that those counseling them be knowledgeable in their treatment and therapy. A gross deficiency in most social work programs as well as many counseling graduate programs is the absence of a required human sexuality course. If the therapist is not lesbian or gay, he or she needs to have a thorough knowledge of and be supportive of the clients he or she serves. Few social work therapists are prepared to deal with sexuality in any depth, much less lesbian and gay sexuality. Therapists who operate under the guise that homosexuality is inferior to heterosexuality or is morally wrong need to state that up front. Therapists need to be aware of their own feelings and assumptions about gays and lesbians and develop inclusive models of sexual treatment that are gay/lesbian positive.

The Pursuit of Happiness

A primary fear of parents regarding their gay or lesbian children concerns their happiness in a society that stigmatizes homosexuality. Is there anyone who has not heard derogatory "fag" remarks and jokes? Gays, lesbians, and their loved ones endure cruel, hurtful words on a frequent basis from thoughtless and ignorant people. Homophobia is fostered by our religious, educational, and legal institutions. Gays and lesbians have lost jobs, been refused housing, denied hospital visitation to their infirmed partners, been beaten, raped, and killed by homophobic heterosexuals or "wanna-be heterosexuals." Families have disowned their lesbian and gay children or siblings. Gays and lesbians have been devalued, been told they will burn in hell, and have been victims of aversion therapy. The roots of unhappiness are not due to sexual orientation but to hatred directed toward those who identify as or are perceived to be gay or lesbian. In spite of overwhelming homophobia, most lesbians and gays eventually state that they are happy. Indeed, research shows gays and lesbians to be as happy as are heterosexuals in their partner relationships.

Counseling concerns in the lesbian and gay population frequently center around depression, suicide, and alcoholism and drug abuse. Thus, along with developing support and self-worth in the coming-out process, issues that affect gays' and lesbians' psychological and physical health may also require treatment. Gay and lesbian hotlines are usually the best source of referral to help avoid organizations that are heterosexist.

Counselor Self-Awareness

To be effective in working with lesbians and gays, the helping professional has to honestly explore his or her deepest and most intimate feelings concerning homosexuality. All people, gay and nongay, have feelings regarding homosexuality. If the counselor or therapist thinks that gays and lesbians are "okay," but is repulsed at the thought of what gays and lesbians do affectionally or sexually, the counselor or therapist is homophobic and erotophobic. Feelings such as these need to be dealt with on a personal level before working successfully with lesbian and gay clients. Because all gays and lesbians have experienced some form of oppression as a result of their sexual orientation, professional helpers need to empathize as well as validate oppression as a reality. By affirming a gay or lesbian client's self-worth within his or her sexual orientation, liberating support from the counselor or therapist helps the client to move toward developing a more positive self-image.

A counselor or therapist takes responsibility for helping the gay or lesbian client address ingrained stereotypes that lead to internalized homophobia. It is necessary for gays and lesbians to reframe their own beliefs about being gay or lesbian. The message becomes that whoever you are regarding your sexual orientation is fine. The goal is to end self-degradation.

This process should enable clients to express deep-seated feelings and emotions that have been hidden from themselves and from others. The helping professional should encourage lesbians or gay persons to examine their deep-seated feelings and emotions that have led to basic assumptions about their own beliefs about sexual orientation as these are directed toward themselves and others who are gay or lesbian. It is important for clients to understand the danger of relying on heterosexist and erotophobic values for self-validation. To become and remain healthy, lesbians and gays must become aware that they cannot afford to accept, often unchallenged by silence, any predisposed set of assumptions. It becomes imperative to desensitize guilt and shame heaped upon those who are gay or lesbian because of their thoughts or feelings or sexuality. The use of humor may be particularly healing with learned guilt and shame. Encouraging a gay or lesbian client to participate in a gay/lesbian support group may help establish cohesiveness and identification with others, and may help reduce a sense of isolation and despair. Supportive, nonthreatening, and affirming touch can also increase positive self-acceptance.

Lesbian, Gay, and Bisexual Therapists

Self-disclosure of one's sexual orientation by a social work therapist to a client is reciprocal to asking the client to share his or her sexual orientation with the therapist. The openly gay or lesbian counselor is in an excellent position to be a role model for one for whom role models are pathetically scarce. The gay or lesbian counselor closeted in a homophobic agency, however, is in a painfully awkward position in treating clients of a like orientation. The client is not, cannot, be bound to confidentiality. Allowing the client to "hold something over" on the counselor is an extremely risky proposition, both psychologically and practically, because the worker's job could be at risk. Probably the best the closeted therapist can do under the circumstances is to leave the door open with a remark such as, "Let's just say I'm very aware of gay/lesbian issues." A display of relevant gay/lesbian brochures such as a flyer for gay/lesbian AA meetings will send a message that this is a safe place to share, even if the sharing is necessarily one-sided.

In any case, the client's sense of compatibility with a particular social worker on the basis of his or her disclosed sexual orientation, or refusal to disclose, is an important consideration for a successful treatment outcome. The practitioner, for ethical reasons, needs to address this issue with the client as early as possible in treatment. Referral to a well-trained, reputable professional can often be a godsend to a client in need of a role model of like orientation or gender. For heterosexual clients for whom homophobia is a major issue, referral to a heterosexual counselor may be the best option. On the other hand, a productive treatment experience with an openly gay or lesbian therapist may help the prejudiced client to examine his or her prejudices and develop self-awareness into their origin. Indeed, characteristics that affect rapport in a counseling setting such as sex, race, age, religiosity, ethnicity, and sexual orientation, as well as personality and the philosophy of the therapist, may be critical.

We conclude this chapter with a consciousness-raising exercise in Box 8.1, especially geared toward the heterosexual reader.

BOX 8.1

Exercise for the Reader

Close your eyes . . . think of the person you have been most in love with . . . imagine that you have gone out for several months . . . for some reason you can't talk about this person or be open about your relationship.

It is Friday afternoon in your residence hall.

People are talking about their dates for the weekend, getting ready. You're in your room, listening to music, thumbing through a magazine. Your roommate comes in with several friends. Your roommate says "I am going out with ________ again tonight. We are going out to dinner, then to the dance." The others mention their weekend plans and talk about whom they are seeing. One asks you: "What are you doing tonight? You're not going to study again, are you?" You reply you do not have any big plans; you're just going to mess around.

They try to fix you up with someone. You reply, "Maybe some other time."

They continue talking about their dates and plans. Pictures of their steadies are on display in their rooms. Whenever you can, you smile, nod your head, and joke with them about love and sex so they won't be suspicious.

You think about your friend, who you've been seeing for three months. You wish you could tell your roommate and friends about the good times you've had and how it feels to be in love. But you know you can't say anything. You cannot put a picture of your friend on your desk or dresser. You cannot tell your roommate or housemates what this person means to you.

Finally, they all leave for their dates. You take a shower, dress, and meet in the front of the hall.

Although you're glad to see each other, you can't hug or kiss each other. You just smile and say hello.

You go to a restaurant for dinner. You sit across from each other rather than on the same side. You can't look too long in each other's eyes. You can't touch each other.

After dinner, you decide to see a movie. You both wanted to go to the dance, but because you can't dance together in public, you opt for a movie. At least in the movie theater, you can sit beside each other. But you can't touch. When you come out of the movie theater, you would like to put your arm around your friend or hold hands, but you can't. Instead, you clamp your hand behind your back.

You wish there were someplace you could go with your friend. You wish you could go to your room, but people might wonder why you always go there, plus your roommate could walk in. You can't even go where other young couples go to neck. You wish you could tell the world about your love, but you're afraid you will be disowned, you will get kicked out of school, your friends won't talk to you, or you won't get the job you want, and all you're doing is loving this person.

Conclusion

Love and intimate companionship are vital for personal happiness and psychological health. This is as true for gays and lesbians as it is for heterosexuals. People who are in stable, loving relationships enjoy greater well-being and longevity. Intimate interactions with significant others serve as buffers against life stressors and provide us with feelings of security, confidence, and self-worth. Heterosexual privilege functions to provide heterosexual couples with a socially supported union. Yet, erotophobic Americans devalue, trivialize, and mock lesbian and gay relationships. So far, Americans have successfully prevented legal unions for gays and lesbians, adding to their stress in the wider world and in those relationships they form. It should not be surprising that lesbians and gays seek therapeutic counseling more often than heterosexuals. (To learn about family counseling, see Chapter 11.)

Although homosexuality has been depathologized, the majority of psychotherapists have been provided minimal guidance for conducting therapy with their lesbian and gay clients. As certified providers of care, social workers are in the forefront to successfully meet the needs of gay and lesbian clients if they can develop their own comfort with sexual orientation and learn to work with the concerns presented by lesbians and gays. To date, most counseling and social work programs are deficient in requiring human sexuality courses and, specifically, those that include therapy and care for gay and lesbian clients.

REFERENCES

The Advocate. (1987, April 1). Making us crazy, 20.

Mirkin, B. (1998). *Bay Windows Newsletter.* Boston, 5.

Weinberg, G. (1972). *Society and the healthy homosexual.* New York: St. Martin's Press.

CHAPTER 9

Social Work with Lesbians in Health Care Settings

There is no better way to subjugate human beings than to silence them. There is nothing more oppressive than denying another's reality.

—Ann Hartman, 1993

A surfeit of suffering endured at any age, but especially in childhood, can breed feelings of powerlessness and despair. Such feelings are rarely conducive to good health. Torn between a desire to be true to themselves and society's desire, even insistence, that they be silenced, lesbians, like gays and bisexuals, are at high risk for problems such as depression, substance abuse, self-destructive sexual behaviors, and suicide. Yet health care providers are often the last ones to realize the connections between physical (and mental) health problems and the sham of masquerading as something you are not ten (or even twenty-four) hours a day. To explore the relationship between lesbian identity and health care needs is the major task of this chapter. (The following chapter will explore health care issues for men.) A second major goal is to argue for a feminist-based strengths perspective for direct social work practice with lesbians who are receiving treatment in traditional health care settings.

Following a discussion of general health concerns, we will look at acquired immune deficiency syndrome (AIDS), a disease with special significance for lesbians in ways that are often overlooked in the epidemiology statistics. We will also look at the connection between homophobia in the society and self-destructive behaviors in the individual, a connection that indirectly compounds the risk of contracting the AIDS virus.

The connection between homophobia and other health problems is more tangible. After reviewing the research on lesbian youth and suicide, depression of lesbians, partner abuse and hate crime victimization, and substance abuse, we will discuss the challenge to social work, both clinically and politically, in providing a supportive treatment environment. Because social workers encounter persons with disabilities on a daily or even hourly basis, one section of this chapter is devoted to this topic. Lesbians with disabilities suffer from dual discrimination and tend to have a double identity; they are seen as disabled in lesbian circles, and as lesbians in groups of disabled persons. This discussion concludes by showing that the goal of personal wellness is achievable through an affirmative approach that draws on the resilience, resources, and positive motivation that are within each person.

Central to contemporary social work theory is the realization that the personal is political and the political, personal. Trained to approach clients holistically and to view the person in the environment, social workers (ideally) help clients find their strengths, strengths that often have emerged out of hardship and that clients never knew they had. In contrast to the medical model, which emphasizes the study, diagnosis, and treatment of disease and illness (Poole, 1995) and which is geared more toward problems and pathologies (Saleebey, 1996), the strengths perspective is built on the concepts of capacities and empowerment. And whereas traditional health care is apt to be managed within a patriarchal system (Trippet & Bain, 1990) that is classist and racist as well, the feminist-based strengths approach strives to be gender and ethnically sensitive.

A major challenge facing health care workers today is the ever present need to address the full array of biopsychosocial factors affecting clients with medical problems. A further challenge is to help create a gay/lesbian-friendly atmosphere in the medical setting, one in which diversity is actively welcomed rather than merely tolerated, and one in which heterosexuality is not taken for granted in the absence of evidence to the contrary.

General Health Concerns

Interweaving her own personal narrative on recovery from a mastectomy with facts from the professional literature, feminist-lesbian author Bricker-Jenkins (1994) recounts the many petty humiliations that she not so much experienced as endured in her hospital patient role. Mercifully, homophobia was not a problem in this sophisticated medical setting; Bricker-Jenkins's partner was accorded the respect of any other close family member. A major source of strain, however, was the near-total lack of validation of her, the patient's, own internal resources. Simple acts of creativity and self-expression ("editing" a pre-op release form, for example) were seen as acts of the utmost defiance by bewildered and harried medical staff. Under circumstances of disfigurement and severe pain, affirmative feminist care would have gone a long way toward alleviating the patient's anxiety and sense of powerlessness. The affirmative feminist model of social work promotes empowerment through full patient participation in the treatment and healing process. Instead of enforcing conformity to the rituals and symbols of the hospital milieu, this model draws upon the patient's (and his or her family's) use of rituals and symbols.

Breast cancer rates are generally higher for lesbians than for heterosexuals (Aguilar, 1995; Bricker-Jenkins, 1994), probably because fewer of them bear children and breast feed, both inhibiting factors in breast cancer development (JAMA, 1996). In general, however, from the little we know about the health of lesbians, we can say that their illnesses are roughly comparable to those of heterosexual women. Compared to other women and to men, lesbians have a low incidence of sexually transmitted diseases such as syphilis, gonorrhea, and chlamydia (JAMA, 1996). The rate of AIDS contraction, except for bisexual women and intravenous drug users, is extremely low. Physical problems commonly experienced by lesbians include bacterial vaginosis, weight problems, and irregular menses. There is some indication, as Trippet and Bain (1990) indicate, that emotional and mental health problems such as depression, alcoholism, and suicide may be more pronounced in this population than are general health problems. Many of these difficulties are not related directly to homosexuality but are a by-product of the stress of living as a sexual minority in a religiously heterosexual society in which one is caught up in pretending to be what she or he is not. In any case, in self-report studies, lesbians are found to avoid health care and rarely to disclose their sexual orientation or behavior to physicians (JAMA, 1996a).

AIDS

According to the most recent information from the Centers for Disease Control and Prevention (JAMA, 1996b), one in every 1,000 U.S. women was infected with the AIDS virus in 1992; this is compared with one in every 160 men. One in 160 black women and one in 400 Hispanic women, compared to one in 3,000 white women, were infected. A New York City study of 1,202 HIV-positive women found that 9 percent were lesbian (Bevier, Chiasson, Garofalo, & Castro, 1992). The greatest risk of HIV infection to all women is from IV drug use and sex with bisexual men. Although cases of suspected woman-to-woman transmission during sexual activity have been reported in the medical literature and in reports from health professionals (Glassman, 1995), very little is actually known concerning the frequency of this type of transmission. In addition, research on women has focused on their role as carriers, with concern centering on prostitutes infecting male clients and on mothers and their babies (Peterson, 1995). The primacy of men and of the fetus have been at the expense of women; the fact that HIV is much more readily transmitted from men to women than the other way around has been entirely overlooked. The lack of knowledge stemming from the gender bias in medical research is a cause of concern. Infections specific to women with HIV, often gynecological in nature, are not widely known. The impaired ability of health care providers to recognize and treat early signs of AIDS in women, and especially of self-identified lesbian women, effectively excludes women from disability programs, social services, and clinical drug trials. The fact that a significant number of lesbians (estimates range from 75 percent to 85 percent, according to Kaufman, Ford, Pranger, Sankar-Mistry, & the Advisory Committee on Women and HIV, 1997) have had and continue to have sex with men (whether out of affection, by coercion, in connection with intoxication, or in order to get pregnant) places this population in a higher-risk category than it would appear on the surface. Lesbian youth are at particular risk for emotional pain related to the coming-out crisis and early relationship problems. Substance abuse and unsafe sexual practices are frequent consequences.

Vicariously through their close association with the gay male community, lesbians have suffered enormously as a result of the AIDS epidemic. The impact on the lesbian world is summarized by Glassman (1995):

> They are health care workers and educators, AIDS activists, workers and volunteers in AIDS service projects. They have been caretakers. They have lost male and female friends and family members to the disease. They suffer from the increased homophobia associated with AIDS hysteria because the non-lesbian/gay world does not distinguish them from gay men. Their choices for donor insemination have become more complicated as has their freedom to explore heterosexual sex. (p. 69)

Youths and Suicide

Among the conditions predisposing young people to attempt or commit suicide are self-hatred, victimization by bullying from peers, a history of family violence, substance abuse, and sexual identity conflicts. Given their common androgynous sex role behavior and tendency to be scapegoated on these grounds, gay and lesbian youths are highly vulnerable on every count. As the literature suggests, conflicts about the disclosure of sexual orientation may influence young people to attempt suicide if they are otherwise predisposed (Friedman & Downey, 1994). Much of the suicidal behavior by disturbed youths is not recognized as such. Thus, gay youths pushed out of their homes because of an "unacceptable" lifestyle may court danger and even death. Joining other "cast-out" youths on the streets, they may gravitate toward illegal drug use and promiscuous sexual activity as a means of survival, ostensibly, but tragically also as a means to death.

Social worker Pederson (1994) provides us with the following case study:

> Jennifer is an eighteen-year-old lesbian, who was infected with HIV at the age of 15, as the result of her only heterosexual sexual experience. During this same time period, Jennifer was abandoned by her mother after many years of intra-familial conflict, which resulted in her being placed in foster care. Soon after, her foster parent refused to allow Jennifer to remain in care, and insisted that Jennifer be removed within hours of learning her HIV status. (p. 138)

The difficulties of lesbian youths are considerable. Among vulnerable adolescents—those who lack stable family and peer support systems—the social worker should be particularly sensitive to the strong likelihood of suicidal ideation and behavior. Although the findings in studies on suicide attempt frequency among gay and lesbian youths have been widely criticized for the lack of a random sample, results consistently show a high rate of attempted suicide among gay males and lesbian teens.

According to a study published by the U.S. Department of Health and Human Services, gay and lesbian youths are two to three times more likely to commit suicide than other youths; 30 percent of all completed youth suicides are related to issues of sexual identity (Gibson, 1989). Due to the disturbing nature of these findings, the results were initially suppressed by the government. Whereas one in ten heterosexual teens attempts suicide, two out of three gay or lesbian teens attempt suicide (Whitlock, 1989). In a survey of 221 self-identified gay, lesbian, and bisexual youths who attended youth groups across the United States and Canada, Proctor and Groze (1994) administered a standard adolescent health questionnaire to the youths. The findings correlated with those of earlier studies that gay and lesbian youths are at high risk for suicide (40.3 percent of their sample had attempted suicide; male/female breakdowns were not given). Youths who attempted suicide reported difficulty in areas of family relations, school performance, peer relations, and self-perception in contrast to gay and lesbian youths who did not attempt suicide.

The findings from this and comparable studies have important implications for teachers, social workers, and families. The creation of a supportive environment for those who are likely to be harassed and the conducting of antioppression workshops to prevent harassment are absolutely essential. Homophobia workshops are invaluable in helping teachers and students to be aware of the way in which irrational fear of homosexuality affects us all. AIDS prevention strategies alone will not suffice; youths will avoid high-risk behaviors only if they care enough about themselves to want to do so. Those who continually are victimized lose their sense of self-worth and respect. Enhanced nurturance and empowerment of youth, accordingly, must go hand-in-hand with AIDS education and prevention efforts if such efforts are to be effective (Durby, 1994). In the public schools, there is a need for advocacy work geared toward the creation of a nonhomophobic school environment; self-identified gay and lesbian teachers can do much by their very presence to offer positive and successful role models for youths who very often feel they are all alone. Additionally, advocacy for the inclusion of sexual orientation information in school sex education is urgent; homosexuality must be presented as a normal variation of human sexuality. School social workers can play a role in setting up support groups for lesbian and gay adolescents and their families. Education about the deadly combination of drug and alcohol use and sexual activity should be provided also. Lesbians, like gay male teens, in short, require a broad-based individual and group "empowerment" education that addresses not only issues of positive role identity but that also facilitates the development of social skills and support systems (Dempsey, 1994).

Lesbians and Depression

Lesbians have one reputed advantage over gay males: They recognize their homosexuality several years later than their male counterparts, most commonly not before the early twenties and then most often in connection with an intense personal relationship (Durby, 1994). Presumably, people have more in the way of personal resources as they get beyond adolescence than they might have had earlier. As a case in point, there is some indication that the suicide incidence for all youth tapers off in adulthood (Hunter & Schaecher, 1995). With adulthood comes greater independence from family & peer groups and more access to the lesbian and gay community, resources, and social support. But not always.

The most comprehensive source for data on lesbian mental health is still the study of 1,925 lesbians from all fifty states who responded to the National Health Care Survey undertaken by the National Institute of Mental Health (1987). The sample was drawn from relevant membership organizations, health and mental health practitioners, and through announcements placed in gay newspapers. The nonrepresentativeness of this sample makes generalizations to the entire U.S. lesbian population difficult. Nevertheless, Bradford, Ryan, and Rothblum (1994) praise this effort for its nonpejorative conceptual framework, which stressed coping mechanisms and diversity rather than deviance and pathology. Because of its broad, psychosocial-based agenda, as these authors further note, the survey could provide implications for mental health treatment and planning.

Relevant to depression, the Lesbian Health Care Survey revealed that 18 percent of the respondents had attempted suicide. Suicide rates among black and Hispanic lesbians were found to be 27 percent and 28 percent, respectively, significantly higher than the white lesbian rate of 16 percent. Thirty-three percent of whites had been physically abused as children or adults, compared to half of black and Hispanic lesbians. Thirty-two percent of the total sample had been raped or sexually attacked, and 19 percent had been victims of incest while growing up. Half of those who received counseling had done so for reasons of sadness and depression. Significantly, 11 percent of the sample were experiencing depression currently, and one third reported having experienced long-term depression at some point in the past.

Despite the grimness of the statistics, it is important to emphasize that lesbian women do not differ significantly from heterosexual women on general psychological adjustment (Friedman & Downey, 1994; Rothblum, 1990). Otis and Skinner (1996), however, drawing on a large sample of lesbians and gay males in a southern state, demonstrated a correlation with severe psychological stress accompanying victimization and depression. Gender differences were pronounced: A sense of helplessness was related to depression in women and internalized homophobia to depression in men. For both genders, an earlier experience of verbal and physical abuse including sexual assault by a male perpetrator significantly affected later emotional health.

In the absence of direct research on depression among lesbians, Rothblum (1990) infers from the correlates of depression in women, namely, alcoholism, suicide attempts, frequent relationship break-up, and a high rate of social stress, that the rate of depression among lesbians is high. An important insulating factor in offsetting depression, however, is membership in a supportive lesbian community. Employment success, generally high for this population, provides further protection against depression.

Greene (1994) offers an analysis of mental health and treatment issues pertaining to ethnic-minority lesbians. In contrast to most ethnic minorities, children who may later discover their gay or lesbian inclinations will already have learned a range of negative stereotypes and attitudes about their future reference group, and not simply from the dominant culture but from their own culture and immediate family members as well. Self-acceptance is greatly complicated by this happenstance. These young people are destined to grow to be something that their loved ones hate and, therefore, to be the victims of prejudice by their own family members. A further complicating factor is that, unlike most other oppressed minority groups, sexual minority members may pass for mainstream and will, therefore, be put under considerable pressure to do so, often with damaging psychological consequences. The dilemma facing ethnic minority lesbians is the same as for all gays and lesbians: how to be yourself and maintain your close ethnic group ties as well. Religiously oriented women may be especially affected by this dilemma.

Lesbians of color often articulate a sense of displacement, a sense of not feeling truly accepted or at home in either the majority lesbian community or in their ethnic community (Leslie & MacNeil, 1995). The lesbian community is dominated by a white, middle-class ethos and a false belief that lesbians, as victims of prejudice themselves and "free spirits," have somehow transcended racism. This belief may be disturbing to ethnic minority lesbians. Then homophobia and heterosexism within the home community keep lesbians on the outskirts of what would otherwise be a protective buffer against society's racism. So if living with one oppressed identity is complex, as Leslie and MacNeil inform us, living with plural oppressed identities can seem overwhelming. And the lesbian of color involved in primary interracial relationships must grapple with being a lover to a member of the oppressive class as well as with the homophobia and antiwhite prejudice of her own community. Although research has largely ignored the mental health problems of black and Latina lesbians, we do know from statistical data that they are at increased risk for suicide attempts as well as for childhood sexual abuse (Rothblum, 1990).

To summarize from what little we know about depression in lesbians, we can conclude that the problem does not seem to be so much organic, at least not any more so than among the general female population, as it is situational. Nor is there any single situation in itself that causes depression among lesbians, but rather a number of factors that in combination promote distress. Although adequate research on lesbian depression is lacking, the one national lesbian health care survey revealed rates of reported depression that were strikingly high. Furthermore, we can conclude from the evidence on correlates of depression—for example, suicide, substance abuse, victimization—that relatively high depression rates would be expected. The finding of a correlation between emotional stress and depression among lesbians would seem to indicate that eradication of homophobia, the provision of affirmative role models, and access to a supportive lesbian community would go a long way toward alleviating emotional distress among members of this group.

Physical Victimization

As a consequence of the gay pride movement, the general public became much more aware of human rights issues and the very presence in their midst of gays and lesbians. With this social resolution came a backlash: society's hostility toward sexual minorities as expressed through legal channels—restrictive legislation—but also through rampant victimization. In his book, *Violence Against Lesbians and Gay Men,* Comstock (1991) provides statistical information on the perpetrators of such crime. A mass campuswide survey of students revealed that 94 percent of the victimizers were male; many of the crimes were hate crimes, but some were committed as acts of anger against family members because of their gayness. Lesbians who were attacked (by family members or strangers) were most often attacked by men; sometimes the attack included rape. The facts on hate crimes against women are presented in Chapter 2.

Lesbian Battering

Until the 1990s, the feminist/shelter movement resisted recognizing the problem of physical violence in woman-to-woman relationships. Activists in both feminist and lesbian social movements feared that recognition of such intimate violence would affirm sexist and homophobic stereotypes (Heer, Grogan, Clark, & Carson, 1998). Today, however, there is an ever-increasing awareness of the presence of physical abuse and violence in lesbian relationships.

What is lesbian battering? As defined by Hart (1986), physical violence abuse alone does not constitute lesbian battering. "*Lesbian battering* is that pattern of violent and coercive behaviors whereby a lesbian seeks to control the thoughts, beliefs, or conduct of her intimate partner or to punish the intimate for resisting the perpetrator's control over her" (p. 173).

Preliminary studies show that 22 percent to 46 percent of all lesbians have been in a physically violent same-sex relationship (Elliott, 1996). Psychologically, battered lesbians experience all the emotions, insecurities, and self-recriminations as do other battered women. Consider the following description from Northwood (1986):

> As a lesbian, my abusive relationship was no different from a heterosexual battering relationship. As a feminist, my principles didn't protect me from the abuse, though they helped

> me to process it. It was as a woman that I was abused and as a woman that I have learned to value myself in my relationships today. (p. 154)

Gentlewind (1986) reports:

> She threw me on the floor. Sitting on me, her knees on my chest, she began to choke me. I couldn't move under her weight. Her choke tightened. Looking up into her menacing leer, I remembered the story she had told me about choking her ex-lover to scare her, to teach her a lesson. Looking her straight in the eye, I whispered, "I don't want to die. Just stop this and get off of me." (p. 42)

These final illustrations pinpoint one uniqueness of lesbian battering—denial by the lesbian community that one woman can victimize another (or that men in gay relationships can be the victims of domestic abuse).

As Cecere (1986) describes the situation:

> If a straight woman shows up with black eyes, swollen lips, and broken arms and a story about walking into doors, falling down stairs, *whatever,* any one of us would assume violence to be the true culprit. But when the same thing happens to our sister, we often don't see it. I was as guilty of this form of denial as anyone. (p. 29)

And as Dziggel (1986) reflects on her earlier relationship:

> I can only speculate about what difference it would have made in my life if there had been a community saying that lesbian battering is real violence, not innocuous fighting among intimates. I can only speculate about what difference it would have made to me had I felt less desolately alone and ashamed. Survivors of lesbian violence must now speak out, for ourselves and our sisters. (p. 69)

Homophobia clearly plays a role in the reluctance of lesbian victims to seek help. Shelter programs, designed for women escaping abuse at the hands of violent men, are often not prepared to address the needs of the victims of same-sex violence. Shelter workers who are lesbians themselves may feel constrained due to homophobia in the community that could affect funding sources to remain closeted (Elliott, 1996). Moreover, many lesbians would be horrified to involve the criminal justice system in getting protection against threats by another woman. And help from family and heterosexual friends may be avoided out of fear of reinforcing stereotypes about the dysfunctional nature of lesbian relationships. Where either the batterer or survivor is a woman of color, racism in the dominant community is compounded by homophobia in the ethnic minority community (Waldron, 1996).

Very little research has been done on lesbian and gay batterers, the perpetrators of the violence. In a unique study of its kind, Farley (1996) examined the profiles of 288 clients who were referred to a gay/lesbian counseling agency specifically for treatment as perpetrators of domestic violence. Intergenerational abuse was found to be prevalent in the backgrounds of abusers. Of 119 female perpetrators whose profiles were studied, 88 percent reported a family history of physical abuse whereas 94 percent reported experiences of childhood sexual abuse. Alcohol and drug use figured in 63 percent of the battering cases. Although batterers represented all ethnic, racial, and economic groups, however, most of the persons referred to that agency had low incomes.

Does the feminist-based strengths perspective have relevance here in terms of its basic precepts (such as that violence stems from the patriarchal, sexist society) or is gender-based theory, as some writers suggest (Island & Letellier, 1991; McNeely & Robinson-Simpson, 1987), irrelevant to the issue of same-sex violence? Indeed, dominant domestic violence theory, which favors, for instance, use of the term *wife abuse* or *wife battering* over the term *domestic violence* to emphasize the predominant male role in perpetrating violence, tends to be heterosexist in practice, if not in intention. Theories, however, as Merrill (1996) suggests, can be modified in order to be appropriately inclusive. His recommendation is for the stress to be on behavior rather than on social identity. Our recommendation is to maintain the emphasis on the violence learned in childhood often at the hands of men (see Farley, 1996) and carried over by the next generation. In any case, there is a need for social work interventions directed toward the unlearning of violence. For the treatment of both batterers and survivors, lesbian-affirmative support services developed for and within the lesbian community are essential. Finally, a lesbian/gay community committed to acknowledging domestic violence is vital to the prevention of violence and protection of lesbians at risk of abuse.

Substance Abuse

For the past fifteen years or so, there has been a growing awareness among gay and lesbian persons that chemical dependency is a major problem in their respective communities, a problem that denies humans freedom and dignity (Kus, 1995). Because of a serious lack of empirically based national data, however, the exact incidence of substance abuse in lesbians is unknown. Studies focusing on women's alcohol and other drug use rarely consider sexual orientation as a variable, whereas studies on lesbian behavior rarely encompass addiction rates. The most commonly cited figure for alcohol-related problems in lesbian women is one out of three (Kus, 1990; JAMA, 1996). A recent survey of two metropolitan areas revealed that marijuana and tobacco use were approximately double among lesbians compared to heterosexual women (Skinner, 1994). However, many of the existing studies are marred by sample flaws including the recruitment of respondents from gay bars (Hughes & Wilsnack, 1994). In the most comprehensive lesbian survey available, the National Lesbian Health Care Survey of 1987 (described by Bradford, Ryan, & Rothblum, 1994), 14 percent of the sample expressed worry about their use of alcohol, and, strikingly, in sharp contrast with heterosexual behavior, alcohol use increased with age. Recognition of the propensity for lesbians to use mood-altering substances, tobacco and alcohol companies have relentlessly targeted lesbians as a lucrative market for their products (Goebel, 1994).

There are several reasons why alcohol use among lesbians would be high. First is the role of the gay bar and women's bars as a key gathering place for coming-out and closeted lesbians. Second is the heavy drinking and active marijuana use among more mature members of this community who function as role models. Third is the interactive relationship among stress attached to living what is regarded as a deviant lifestyle, relationship strain in the absence of public role models, and problems related to internalized homophobia, especially among lesbian youths. Finally, the fact that fewer lesbians than straight women are taking care of children gives them more freedom to party and indulge in substance use than persons tied down by parenting roles. People who feel good about themselves take care of themselves as do most lesbians, but people who don't are inclined to jeopardize their health through the use of mood-altering substances.

Due to the unique needs of this special population and the need for lesbians, like other women, to deal with issues related to victimization and sexuality in a safe and understanding environment, a lesbian-affirming treatment atmosphere is essential. Unfortunately, substance abuse providers tend to hold traditional attitudes toward women's sex roles and to lack training in gay/lesbian dynamics (Underhill, 1991). A feminist, nonheterosexist model is appropriate in order to empower lesbians to make the personal adjustments (in thinking and behavior) necessary for recovery. For lesbian alcoholics in need of inpatient treatment, referral to a lesbian-friendly treatment center such as the Pride Institute in Eden Prairie, Minnesota, or the Gables Recovery Home in Rochester, Minnesota, is appropriate. The expense, however, may be prohibitive for the client who lacks generous insurance coverage for inpatient treatment. Gay/lesbian self-help groups such as Alcoholics Anonymous (AA) are widely available even in small cities across the United States. Since the 1980s, in fact, as vanGelder and Brandt (1996) indicate, alcohol, the mainstay of all bars, lost ground within the lesbian community. Suddenly according to these authors, there was a stronger AA crowd than a drinking crowd; lesbians attending the annual October Women's Weekend had a choice of seven Twelve Step meetings per day.

Lesbians Who Are Disabled

Defined as disabilities are various conditions that range from a permanent physical or mental impairment to a chronic health disorder. Estimates are that one in ten Americans has a disability; disabilities increase with age (Rothblum, 1994). The impairment may be visible or invisible to others. Disabled persons, like gays and lesbians, are socialized in the art of concealment—concealing their condition as much as possible so as not to be discriminated against. But in doing so, they only perpetuate the discrimination. In fighting to appear normal, disabled persons are denying an important part of their reality and effectively disempowering themselves, politically as well as personally.

Corbett (1994) analyzes the similarities and differences between gay pride and disability politics. There is the collective experience of social stigma and internalized oppression, but, regarding those who are disabled, there is the cultural dissonance produced by an idealized physical persona and the rejection of bodily imperfections, which permeates all parts of society. Relating to able-bodied women who tend to be objectified as sexual objects, women with disabilities are often desexualized; they are not even expected to get married or have children (Rothblum, 1994). In contrast, sexuality is seen as a central issue in relation to lesbian and gay persons. So the disabled lesbian becomes, in effect, a study in contradictions. As one disabled lesbian (Boston Women's Health Book Collective, 1992) puts it: "People on the street will deal with my disability sometimes, but no matter how butch I am or what buttons I have on, they won't deal with me as a lesbian" (p. 195).

The discrimination experienced by gay and lesbian people with disabilities, according to Wohlander and Petal (1985) is threefold: homophobia among peers in the disabled community, devaluation and denial of potential in the gay/lesbian community, and some of each from the able-bodied, straight world. Providing social work services to disabled lesbians requires a sensitivity to the challenges of dual membership in minority groups.

Social workers in health care settings need to recognize every individual's right to be viewed as a sexual being, whether homosexual or heterosexual. In this way they can help clients, in the words of Corbett (1994), to see:

- The value of coming out to pave the way for others;
- The importance of our shared pride, when our history is one of persecution and extermination;
- Our disability and sexuality as just part of who we are and to celebrate our whole self, in all its varied dimensions. (p. 356)

Social Work Roles

In this chapter, we have provided a broad overview of many of the issues pertinent to lesbians and health care. Some of the most difficult challenges that lesbians face and that may bring them to the attention of social work services at a hospital or health care center include general health concerns, AIDS, suicide attempts, depression, physical injuries from assault, substance abuse problems, and general disabilities. Many of these challenges are closely bound up with the emotional stress of pursuing a nonheterosexual lifestyle in an inhospitable social environment. The need for social work intervention is paramount to help pave the way for lesbians to get the support services they need for their health and personal empowerment. Now we will consider three roles of the social work—broker, advocate, and clinician—and how they apply to the uniqueness of the population and the setting.

Brokering

In her or his role as social worker, the broker helps clients receive the community services that they need. Health care practitioners who have a thorough knowledge of the variety of community resources available can refer lesbians with health and mental health problems to self-help and other support groups in which they can receive invaluable psychological and practical guidance. For ethnic minority clients with drinking problems or AIDS, for instance, help in rebuilding the extended kinship network can buffer the effects of negative life stressors and isolation. For the chronically or disabled lesbian, referral to an appropriate professional, agency, or organization may be in order. Information can be found in many of the lesbian travel guides that list health clinics, religious groups, and local organizations catering to lesbian clientele. Where appropriate services do not exist, social workers can play an instrumental role in establishing crucial links and networks between health care agencies and major volunteer efforts in the community.

Advocacy

Interceding on behalf of clients both within the health care setting and in the wider community is a vital aspect of social work with lesbians. In order for lesbians to become politically active and to collectively name and confront their suffering in ways that are healing and preventive, they must feel safe; and they can feel safe only in an atmosphere of social and legal acceptance. Providing sensitivity training in hospitals, lobbying politicians to expand financial and medical coverage, conducting homophobia workshops for local women's shelters and substance abuse agencies, writing and distributing pamphlets with facts on legal medical rights and the importance of power of attorney for partners are just a few of the ways that social workers can help ensure that lesbian patients receive the respect and care that they deserve. The importance of conducting empirical research on health care concerns of women and lesbians in key areas such as sexual abuse, suicide, and domestic violence also should not be disregarded.

Clinical Intervention

Psychological woundedness prevents lesbians from acting collectively to alleviate their pain and even from acknowledging the very existence of pain and suffering. Social workers, in the role of clinician, can do much to engage clients in holistic strategies for healing that will break this cycle. Counseling (individual and group) from a nondeficit, nonpathological perspective can help lesbians find their strengths and in so doing even experience a political awakening of sorts. Utilizing feminist empowerment strategies, social workers can reconnect people to the health within themselves and in their environment so that together they—social worker and client—might engage in a collaborative effort toward personal and social growth. Assuming that our clients are either exclusively heterosexual or homosexual inhibits our ability to provide relevant information concerning sexually transmitted diseases. Instead of relying on labels, we need to focus on behaviors as the key to effective safe-sex counseling. Sexual activities among women that can pose a health risk include fisting, sadomasochistic sex, sharing sex toys, unprotected sex with men, amateur tattooing, sharing injection equipment, and alternative insemination (Kaufman et al., 1997). Social workers need to stay abreast of recent empirical studies concerning risk factors for women and share this information with clients.

Conclusion

In a political atmosphere of virulent political attacks on anything connected with sexual diversity and a health care atmosphere of harsh curtailment in social services, especially nonstandard or controversial services, the challenge to social workers with a feminist-based strengths perspective is considerable. The analysis of social worker roles in the final portion of this chapter gives credence both to the view that there is a lot of work to be done and that social workers attached to hospitals and other health care agencies are in a unique position to do it.

We have seen evidence presented for the strong interplay between homophobia in the society (homophobia ranging from direct persecution to subtle neglect and requirements for keeping one's orientation silent) and health problems in the individual. These problems include but are not limited to suicide during adolescence, unhealthy substance use and high risk-taking behaviors, depression, and stranger/relationship victimization. As investigators, educators, healers, role models, and advocates, social workers can alleviate if not totally prevent such outcomes. The next chapter addresses the unique health and mental health concerns of gay males.

REFERENCES

Aguilar, M. (1995). Women and health care. In the *Encyclopedia of social work* (19th ed., pp. 2539–2551). Washington, DC: NASW Press.

Bevier, P., Chiasson, M., Garafalo, E., & Castro, K. (1992, July). Women who have sex with women and multiple risks for HIV at a New York City STD clinic. VIII International Conference on AIDS. Abstract #PO.C. 4662, Amsterdam.

The Boston Women's Health Book Collective. (1992). *The new our bodies, ourselves.* New York: Simon and Schuster.

Bradford, J., Ryan, C., & Rothblum, E. (1994). National lesbian health care survey: Implications for mental health care. *Journal of Consulting and Clinical Psychology 62* (2), 228–242.

Bricker-Jenkins, M. (1994). Feminist practice and breast cancer: "The patriarchy has claimed my right breast. . . ." *Social Work in Health Care 19* (3/4), 17–42.

Cecere, D. (1986). The second closet: Battered lesbians. In K. Lobel (Ed.), *Naming the violence: Speaking out about lesbian battering* (pp. 21–31). Seattle, WA: Seal Press.

Comstock, G. D. (1991). *Violence against lesbians and gay men.* New York: Columbia University Press.

Corbett, J. (1994). A proud label: Exploring the relationship between disability politics and gay pride. *Disability and Society 9* (3), 343–357.

Dempsey, C. (1994). Health and social issues of gay, lesbian, and bisexual adolescents. *Families in Society 75* (3), 160–167.

Durby, D. (1994). Gay, lesbian, and bisexual youth. *Journal of Gay and Lesbian Social Services 1* (3/4), 1–37.

Dziggel, C. (1986). "The perfect couple." In K. Lobel (Ed.), *Naming the violence: Speaking out about lesbian battering* (pp. 62–69). Seattle, WA: Seal Press.

Elliott, P. (1996). Shattering illusions: Same-sex domestic violence. *Journal of Gay and Lesbian Social Services 4* (1), 1–8.

Farley, N. (1996). A survey of factors contributing to gay and lesbian domestic violence. *Journal of Gay and Lesbian Social Services 4* (1), 35–42.

Friedman, R., & Downey, J. (1994). Special article: Homosexuality. *New England Journal of Medicine 331* (14), 923–930.

Gentlewind, C. (1986). Will it never end? In K. Lobel (Ed.), *Naming the violence: Speaking out about lesbian battering* (pp. 41–47). Seattle, WA: Seal Press.

Gibson, P. (1989). *Report of the secretary's task force on youth suicide: Vol. 3, Prevention and interventions in youth suicide* (pp. 110–142). Washington, DC: U.S. Department of Health and Social Services.

Glassman, C. (1995). Lesbians and HIV disease. In G. Lloyd & M. A. Kuszelewicz (Eds.), *HIV disease: Lesbians, gays and the social services* (pp. 61–74). New York: Haworth.

Goebel, K. (1994, November/December). Lesbians and gays face tobacco targeting. *Prevention Pipeline,* pp. 105–107.

Greene, B. (1994). Lesbian and gay sexual orientations. In B. Greene & G. Herek (Eds.), *Lesbian and gay psychology: Theory, research and clinical applications* (pp. 1–24). Thousand Oaks, CA: Sage.

Hart, B. (1986). Lesbian battering: An examination. In K. Lobel (Ed.), *Naming the violence* (pp. 173–189). Seattle: Seal Press.

Heer, C., Grogan, E., Clark, S., & Carson, L. M. (1998). Developing services for lesbians in abusive relationships: A macro and micro approach. In A. Roberts, *Battered women and their families* (2nd ed.). New York: Singer.

Hughes, T., & Wilsnack, S. (1994). Research on lesbians and alcohol: Gaps and implications. *Alcohol, Health and Research World 18* (3), 202–205.

Hunter, J., & Schaecher, R. (1995). Gay and lesbian adolescents. In the *Encyclopedia of social work* (19th ed., pp. 1055–1063). Washington, DC: NASW Press.

Island, D., & Letellier, P. (1991). *Men who beat the men who love them.* New York: Harrington Park Press.

JAMA. (1996a). Health care needs of gay men and lesbians in the United States. *Journal of the American Medical Association 275* (17), 1354–1359.

JAMA. (1996b). Prevalence of HIV infection in the United States, 1984 to 1992. *Journal of the American Medical Association 276* (2), 126–131.

Kaufman, H., Ford, P., Pranger, T., Sankar-Mistry, P., & the Advisory Committee on Women and HIV (1997). Women who have sex with women. *The Social Worker 65* (3), 77–85.

Kus, R. (1990). Alcoholism in the gay and lesbian communities. In R. Kus (Ed.), *Keys to caring: Assisting your gay and lesbian clients* (pp. 66–81). Boston: Alyson.

Kus, R. (1995). Introduction. In R. Kus (Ed.), *Addiction and recovery in gay and lesbian persons* (pp. 1–3). Binghamton, NY: Haworth.

Leslie, D., & MacNeil, L. (1995). In J. Adleman & G. Eguidanos (Eds.), *Racism in the lives of women: Testimony, theory, and guides to antiracist practice* (pp. 161–171). New York: Harrington Park Press.

McNeely, R., & Robinson-Simpson, G. (1987). The truth about domestic violence: A falsely framed issue. *Social Work 32,* 485–490.

Merrill, G. (1996). Ruling the exceptions: Same-sex battering and domestic violence theory. *Journal of Gay and Lesbian Social Services 4* (1), 9–21.

National Institute of Mental Health. (1987). *National lesbian health care survey.* Washington, DC: U.S. Department of Health and Human Services.

Northwood, B. (1986). She never really hit me. In K. Lobel (Ed.), *Naming the violence: Speaking out about lesbian battering* (pp. 148–154). Seattle, WA: Seal Press.

Otis, M., & Skinner, W. (1996). The prevalence of victimization and its effect on mental well-being among lesbian and gay people. *Journal of Homosexuality 30* (3), 93–121.

Pederson, W. (1994). HIV risk in gay and lesbian adolescents. *Journal of Gay and Lesbian Social Services 1* (3/4), 131–147.

Peterson, J. (1995). HIV/AIDS: Women. In the *Encyclopedia of social work* (19th ed., pp. 1325–1329). Washington, DC: NASW Press.

Poole, D. (1995). Health care: Direct practice. In the *Encyclopedia of social work* (19th ed., pp. 1156–1167). Washington, DC: NASW Press.

Proctor, C., & Groze, V. (1994). Risk factors for suicide among gay, lesbian, and bisexual youths. *Social Work 39* (5), 504–512.

Rothblum, E. (1990). Depression among lesbians: An invisible and unresearched phenomenon. *Journal of Gay and Lesbian Psychotherapy 1* (3), 67–87.

Rothblum, E. (1994). Lesbians and physical appearance. In B. Greene & G. Herek (Eds.), *Lesbian and gay psychology: Theory, research, and clinical applications* (pp. 84–97). Thousand Oaks, CA: Sage.

Saleebey, D. (1996). The strengths perspective in social work practice: Extensions and cautions. *Social Work 41* (3), 296–305.

Skinner, W. F. (1994). The prevalence and demographic predictors of illicit and licit drug use among lesbians and gay men. *American Journal of Public Health 84,* 1307–1310.

Trippet, S., & Bain, J. (1990). Preliminary study of lesbian health concerns. *Health Values 14* (6), 30–36.

Underhill, B. (1991). Recovery needs of lesbian alcoholics in treatment. In N. Van Den Bergh (Ed.), *Feminist perspectives on addictions* (pp. 73–86). New York: Springer.

vanGelder, L., & Brandt, P. R. (1996). *The girl next door: Into the heart of lesbian America.* New York: Simon and Schuster.

Waldron, C. M. (1996). Lesbians of color and the domestic violence movement. In C. M. Renzetti & C. H. Miley (Eds.), *Violence in gay and lesbian domestic partnerships* (pp. 43–53). Binghamton, NY: Haworth.

Whitlock, K. (1989). *Bridges of respect: Creating support for lesbian and gay youth* (2nd ed.). Philadelphia: American Friends Service Committee.

Wohlander, K., & Petal, M. (1985). People who are gay or lesbian and disabled. In H. Hidalgo, T. Peterson, & N. J. Woodman (Eds.), *Lesbian and gay issues: A resource manual for social workers* (pp. 38–42). Washington, DC: NASW Press.

CHAPTER 10 Social Work with Gay Males in Health Care Settings

For many gay men death is not a metaphor but a painful reality, as a generation succumbs to the effects of a deadly virus. How to make sense of such horror? How to suggest that in the center of such destruction lies the seed for future awakening?

Mark Thompson, 1987, *Gay Spirit*

Oppression is not conducive to good health. Directly through discrimination and indirectly through anticipating discrimination, homophobia and heterosexism present barriers to gay males seeking health care. Social workers in health care settings are in a key position to influence medical staff to accept the legitimacy of gay lifestyles and to be cognizant of the full array of biopsychosocial variables impinging upon the health of an individual. One of the characteristics of social work practice that distinguishes it, at least ideally, from the medical approach is concern with the social context within which health problems emerge. Gay men with health problems and physical and mental disabilities suffer from dual discrimination and tend to have a double identity, as diseased or disabled in some circles, and as gay in others. Social workers may encounter persons with disabilities in the normal course of their practice. These clients are as apt to be gay as anyone else and need an atmosphere that is open to their concerns about sexuality.

Related to the social context (the stigma, discrimination), and inseparable from it, is the psychological context. That health and self-acceptance are intrinsically linked is one of the underlying assumptions of this chapter. That care and prevention are often far more effective than cure (or attempted cure) is another basic assumption. These assumptions are informed by contemporary social work theory, which perceives society and self in constant and dynamic interaction. The impact of society's heterosexism, for example, can have an impact on the self through self-destructive behaviors relating to personal wellness and health. Internalized homophobia brings an effect to bear on AIDS, both in transmission (related to personal risk taking) and in its treatment. Because the major health care concern of gay men clearly is the impact of the AIDS epidemic, an in-depth discussion of AIDS—transmission and treatment—is the focal point of this chapter.

The connection between homophobia and other health problems is even more tangible with regard to suicide, hate crime victimization, and domestic violence. We will explore the relevant research on these matters and discuss the challenge to social work, both clinically and politically, in providing a supportive treatment environment. This chapter concludes by showing that the goal of health realization is achievable through an affirmative approach that draws on the resilience, resources, and positive motivation that are within each person.

In an article entitled "Heterosexism: Redefining Homophobia for the 1990s," Neisen (1990) argues that the concept of homophobia should be replaced by the interactive constructs of *heterosexism* of the society and *shame* by the individual. Heterosexism, as we have seen in Chapter 2, is the continued promotion by major societal institutions of a heterosexual lifestyle while simultaneously subordinating other (e.g., gay, lesbian, bisexual) lifestyles. Sense of shame occurs in the individual as a response to the public condemnation, whether anticipated or real. These constructs can be effective therapeutic tools for clinicians working with heterosexual, homosexual, or bisexual clients. Therapeutic uses of the constructs focus on establishing a connection between sex role stereotypes and antihomosexual sentiment, assisting gay and lesbian clients in the coming-out process, articulating how oppression leads to shame about one's homosexuality, and working with persons with acquired immunodeficiency syndrome (AIDS).

Gay Men and AIDS

Diseases associated with particular lifestyles, such as heart disease, cancer, stroke, and, most recently, AIDS, are major threats to life expectancy in modern societies. Therefore, decisions about whether or not to live in a healthy manner are central to day-to-day living and constitute a major form of contemporary lifestyles. AIDS deaths fell 44 percent nationwide in 1997, and the number of new AIDS cases also has begun to drop, new statistics show. AIDS deaths dropped from 21,460 in the first half of 1996 to 12,040 during the same period the following year. The falloff has its roots in new drugs rather than in healthy lifestyles (Sternberg, 1998).

Called protease inhibitors, these medicines prevent the virus from making copies of itself, virtually clearing the virus from the blood. As a result, HIV-infected people are less likely to progress to full-blown AIDS and show up in reporting statistics.

There is still no significant decline in new infections with HIV, the AIDS virus, which spreads to roughly 40,000 new people a year. Because of lack of new federal funding for prevention efforts, we can expect to see no serious reduction in HIV transmission rates (Painter, 1998).

CDC epidemiologists favor a national program of "name-based" HIV tracking, a strategy that raises concerns about breaches of privacy. Some states already report HIV cases by name and there have been no government leaks of private information so far.

Before diagnosis, individuals had to find ways to cope with uncertainty about their risk of contracting AIDS and about their initial symptoms. After diagnosis, they have to find answers to their questions about why they contracted the disease, whether they would be able to function in the short run, whether their illness would kill them, and whether they would be allowed to live and (if death was unavoidable) to die with dignity. The data suggest that persons with AIDS respond to the uncertainties of their illness by attempting to assert as much control as possible over their lives, through such divergent strategies as seeking and avoiding knowledge about their illness.

PWAs (Persons With AIDS) are more likely to feel guilty about the behaviors that led to their becoming ill. Thus, when faced with uncertainty about why they became ill, they are more likely to conclude that it was a deserved punishment.

PWAs are more likely to face difficulties in obtaining an accurate diagnosis. Like other illnesses, AIDS can be difficult to diagnose because it is rare and causes multiple symptoms. These problems are exacerbated because physicians often deliberately (although sometimes unconsciously) avoid questions or actions that would lead to diagnosis.

PWAs face greater uncertainty than other ill persons in predicting how their illness will affect their lives; AIDS causes more extensive and less predictable physical and mental damage than most other illnesses.

Social Work Practice

Those who care for or care about PWAs must recognize that PWAs have a strong need to find a logical explanation for their illness. Physicians, social workers, and AIDS activists must learn that although talking in terms of "risk behaviors" can be useful in discussing the possibility of AIDS with persons not yet infected, it can reinforce guilt feelings among those who have AIDS and, thus, can increase their emotional difficulty. Family members and friends, as well as health care workers, must learn to ascertain whether PWAs are blaming themselves and to intervene in such instances, or at least to refer them for counseling. Those who work with PWAs need to learn how psychosocial factors affect PWAs and to develop ways of responding to PWAs' emotional as well as physical strengths.

According to Janis (1983), people can handle stressful situations most effectively if they feel that they are in control of their lives. To achieve this goal he proposes "stress inoculation," in which people (1) are given information about what to expect, which is realistic but allows them to maintain optimism; (2) are encouraged to identify possible actions that can help them to survive and to find internal and external resources that would allow them to take those actions; and (3) are helped to develop their own plan for responding to their situation. Social workers, working with PWAs and their families, can play a major helping role by listening to people, responding to their needs, and validating their feelings. Although some hospitals are beefing up their social work departments for counseling persons diagnosed as HIV positive, unfortunately, other medical establishments are eliminating such programs under the guise of cost-efficiency requirements.

Health Care Provision

When one considers the impact of the fundamental changes taking place in health care, the implications are disturbing. We are talking here of massive accountability reckoning, budget cuts, and downsizing as a result of managed care affecting the most professionally trained nurses and social services staff. At the hospital in Philadelphia, for example, where Boes worked largely with the homeless and persons afflicted with late-stage AIDS infections, the entire social work department recently has been eliminated. What happens when uncertainty is so prevalent, when the medical model has been replaced with a business-oriented model? How will institutionalized systems of accountability affect autonomy and self-identity? How will training of health care professionals be affected by shorter hospital stays and by the lack of control that characterizes ambulatory settings (Gallagher & Searle, 1989)?

Some clues are provided by Mizrahi's (1986) identification of structural strains: between cost containment and the emphasis of academic medicine on using every diagnostic test and trying every treatment that might work; between responsibility for a heavy caseload of patients and the desire to focus on "cases" from which physicians can learn; between the extraordinary benefits of powerful new drugs or procedures and their potential for harm. Mizrahi also notes important limitations under which the house staff work: that the hospital receives persons rejected or released from the rest of the private health care system; that primary and rehabilitative services are neglected in the neighborhood because all resources focus on the one large academic medical center; and that the hospital lacks enough beds to serve "the enormous volume of sick patients." Mizrahi finds hospital care a combat zone. She cites Resident McGee who tells her, "You start regarding them (patients) as the enemy and you really don't care." And Resident Edwards who says, "They get you before you get them. . . . They destroy you and you don't even want to deal with them."

As Fox (1989) concludes in her earlier overview of health care trends, conditions are deteriorating. Some trends mentioned, which have grown worse in recent years, include pressures to contain costs, the briefer and shallower experiences received by trainees because patients leave the hospital more quickly, the growing prevalence of very old hospitalized patients who are chronically ill and disabled, the systematic though unintentional downgrading of patient-oriented clinical training, and the demoralization of medical faculty.

These and recent developments, such as the increase in AIDS patients at academic centers, the shortage of nurses, and the pressures to increase productivity by altering the division of labor, need to be seen as important areas of concern.

Contextualizing Risk Factors

Epidemiology draws on the skills and expertise of professionals from many fields, including medicine, public health, nursing, biology, statistics, anthropology, and psychology. Epidemiologists are like detectives; they investigate what causes groups to become sick or injured and devise solutions.

The study of contextualizing risk factors goes beyond proximate causes, such as unprotected sexual intercourse, sedentary lifestyles, or needle exchange, to understand how people's life circumstances contribute to unhealthy behavior and possible disease exposure. Ultimately such an epidemiologic conceptualization allows for broad-based social interventions and enhances the potential for substantial health benefits for the general population.

Proximate or individually based risks provide only a partial etiological picture of the cause of important health problems, such as infant mortality, chronic illness, and AIDS. Inclusion of social conditions completes the portrait and deepens our understanding of health and illness among human populations.

Bareback Sex

Riding bareback, skin-to-skin sex, and *raw* are the titillating new terms used to describe anal intercourse without rubbers. This form of behavior borders on suicide.

What we have learned in the past decade is that efforts to keep gay men from engaging in unsafe behavior must be consistent and constant. Our AIDS service organizations and local health departments must step up their efforts to be loud and clear in the message of condoms for every act of anal intercourse, particularly when advancements in treating HIV are in the news. What with protease inhibitor ads depicting PWAs as rock-climbing hunks, we must not lose touch with the reality of AIDS. A healthy dose of fear must be placed back into the HIV prevention equation, as it becomes increasingly apparent that the drug cocktails are not a cure. With the huge pool of HIV-positive men in the gay community, odds are high that those who are not using condoms during anal intercourse will eventually become infected.

As T-cells (the immune system's main infection fighters) drop, people start to develop eczema, folliculitis, and, most maddeningly, itchy skin. Many days people scratch themselves to the point of bleeding. More unsightly will be the molluscum—a small raised tumor on their face, neck, buttocks, or other body parts—people may develop.

If there is one common affliction for all people who have HIV, it is periodic diarrhea. People who are HIV positive can get quite sick from many of our municipal water supplies right here in the United States. Many gay men are exposed to genital warts, but often a healthy immune system will help keep them at bay. Without an immune system that functions properly, things like anal condyloma (warts) will start appearing.

To practicing gay men bent on taking chances, we are tempted to urge, "Please, don't take the first sign of good news on the AIDS front and turn it into something it's not." What we have now are a few difficult to tolerate and exorbitantly expensive drugs that have been used to help some people temporarily gain a part of their immune system back to fight the diseases of AIDS. With any luck, it will buy them a few more months or years before they stop maintaining good health. Then, most likely, the skin problems will return, the Kaposi Sarcoma lesions, the dementia, the incontinence, the fevers, the nausea, the brain tumors, and so on.

Grabbing a condom and some lube before entering or being entered by someone is not that big a deal. But if people insist on skin-to-skin sex, once infected with HIV, they can look forward to a future of molluscum, Kaposi's sarcoma, diarrhea, uncontrollable herpes, and other maladies related to immunosuppression, ultimately leading to a painful, difficult death.

The following guidelines represent safe-sex practices based on our knowledge at the present:

1. Sexual abstinence.
2. Have a mutual monogamous relationship with an HIV-negative partner (the greater the number of sexual partners, the greater the risk of meeting someone who is HIV infected).
3. If the sex partner is other than a monogamous partner, use a condom.
4. Do not frequent prostitutes—too many have been found to be HIV infected and are still "working" the streets.
5. Do not have sex with people who you know are HIV infected or are from a high-risk group. If you do, prevent contact with their bodily fluids.
6. Avoid sexual practices that may result in the tearing of body tissues (e.g., penile-anal intercourse).
7. Avoid oral-penile sex unless a condom is used to cover the penis.
8. If you use injection drugs, use sterile or bleach-cleaned needles and syringes and *never* share them.
9. Exercise caution regarding procedures such as acupuncture, tattooing, ear piercing, and so on, in which needles or other unsterile instruments may be used repeatedly to pierce the skin and/or mucous membranes.
10. If you are planning to undergo artificial insemination, insist on frozen sperm obtained from a laboratory that tests all donors for infection with the AIDS virus.
11. If you know that you will be having surgery in the near future and you are able to do so, consider donating blood for your own use.
12. Don't share toothbrushes, razors, or other implements that could become contaminated with blood with anyone who is HIV infected, demonstrates HIV disease, or has AIDS.

Social Dimension of Healing

The social dimension of healing is often overlooked in research. Belief systems and certain symptom complexes are defined as social constructions (Comaroff, 1982; Csordas, 1983; McGuire, 1988) but use of this mode of analysis to document outcome experiences and healing events is less common. The importance of this approach to the study of healing is to understand how clients view their illnesses or life situations, and how they interpret their resolution, transformation, or continuation. Thus, social contexts influence cognitive representations, which in turn may help persons in such groups "get well."

Generally, healing options can lead and will be employed at any time during the course of an illness. At first signs or symptoms of an emotional or physical problem, some individuals seek options other than mainstream medicine. In other instances, people use healing options concurrent with or instead of conventional medical care. At still other times, they turn to healing options after traditional medicine has failed to cure mental, chronic, or terminal illnesses. In this sense, healing options constitute a treatment of last resort.

Healing is a socially constructed event dependent on how individuals view and interpret their physical and emotional problems. Any comprehensive study of health and illness must, therefore, consider how social factors impact the use of options that diverge from mainstream care.

Individuals use healing options because practitioners are friendly, considerate, sensitive, nonthreatening, affordable, and geographically accessible. Additionally, they share similar cultural values and traditions, spend time with their patients or clients, instill optimism and hope, and exercise a more holistic style in treating suspected causes of emotional and physical maladies. Most of all, they are perceived as supportive and helpful whether their remedies succeed or not.

Medical Treatment of HIV

The success of combination HIV drug therapy has led to federally established treatment guidelines that are constantly being revised as new drugs and studies emerge. Federal data show a three-drug combination therapy (also called HAART, for highly active antiretroviral therapy) can reduce HIV activity to below-detectable levels in blood and provide a clinical benefit to many patients by increasing T-cell counts and preventing the onset of HIV-related opportunistic infections.

Despite the high costs of combination therapies, the good news can be measured economically. Reports suggest that HAART is cost-effective because it reduces the amount spent on treating patients with HIV-related illnesses. A study released in January 1997 by St. Vincent's Hospital and Medical Center in New York (a Greenwich Village facility with a high AIDS caseload) showed a 10.5 percent decrease in admissions from 1995 to 1996, along with shorter hospital stays and a striking 24 percent decrease in the hospital's average monthly AIDS census. At the same time, the number of HIV-related ambulatory visits dramatically increased, as did inpatient pharmacy costs. This trend has been mirrored in other studies across the country.

For now, it's almost impossible to document the impact of HAART on every opportunistic infection, but several important studies have tracked the major ones. Preliminary data in July 1997 from a CDC study called the Adult Spectrum of Disease Cohort showed that from 1994 to mid-1997, there was a sharp drop in the incidence of pneumocysts carinii pneumonia (PCP), mycobacterium avium complex (MAC), esophageal candidiasis, and wasting syndrome. In September 1997 Johns Hopkins researchers released results of a five-year study showing that in 1996, use of HAART was linked with decreased rates of cytomegalovirus (CMV), toxoplasmosis, and MAC. This news is particularly relevant because these opportunistic infections can affect the brain, an organ that is difficult to treat because few HIV drugs penetrate the blood-brain barrier. For now, front-line researchers caution that individuals on HAART remain vulnerable to HIV-related brain infections.

Looking ahead, there are other reasons to be worried. In September 1997 French scientists at the Hopitâl Pitie-Salpetrière reported that although CMV cases had declined due to

HAART therapy from 1995 to 1996, fourteen patients with low T-cell counts had still developed CMV infections. The French research suggests that for now HAART therapy should not be a substitute for CMV preventive therapy in individuals with low T-cell levels; experts continue to advocate preventive therapy when a patient's T-cells fall below 300.

Racial/Ethnic Aspects

The continuing decline in AIDS deaths in the United States has caused some experts to declare that we have turned a corner in the epidemic, due largely to new therapies. Although true, this is masking a rapid rise in HIV infection in minority populations. As economic and cultural factors hinder the access of minorities to HIV education and medical care, HIV is making new inroads to these lower-income communities. Youth are at greater risk; up to 50 percent of new infections are in people under age twenty-five.

By the close of 1996, the Centers for Disease Control and Prevention reported that the number of AIDS cases had dropped among gay men. Among minority youths, gay and bisexual teenagers are particularly at risk. Advocates now warn that unless targeted prevention and comprehensive treatment efforts are aimed at minority communities, the HIV epidemic here may come to resemble that in developing countries.

An underlying reason for the present racial/ethnic disparity has to do with the AIDS-care infrastructure, which was largely created by the gay and lesbian community at the onset of the epidemic. As the epidemic has shifted, larger HIV agencies across the country have expanded their outreach efforts. But they are often not located in poorer, minority neighborhoods, so those at highest risk aren't getting AIDS services or treatment education. Meanwhile, cuts in government funding have caused a shortage of minority-run services in many at-risk communities.

Looking ahead, prevention advocates say that education efforts must be specifically targeted to reach affected groups. Training peer educators and providing culturally sensitive materials are two examples of strategies that can help improve access to care and to HIV therapies within minority communities. But advocates must focus on the socioeconomic barriers that limit access to the health care system for certain populations, and on psychosocial factors that underlie risky behavior.

Indeed, successful HIV outreach must be placed firmly in the context of real-world issues such as poverty, homelessness, drug addictions, sexual abuse, sex work, and mental illness, say advocates. That means offering HIV counseling, resources, and medical care in places where people are already getting help for other problems: community organizations, methadone and substance abuse clinics, homeless and runaway shelters, and street programs. It also means increasing support for local and minority-headed HIV programs run by trained peer educators, counselors, and physicians with established ties to at-risk communities. Such innovative strategies can help bridge the gap in HIV care for the most affected populations. No prevention approach will be effective, however, without attention to the role substance abuse plays in increasing gay men's susceptibility to contracting AIDS and other diseases.

Before we go on to consider substance abuse as a gay male health issue, see Box 10.1 for an informative and moving interview with a person in the final stages of the AIDS virus.

BOX 10.1

Interview with My Brother

Tami: When were you diagnosed as having HIV?

Ken: May 1991.

T: What made you get tested?

K: I had an allergic reaction and had to have blood drawn for a test.

T: How did you deal with the results?

K: Didn't bother me. I went on with my life. I actually expected it.

T: Do you know how you contracted the virus?

K: No. Well . . . sex.

T: How did your friends, family, and partner deal with the news that you were HIV-positive? Did you tell them right away?

K: Mom was upset at first. She followed up with support though and is now the strongest in supporting me. Some of the rest of the family doesn't know. Randy [his older brother] wouldn't handle it well, and so I will not tell him . . . It's better this way. We still talk as if there is nothing wrong. It did take me a while to tell the family because I was scared of their response, especially Dad's. He is okay with it now. Brian [his partner] is still not sure how to deal with it. He pretty much just ignores it. The disease is passé with my friends because a lot of them have it. We all support each other.

T: When did you first begin to become sick or ill due to this disease?

K: There has been nothing major accredited to it yet. Well, except for Chronic Obstructive Lung Disorder. Also, I have had chronic fatigue, pains and cramps, night sweats, and fever since the beginning.

T: What kind of treatment have you been through?

K: Lots of medicine. I started on the natural protocol of AZT, DDI, and DDT. These weren't working so I was removed. Now I am taking 34 pills a day. The medicines are Norvere (a protease inhibitor), Beclovent (for lung disease), Percoset (for pain), Prophylaxis (so I don't get pneumonia), Epovir, Acyclovir, Zerisept, and Zerot. There are others too, but that's what I can remember right now.

T: How have you been feeling lately?

K: I recently had surgery for my neck. The recovery was only supposed to be a few days, and it has been about a month. I have a fever and rash from the antibiotic. It did not interact well with the AIDS medicine . . . My body rejected it. I feel like hell. It's one thing after another. My T-cell count is very close to zero. My viral load is 357,000 . . . It's supposed to be zero.

T: What does viral load mean?

K: How much of the virus is in a million parts of your blood. Otherwise I seem to have been doing well. No opportunistic infections. My body is ignoring the disease for the most part. Lately there have been setbacks, but I still have it under control.

T: Have you been treated any differently since being diagnosed? Experienced any discrimination?

K: No, not in the Washington, DC area. You learn to not tell people . . . especially in a straight environment. In the gay community here, it is not stigmatized.

T: Can you tell me about any "benefits" you've received such as Social Security or insurance?

K: I am receiving Social Security disability. I have been on it for about 2½ years now. It only took one time at the Social Security office to get it and I never have had to go back. It was smoother than it should have been. Most people have a real hard time. It is not enough money to live on. I get $697/month. One medicine costs $52,000/year. I only pay $20 for each prescription, but it really adds up. My wages were insured, so I always will get 60% of the wages I was earning when I left. The problem with getting benefits is telling them more than they need to know. Relax and go to the doctor first for a statement. My life

(continued)

BOX 10.1 Continued

insurance is a retirement plan from my prior job. I have about $78,000. It's nice to see on paper. I am going to sell them soon and invest while I still have time.

T: Do you ever think about death or dying?

K: Not really. Sooner or later everyone dies. What has changed is the feeling of how you're going to get there. I'm more worried about the illnesses and sickness before than I am about the actual dying part. I do know that I want to be cremated and I know where all of my ashes are going.

T: What about religion . . . ?

K: I am Catholic. I was born a Catholic and I will die a Catholic. I do not practice being one. I have made peace with God in my own way.

T: Do you have anything else you'd like to add or any words of advice for others?

K: Be careful of doctors. Many claim they know how to treat AIDS, but only want insurance money. I just fired my doctor. He just wanted to barely keep me alive and was very negative in my outlook. Do research on doctors. You should fire them if you doubt anything. You must have a good knowledge of your disease . . . It saves time and effort.

Insurance companies need to do more. Once you are diagnosed as terminal, insurance companies can waive paying your bill. A caseworker friend of mine said that at his AIDS clinic, in 60% of cases people are left devastated. A single white male in Virginia gets only $9/month for food stamps. This does not allow you to survive AIDS.

Stay as positive as you can. Don't let it (the disease) run your life, run it. Once it gets control of you it's over.

There is too much research being done. There needs to be help for those of us who already have the disease. It is a government genocide of those with AIDS. This is a plague and it needs to be dealt with on a here-and-now basis.

K: Have you had any contact with a counselor or social worker?

T: No. I am not ready for one yet. I will not go to a psychiatrist or psychologist though . . . they have no business treating AIDS patients. I have my own support system. I have heard from others that they, social workers, that is, do care and do help them out in getting the things they need to live, cope with, and survive the disease.

T: Thank you very much for doing this interview for me.

K: No problem. It was good for me to talk about it, especially to someone who understands the situation.

Two days after this interview, Ken was hospitalized for a very high fever and weakness. He was then diagnosed a week later with MAC, an opportunistic infection.

Source: By Tami Huff. Printed with permission of Ken Huff and Tami Huff, BA in Social Work, University of Northern Iowa.

Substance Abuse

Abuse of alcohol and other drugs has long been noted as a problem in the gay community. Although it is hard to arrive at an accurate estimate of the percentage of gay men who suffer from substance abuse due to the difficulty of obtaining a random sample of gay men, all the research confirms a high incidence of alcohol and other substance abuse; estimates range from 20 percent to 35 percent (van Wormer, 1995; Warn, 1997). Gay bars and clubs are central to the social fabric of gay life; cocaine and methamphetamines and other dangerous drugs are readily available in after-hours clubs frequented by gay men (Warn, 1997). A skimming of the ads in gay and lesbian magazines reveals a marketing blitz of hard liquor advertising that is unconscionable.

Approximately 4 percent to 5 percent of heterosexual drug injectors are HIV positive. About 40 percent of men who have sex with men and shoot crystal meth are HIV positive, according to a study by Clay (1997). Clay discovered in interviews with meth users in Washington state that crystal meth is used as a powerful sexual facilitator, a means of overcoming sexual fears and reservations. When people are influenced by such strong chemicals, safe-sex practices, needless to say, are thrown to the wayside.

In a sample of 340 gay men from the Cleveland area, Ghindia and Kola (1996) found that alcohol was the drug of choice and that cocaine use was prevalent among those aged twenty-five through thirty-nine. Unique to this population compared to heterosexual men is that heavy alcohol consumption and associated problems continued across the life span rather than diminishing with age. One possible explanation for homosexual men is that they do not "settle down" as readily and are freer to spend more time drinking. Another factor relating to their substance abuse is the tendency of sexual minorities to use mind-altering chemicals to break down their sexual inhibitions; such inhibitions or hang-ups are related to sexuality that is out of step with societal norms (Warn, 1997). In substance abuse treatment, one of the biggest challenges to sobriety for gays and lesbians entails learning how to initiate same-sex encounters without the aid of alcohol as a "social lubricant."

Gay and lesbian alcoholics and other substance abusers most often find themselves in predominantly heterosexual treatment centers. Because of the homophobia present in the typical treatment group, few gays and lesbians will want to take the risk of disclosing their sexual orientation. To encourage private sharing in individual sessions, the counselor will find it helpful to display literature about gay/lesbian AA meetings. To meet the needs of sexual diversity, every large agency should make a point of having one or more openly gay or lesbian counselors on the staff.

Pride Institute, a thirty-six-bed facility in Eden Prairie, Minnesota, near Minneapolis is a gay-specialized treatment center. Its unique program addresses issues such as internalized homophobia, low self-esteem, coming out to family and friends, same-sex sexuality, early childhood sexual abuse, and safe-sex practices in addition to addictions education and treatment. Insurance payment plans, however, are reluctant to cover such intensive inpatient treatment due to cost-saving managed care restrictions. In any case, gay and lesbian Twelve-Step meetings provide gay and lesbian substance abusers with sober support networks and an opportunity for complete openness.

Hate Crimes

Feminine men thrown into a jail cell, cross-dressers, adolescent gays at school: These are examples of males who are prone to be physically attacked and possibly even killed. The scapegoating of this sexual minority, discussed in some depth in Chapter 2, creates a major health risk, physically and mentally, for the survivors and victims of this terrifying kind of abuse. The Hate Crimes Prevention Act of 1998 removes the overly restrictive requirements the FBI previously had to investigating and prosecuting hate crimes based on race, religion, national origin, and color. Furthermore, for the first time in history, hate crimes against gays and lesbians as well as gender-based hate crimes and hate crimes against the disabled are now a violation of the federal law. According to the FBI's Uniform Crime Reports of 1996, hate crimes committed against a person because of the victim's real or perceived sexual orientation make up the third largest reported category, following race and religion, respectively. But despite the frequency of hate crimes committed on the basis of sexual orientation, thirty states still do not have much needed hate crime laws that cover sexual orientation as a category.

Suicide Risk

Sometimes society's hatred is turned within. Remafedi, French, Story, Resniek, and Blum (1998) in their study on the relationship between suicide risk and sexual orientation found that there is evidence of a strong association between suicide risk and bisexuality or homosexuality in young males. A Canadian study conducted through the University of Calgary's renowned center for the study of suicide interviewed young adult men who answered questions on portable computers (King, 1996). Results were startling in that gay and bisexual subjects were found to have nearly fourteen times the suicide risk of heterosexual males. Celibate males were found to have the highest rates of attempted suicide. The sample size for celibate males, however, was extremely small. The Canadian study is unique in that it is based on a cross section of young males, not on a sample of persons already known to be gay. The researchers, Christopher Bagley and Pierre Tremblay, are social work faculty at the University of Calgary.

Religious fundamentalism was seen to be associated with a risk of suicide in gay males, presumably because of unresolved feelings of guilt. In their work in a psychiatric clinic, in the early years of the AIDS epidemic, Flavin, Franklin, and Frances (1986) were disturbed to find that several suicidal gay patients had deliberately tried to contract AIDS as an indirect way of killing themselves. In helping gay men come to terms with their sexuality, a strengths approach is essential. Strategies of gay-positive counseling are described in full in the following chapter. For more details on this study, see Chapter 2.

Domestic Assault

Gays and lesbians are more likely to physically injure one another than to be victims of hate crimes, according to a study released by the National Coalition of Anti-Violence Programs and cited in *The Advocate* (1996). The numbers, based on reports from gay organizations in six cities, are indicative of a serious although often unreported incidence of domestic male violence.

With two men in a relationship, conjecture Island and Letellier (1991) in their book aptly entitled *Men Who Beat the Men Who Love Them,* it is possible that domestic violence occurs more frequently in the gay community than in straight America. In any case, the fact of gay men's violence forces us to admit that many men are victims, sometimes passive victims, of dangerous power plays. Yet, as Island and Letellier indicate, there is a dearth of research on this topic and few agencies specialized to deal with it. Even more alarming is the near-total absence of agencies set up to provide services to gay male batterers.

One treatment center set up to deal with this problem is located in the Seattle area. Farley (1996) studied over 200 clients referred for what he calls "perpetrator treatment." His finding was that intergenerational abuse patterns were common, with a high incidence of alcohol abuse reported in the families of origin of the perpetrators as well as heavy substance abuse among themselves.

Byrne (1996) describes an innovative and highly practical model for treatment—didactic and long-term individual and group therapy—for gay batterers in Washington, DC. The majority of gay males referred to Byrne, as he notes, have manifested a negative self-concept related to being homosexual as well as negative feelings about their personhood in general. A critical question posed to such clients is: How is it that you are hurting so badly and experiencing such pain that you are abusing your partner? Another theme reiterated frequently is that positive change is possible. Treatment is strengths oriented, rare among work with violent men; Byrne's goal is to create, nurture, and strengthen the individual's capacity to maintain healthy intimate relationships. Written contracts of nonviolence are drawn up. Three rules that are included in any safety plan to protect the partner are to not drink, use drugs, or drive a vehicle when angry. Appropriate time-out procedures are taught.

Méndez (1996), similarly, describes an innovative program at the New York City Gay and Lesbian Anti-Violence Project. Knowledge of immigration issues is essential, as Méndez argues, for effective services to a diverse population. A common form of psychological abuse of gay batterers is to use the undocumented status of the victim as another weapon of power and control. Latinos can be recruited as volunteers through ads in the mainstream Spanish-speaking press. A Latina/Latino domestic violence support group can be very helpful to lesbian and gay male victims of domestic violence.

Conclusion

A slow, uneven increase in social accommodation and legal protection for gay men and lesbian women characterizes the American scene. Centuries-old state laws criminalizing same-sex genital contact have fallen one by one in half the states; enforcement is less vigorous in those remaining. Decades-old restrictions on admitting gay and lesbian foreigners into the country have been repealed.

Efforts by homosexual men and women to enjoy the civil rights of heterosexuals continue, exemplified by the fight to join the military and to marry. For the first time, the military is being seriously challenged on its policy of excluding practicing gays and lesbians. For the first time, similarly, a state has considered seriously the right of two same-sex persons to marry.

Hesitantly, courts are acknowledging the capacity of homosexuals to be effective parents who do not compromise the best interests of the children. The definition of *family* is evolving. Same-sex partners with children have become more visible and increasingly recognized by the law.

Some inroads are being made to guarantee openly gay and lesbian people equal opportunity both in securing employment and in working in an environment free from harassment. Canadian federal law has been much more advanced than U.S. law, however, in this regard. People are becoming increasingly open to colleagues and relatives about their sexuality.

Public opinion, especially among younger persons, is more accepting of gays and lesbians, although discrepancies exist between regions of the country. At the same time that lesbians and gays are achieving greater visibility and unprecedented gains in civil rights, however, and maybe because of it, they are being victimized by increased violence and oppression by organized factions from the religious right.

Countering this heightened acceptance has been a recent backlash brought by those claiming to be protectors of "traditional family values." We will hear more about this in the next chapter. Although court decisions protecting homosexuals may not alter public opinion, they are applying the brakes against enforcement of new discriminatory laws. And, although some individuals continue to beat and kill in consequence of the victim's sexual orientation, the law has taken a firm stand against the crimes of hate.

The HIV epidemic, blighting hundreds of thousands, although devastating, has bonded the gay community. Furthermore, it has not yielded the feared isolation, scapegoating, and branding of homosexuals as the new lepers. This too reflects an evolution of the social and legal status of gay and lesbian citizens in the United States and Canada.

All-or-nothing approaches, which ignore the evolved and ambiguous sexual realities of everyday life, will not reduce the transmission of HIV, but indeed may increase it by enforcing and reinforcing guilt and a lack of self-efficacy with each and every slip; moreover, as a grand and fatal finality, such approaches give more virulent HIV strains a helping hand. Reducing transmission—not eliminating transmission—is truly our only hope at this stage of the epidemic. To realize this feat is no small endeavor and would be the noblest of accomplishments. It requires the pragmatic and steadfast efforts of individuals, communities, professionals, and governmental agencies; and furthermore, any such endeavor must consider the amorphous and unpredictable world of sexual pleasure, a fuzzy world to which HIV has so well adapted.

If we are wise enough to view the world as it really is, as a fuzzy world, we can learn to see how the big picture and the little picture connect in the overall scheme of things—where daily human experience is acted out and pleasure is savored, where viruses may evolve but human behavior can be changed, and yes, where people, including gay men, sometimes have sex without a condom, but then, later, regret their mistakes, try to do better, and spread the word to others.

REFERENCES

Byrne, D. (1996). Clinical models for the treatment of gay male perpetrators of domestic violence. *Journal of Gay and Lesbian Social Services 4* (19), 107–116.

Clay, C. (1997, Spring). Bisexual crystal injectors in Seattle. *Harm Reduction,* pp. 18–19.

Cline, R., & Johnson, S. (1992). Mosquitoes, doorknobs, and sneezing: Relationships between homophobia and AIDS mythology among college students. *Health Communication 4* (4), 273–289.

Comaroff, J. (1982). Medicine: Symbol and ideology. In P. Wright & A. Treacher (Eds.), *The problem of medical knowledge.* Edinburgh: Edinburgh University Press.

Csordas, T. (1983). The rhetoric of transformation in ritual healing. *Culture, Medicine and Psychiatry 7,* 333–375.

Farley, N. (1996). A survey of factors contributing to gay and lesbian domestic violence. *Journal of Gay and Lesbian Social Services 4* (1), 35–42.

Flavin, D., Franklin, J., & Frances, R. (1986). The acquired immune deficiency syndrome (AIDS) and suicidal behavior in alcohol-dependent men. *American Journal of Psychiatry 143* (11), 1441–1442.

Fox, R. (1989). *The sociology of medicine.* Englewood Cliffs, NJ: Prentice-Hall.

Gallagher, E., & Searle, C. (1989). Content and context in health professional education. In H. Freeman & S. Levine (Eds.), *Handbook of medical sociology.* Englewood Cliffs, NJ: Prentice-Hall.

Ghindia, D., & Kola, L. (1996, November). Gay male substance abuse examined. *Issues of Substance, 8,* 11.

Island, D., & Letellier, P. (1991). *Men who beat the men who love them.* New York: Haworth.

Janis, I. (1983). Stress inoculation in health care: Theory and research. In D. Meichenbaum & M. Jaremko (Eds.), *Stress reduction and prevention.* New York: Plenum.

King, M. (1996, November 12). Suicide watch. *The Advocate,* pp. 41–44.

McGuire, M. (1988). *Ritual healing in suburban America.* New Brunswick: Rutgers University Press.

Méndez, J. (1996). Serving gays and lesbians of color who are survivors of domestic violence. *Journal of Gay and Lesbian Social Services 4* (1), 53–59.

Mizrahi, T. (1986). *Getting rid of patients: Contraindications in the socialization of physicians.* New Brunswick: Rutgers University Press.

Neisen, J. (1990). Heterosexism: Redefining homophobia for the 1990s. *Journal of Gay and Lesbian Psychotherapy 1* (3), 21–35.

Painter, K. (1998, October 8). Drugs cut AIDS deaths nearly in half. *USA Today,* p. 1A.

Remafedi, G., French, S., Story, M., Resnick, M., & Blum, R. (1998, January). The relationship between suicide risk and sexual orientation: Results of a population-based study. *American Journal of Public Health 88,* 57–60.

Sternberg, S. (1998, February 3). AIDS deaths, new cases show decline. *USA Today,* D1.

Thompson, M. (1987). *Gay spirit: Myth and meaning.* New York: St. Martin's Press, Introduction.

van Wormer, K. (1995). *Alcoholism treatment: A social work perspective.* Chicago: Nelson-Hall.

Warn, D. (1997). Recovering issues of substance-abusing gay men. In S. L. A. Straussner & E. Zelvin (Eds.), *Gender and addictions: Men and women in treatment* (pp. 387–410). Northvale, NJ: Jason Aronson.

CHAPTER

11 Working with Families of Lesbians, Gays, and Bisexuals

Each family is special. The most important thing about a family is that all the people in it love each other.

Lesléa Newman, 1994, *Heather Has Two Mommies*

Lesbians, gay males, and bisexuals come to family therapists for all the reasons straight people do; they come to work on family of origin issues, communication problems, and a family member's alcoholism or mental illness. But they also come with unique concerns related to their sexual identity: blended family complications, child custody problems (especially for lesbian mothers), the desire to open up communication channels with estranged relatives, issues pertaining to same-sex sexuality, and loss of a loved one who died of AIDS. Heterosexuals, too, seek family therapy for matters related to homosexuality, for example, concern over gender-appropriate behavior in a young son, the shock of learning an offspring is gay or lesbian, or the even more shocking discovery that a spouse is having an affair with someone of the same sex.

Two key principles attract sexual minority clients and their families to seek professional help: the promise of confidentiality, and the tradition of nonjudgmental acceptance. Perhaps for these reasons, and due to a reluctance to talk of these matters to family members, friends, or clergy, gays and lesbians are more likely than are heterosexuals to see a therapist (Liddle, 1997). Often gays, lesbians, and bisexuals seek out a psychotherapist for individual therapy when they need to see someone skilled in the dynamics of intensive family work. Often, also, they seek out a specialist in the area of their concern—mental health, alcoholism, and the therapist simply takes for granted that the client is heterosexual. African Americans seeking assistance related to their sexuality are likely to find few, if any, therapists of color with relevant training (Greene, 1994).

"Homosexuality: Are We Still in the Dark?" This is the theme of a specialized issue of *The Family Therapy Networker.* In her article of the same title, Markowitz (1991) bemoans the paucity of gay and lesbian content within family therapy circles. Laird (1995) concurs:

Until very recently, she claims, the lesbian or lesbian-headed family has been virtually unheard of in the family therapy field, and the gay family nonexistent. And the parents of gays and lesbians haven't been given much understanding either.

A strongly adhered to misapprehension within family therapy is that sexual minority clients will only seek out known gay and lesbian therapists. And, indeed, a national survey of 392 gay men and lesbians who had engaged in therapy revealed that 41 percent did select self-identified gays, lesbians, or bisexuals (Liddle, 1997). And lesbians tended to prefer female over male therapists. Despite these preferences, however, it is obvious that all practitioners will be dealing with sexual diversity and complicated family arrangements. Laird estimates, in fact, that family therapists can expect to see two cases per week involving lesbian or gay issues. The need for therapist knowledge about these issues is obvious.

Following an overview of gay, lesbian, and bisexual issues relevant to family counseling, this chapter will concentrate on working with three populations: parents who are gay, lesbian, bisexual, or transgender; parents of gay, lesbian, and bisexual children; and couples dealing with relationship issues. Guidelines for affirmative counseling under diverse situations will be provided.

Overview

Two major biases pervade the literature and practice ideology concerning gay and lesbian families. The first one is the pathology bias, the error of exaggerating the difficulties of living as a gay or lesbian family in a heterosexist society. A major principle of practice with lesbian, gay, and bisexual parents is not to assume the sexual orientation of the parents is the problem (Appleby & Anastas, 1998). Knowing only the nature of the sexual bonding gives social workers and other practitioners little information about the family's personality components, cultural affiliations, or economic hardships. Markowitz (1991), for example, describes how upon going into therapy to deal with unresolved anger toward her dying alcoholic father, the therapist failed to get beyond a nonissue of coming out to her father.

The second major bias in the practice field is the therapist who, at the other extreme, believes that sexual identity makes absolutely no difference, so why should gay or lesbian clients keep harping on their sexuality? After all, they can keep this aspect of their lives private just like heterosexuals do. Hardman's (1997) survey of British social workers revealed that many respondents holding liberal humanist attitudes failed to acknowledge the lesbian context in their assessments and interventions. In the absence of theoretical guidance, the social workers' insistence that "the problem is the problem" caused them to lose sight of their clients' uniqueness. The conventional wisdom in the family therapy world is to concentrate on boundary and communication issues and to stress the importance of constructing clear boundaries between family members. Yet, as for all minority groups living in a hate-filled environment, the particular familial arrangements that develop may have positive dividends for survival. And the high level of fusion in lesbian relationships, labeled as *enmeshment* by family therapists, may serve important compensatory functions.

Both tendencies in social work practice—exaggerating or ignoring differences—are associated with a failure to recognize the tremendous diversity within gay/lesbian experience, diversity by class, race, ethnicity, or personality. Speaking of the African American gay experience, Hardy (1997) observes that therapists who fall into the trap of only wanting to emphasize the positive do a disservice to clients because it's like telling an abused child to stop thinking about the beatings and return to play.

In this chapter, we will try to hit on a happy medium between praise and despair regarding alternative family forms. With the strengths approach as our guide, we will be looking for resilience in whatever form it takes. Like Laird (1993), we will learn of "the special strengths of this invisible minority, strengths that, at least to some extent, come from standing at the margins and from having to be particularly alert to and critical of prevailing cultural and political discourses" (p. 210).

Today the prevailing winds are blowing from every direction all at once; the focal point of the storm is the family. Whereas politically ambitious politicians seek to restrict gay/lesbian behavior and civil rights, especially in regard to the right to marry and adopt children, lesbian and gay militance has come increasingly to direct attention toward winning domestic partner benefits and all the rights pertaining thereof.

In Canada, according to some gay and lesbian commentators, this may be the time to be out of the closet (Dwyer, 1997). Parliament recently outlawed discrimination based on sexual orientation; many employees now offer same-sex spousal benefits. In the classrooms of Canada, however, the harassment of seemingly gay students continues unabated. And instead of taking initiatives to curb such violence, school boards such as one in British Columbia are banning pro-gay and lesbian library material. In other parts of the country, however, such as Toronto, many effective antihomophobia programs are being offered.

Over the past decade any movement in one direction—for example, recognition of the gay/lesbian presence in art or politics—has been countered by a surge of activity from the opposite direction. The war being waged against gays and lesbians today, as mentioned earlier, is being waged on the family front. Even people who seem ready to accept homosexuality as a given have difficulty with the idea of gays, lesbians, or bisexuals gaining recognition as married partners or parents. And yet, today, as Laird and Green (1996) note, an increasing number of lesbians are choosing to give birth to or adopt children whereas gay men are choosing to build families through the use of surrogate mothers. Research consistently reveals that the children of gays and lesbians do as well as the offspring of traditional parents on the standard mental health measures. Such children, moreover, have definite advantages when it comes to flexibility and tolerance. Writers in the family therapy literature would do well to explore the strengths of such family forms as well as their problems. Not only are gays and lesbians forming couples and family relationships that are viable and healthy but, in many ways, as Laird and Green further indicate, they are forging creative couple and family relationship models that have much to offer all couples and families.

The desire for family is universal. So strong is this inclination among women that even under conditions of imprisonment, inmates will often relate to each other in terms of surrogate family roles. (See Chapter 2 for a description of these institutional family forms.) That gays and lesbians are family oriented, as well, is revealed in the gay theme song of the movie *The Birdcage,* "We Are Family." It is further echoed in the lesbian/gay code words for determining if another person is a member of the tribe. "Is she family?" it is asked.

All too often the mental health literature views gays and lesbians in isolation. If family matters are mentioned at all, it is often in terms of presumed family of origin causative factors.

In the remainder of this chapter we will explore the experiences of gays, lesbians, and bisexuals as life partners, as parents, as children, and as members of intimate relationships.

Working with Gay, Lesbian, Bisexual, and Transgender Parents

To be a family headed by a same-sex couple in a heterosexist society is to wrestle with weighty issues at every turn: childbearing and/or child custody arrangements; when and how to come out to children; how much to tell people at church, school, work, or in the neighborhood. How do you walk the fine line between discretion and openness in dealing with the outside world, in other words? Issues of extended family acceptance, of gender socialization of the children, and internalized homophobia in one or both partners can undermine the healthiest of same-sex relationships. Forced to shape their own rituals and traditions, these unorthodox families are blazing the trail for themselves and others.

Lesbian-Headed Families

Although there are no reliable statistics on the exact numbers, estimates are that there are between 1.5 to 5 million lesbian families with children (Appleby & Anastas, 1998). These families occur in many forms. Until recently, most of the children were products of prior heterosexual marriages (Laird, 1995). The present-day trend is for the lesbian couple to choose to be foster parents or to adopt children or perhaps, more logically (although not less controversially), for one or both partners to get pregnant. Often the pregnancy takes place through medically sponsored donor insemination. Before the advent of the AIDS pandemic, informal arrangements were often made, the common choice of donor being a gay male friend of the family. This course, which was far less expensive than going through a sperm bank, could be done in the privacy of the home. However the procedure was done, the process offered the gay male the opportunity to parent and at the same time provided the child with a male parent figure. Moreover, it sealed in an impressive way the sister/brother bonding of lesbian and gay man. Unfortunately, publicized incidents in which both mother and child contracted the AIDS virus in this manner has considerably reduced the numbers of women choosing this option (Weston, 1991).

Laird reports an alternative arrangement in which the sperm donor is related to the nonbiological lesbian parent or "co-mother." In this way, each woman is biologically kin to the child. An increasingly common arrangement is for an anonymous donor obtained from a sperm bank to provide the sperm; this approach minimizes the likelihood of future legal or social connection between the mother or her child and the donor (Appleby & Anastas, 1998). Hare (1994) describes the situation of both women getting impregnated from the same unknown donor, making the children biologically half-siblings to each other.

In New York City, Beth Israel Health Care System has opened Gay Women's Focus, the first hospital-based lesbian health care practice in the nation (*The Advocate,* 1998b). The practice, which is lesbian run, will provide basic gynecological services as well as artificial insemination and mental health referrals. And in Northampton, Massachusetts, a town described in *Newsweek* as a "lesbian mecca" (Kantrowitz & Senna, 1993), there are lesbian parenting classes and day-care centers for children of lesbian mothers. Newman, one of the more famous residents, authored the controversial book *Heather Has Two Mommies* to meet the need for a storybook to reflect an alternative family focus.

In an issue of *Newsweek* featuring a loving lesbian couple on the cover, Salholz (1993) describes the modern vital "sex positive" scene in today's "extraordinarily diverse lesbian culture," which includes a thriving sexual paraphernalia shop in San Francisco. However:

> Others don't have the energy to party—they're the "vanilla lesbians," home with their kids. There have always been lesbian parents, but in previous decades they tended to be women who discovered their sexuality some time after marriage and motherhood. Increasingly, there are lesbian couples who are becoming mothers together. Eileen Rakower, 33, and her partner each had a child by artificial insemination from the same unknown donor. "We have created a family this way, as out lesbians," says Rakower, a lawyer. Interestingly, some of the deepest resistance the two women encountered came from older homosexuals. "What we saw," she says, "was a real self-doubting, self-hatred. We don't get that anymore from people who know us and know our kids," now 4 years old and 20 months old. (p. 59)

Myths of Lesbian Families

Myth 1 Children of Lesbian Mothers Will Grow Up to Be Homosexual. The fear perpetuated by the general public is that children reared by lesbian mothers (or gay fathers), because they lack normative role models for "gender-appropriate" behavior, will be confused. The research which has been done, predominantly on the more numerous lesbian-headed families, however, consistently has found that children reared in lesbian homes were every bit as well adjusted as comparable children reared by heterosexual mothers (Appleby & Anastas, 1998). In a rare, fourteen-year-long British study of the offspring of eighteen lesbian mothers (most of whose children were a result of an earlier marriage), Tasker and Golombok (1997) studied the effectiveness of lesbian mothers as parents. This study, conducted at a research center at the City University of London, found that the children from lesbian households emerged every bit as well adjusted as their peers in the comparison group raised in heterosexual homes. As adolescents, they were not teased by peers any more than the youths in the comparison sample about their parents' sexuality, but they were teased to a greater extent about their own sexuality. In the end, they often expressed pride about their mothers' openness regarding their family structure. Notably, more children from the lesbian families engaged in same-sex sexual contact. Two women out of the twenty-five grown children identified themselves as lesbian compared to zero from the comparison families. As the sample size was too small for generalization, more extensive research is clearly indicated. In other comparable studies, equally small scale, but involving hundreds of children sum total, the children's sexual orientation was found overwhelmingly to be heterosexual.

In Australia, similarly, reports on the children of gays and lesbians are encouraging. According to a study released by Charles Sturt University, children of gays and lesbians perform better than others in social studies classes and are more likely to respect authority and to assist with chores (*The Advocate,* 1996). In their survey of the literature on lesbian families, Appleby and Anastas draw the interesting conclusion that where the lesbian mother co-parents with her partner, the children tend to do exceedingly well. When the child has a biological father with an intolerant attitude, however, his or her self-esteem may suffer.

As with all blended stepfamilies, sometimes the desired closeness does not take place when woman-headed families merge. Ariel (1997) describes the following complex situation:

> The relationship between my sons and Linda was somewhat problematic. She never became a true second parent to my children, even though she lived with them for more than 10 years. In my mind, probably the most compelling reason for this was the loyalty my children had to their father, even though he had not chosen to be a significant part of their daily lives. (p. 8)

In her chronicle, *Family Values: A Lesbian Mother's Fight for Her Son,* Burke (1994) recounts her ordeal gaining adoption rights to her nonbiological son, conceived by her partner. The tremendous love shared by these mothers (Mama Phyllis and Mama Cher) shines through the pages of this book. In one memorable but disturbing scene, the social worker doing the adoption intake is clearly baffled by the lesbian parenting. "What are you going to do for Father's Day?" she asks (p. 215).

Myth 2 Lesbian Families Are Socially Isolated. In her exhaustive, participant-observation study of lesbian and gay families in the San Francisco Bay area, anthropologist Weston (1991) details the mutual aid network of households united by a sense of kinship. What Weston collectively calls "gay families" entails intricate kinship ties whereby adults characterize themselves as aunts or uncles to unrelated children. Participation in the extension of gay kinship is widespread, with the brother and sister role, regardless of age difference, being the most common. These chosen family ties, as Weston argues, are by no means a replacement for relations with one's biological families, but instead are enjoyed in addition to continuing bonds with blood relatives. Most of the lesbian women interviewed by Laird (1996), similarly, were found to both maintain connections with blood families *and* to have forged new and meaningful extended networks of friends that behave like close extended families. And a fascinating phenomenon, most pronounced among lesbians, is to include ex-lovers as members of the chosen family circle. As Weston (1991) observes:

> Flexible boundaries released chosen families from the genealogical logic of scarcity and uniqueness that, for example, would limit a child to one mother and one father. Unlike nuclear families, gay families were not intrinsically stratified by age or gender. Their capacity to continue to embrace former lovers represents another strength. (p. 196)

Myth 3 It Is Best for Children If Their Lesbian Parents Keep the Nature of Their Relationship a Secret. The emergence of openly lesbian couples is a relatively new phenomenon. In days gone by, the thinking would have been to protect the children from the knowledge of homosexuality in their parents at all costs. In "Memoirs of a Lesbian Daughter," Garnett (1994) writes both from the standpoint of a lesbian and as one who was brought up by two lesbians. The true nature of the relationship, however, became apparent only after her mother's death.

> Rachael, my mother, was pregnant with me when she met Evelyn, the woman who was to become her lover, and who was to be my "Aunt Evelyn" forever after . . . Strange as it may

> sound today, Rachael and Evelyn did decide that I was never, ever to know what was going on between them so that I could have a "normal" upbringing . . . They told everyone they were sisters despite the fact that Rachael was very dark (and the other red-headed) . . . In its broadest sense, what this kind of lying does is teach you that what you perceive may, or then again may not, be true, and being unable to trust the evidence of your eyes can make you feel almost schizophrenic . . . What it did do was make one a chronic liar as a child . . . (pp. 315–316, 323)

The harm in family secrecy of this sort is emphasized by Sanders (1993) in his chapter in the book, *Secrets in Families and Family Therapy.* Blindly accepting familial expectations to keep one's love secret, notes Sanders, can be life restricting and even life erasing. This attempt to pass as a member of the majority results in an all-consuming effort to manage information when around members of the majority (Schope, 1998). The secrecy that can be so toxic to gays and lesbians is often exacerbated by therapists who seek to minimize any differences that emerge, and who somehow give clients the message that they must keep "this thing" quiet, especially if there are children in the picture. Such family secrecy, as Sanders indicates, shields the family not only from imagined pain but also keeps this unit removed from vital social and community resources. Sanders cites the case of Denise, a married woman with a lesbian identity who found peace and community through coming out to her United Church of Canada minister and being referred to a gay/lesbian-oriented congregation. Despite her older child being angry at not having been told sooner, both of her children eventually came to accept their mother and her partner in life.

When lesbian and gay couples set up housekeeping and begin to combine their resources (and children and pets), the nature of their relationship will certainly be questioned by outsiders. Children will likely overhear talk about this arrangement, which is apt to be highly negative. Often, as with "the facts of life," children know the truth years before their parents tell them. One can only wonder what this does to the level of trust and communication in the family. In an almost anticlimatic scene from the autobiography of Colonel Margarethe Cammermeyer (1994), *Serving in Silence,* the colonel, facing dismissal from the U.S. Army, decides to tell her sons of her lesbianism. Her sons, however, know already. " 'Did you know,' I asked, 'because of something Harvey [her ex-husband] said?' 'No,' he explained, 'it was just how you were. We aren't dumb, you know' " (p. 247).

To prevent children from discovering their lesbian mother and her partner's sexuality through the rumor mill and from feeling that they have been deceived by the secrecy, therapists can help their lesbian clients feel more comfortable about "being who they are." To resolve such issues and to compare notes with others in a similar situation, family therapists Dahlheimer and Feigal (1991) recommend multiple family groups as the treatment of choice for blended families. Breaking the isolation, normalizing family issues, and affirming the legitimacy and sense of family of these households are all benefits of such multiple group work. However, only large cities are likely to have enough same-gender families with children to make such specialized groupings a possibility. In any case, when lesbian mothers make a shift from heterosexual to homosexual in their children's eyes, many children react with denial or anger. The road to final acceptance may be long and difficult. Parents can be prepared not to expect automatic acceptance and to nurture their children's growth toward acceptance of their mother's lesbian identity.

In her in-depth study of thirty-seven lesbian mothers, in the San Francisco Bay area, psychologist Charlotte Patterson (1996) focused her attention on mothers whose children were conceived or adopted within the context of a lesbian relationship, not the product of a previous marriage. We might consider these children as representative of what is sometimes popularly called the "lesbian baby boom." After conducting a battery of psychological tests, Patterson found that both lesbian mothers and their children scored in the normal range on assessments of mental health. Moreover, when asked about social activities, these mothers and their children reported having a wide range of contacts with their extended families, neighbors, teachers, and friends at school. The reader is invited to ponder the wonderful impact of the lesbian mothers' openness before a whole classroom of children, their parents, and teachers, how much their favorable contact with an openly lesbian-headed family might do for them all.

The opportunity to forge new pathways to family living can be conceived as just that—an opportunity to be creative and courageous. In a powerfully moving passage, Laird (1996), professor of social work and well-known author, describes the wedding of her son Duncan and his bride, both young social workers:

> Although the *New York Times* would not allow Ann's name to be included in the engagement announcement, Ann's [her partner of 30 years] and my names were on the wedding invitation, along with the names of our daughter-in-law's father and stepmother. The wedding ritual was wonderfully expressive of the cultures of both families . . . The fact that both Ann and I walked Duncan down the aisle, wished him well, and danced together at his wedding modeled—for younger lesbians and for the straight world—one way that lesbian relationships can be enacted in the larger family context and how central rituals can be adapted to express particular definitions of kinship. (p. 89)

For an in-depth interview with a young woman from Iowa who wrestled with the problems of her mother's coming out while she was also coping with the usual difficulties of a parents' divorce, read Box 11.1.

Van Voorhis and McClain (1997) describe helpful intervention strategies to support mothers taking the courageous step of self-disclosing to their children. The guidance includes enabling mothers to help their children face the homophobia to which they as family members of a lesbian will almost certainly be subjected. Social workers can reassure mothers that children brought up in even the most unconventional of situations can demonstrate surprising resilience, perhaps *because of* rather than *in spite of* their difference. The clinical use of narratives, written and edited by the children, can help children recognize their own resilience in their efforts to transcend their circumstances or, better yet, to appreciate them. Such families can be helped in therapy to cope with the daily cruelties inflicted by a heterosexist society through an approach that captures the strengths and abilities that will help these children and their parents prevail.

Unfortunately, the widespread portrayal of such family arrangements as damaging and as a threat to family values creates an unnecessary source of stress. In the Latina lesbian family, extended family pressure to remain in the closet is a major stressor. In an interview sample of thirty-five Latina lesbian women in treatment for substance abuse, Reyes (1998) found that only two women experienced acceptance from their relatives when they disclosed that

BOX 11.1

Interview with Stacy Wilson

Q: What is it like being brought up in this world with a lesbian mother?

A: Well, actually I was raised by my mom until I was in 6th grade. During that time she had two partners. She and my dad divorced when I was in 4th grade, so I really did not get along with my mom—or her partners. I don't know what that was about. I mean I'm sure it had to do with my age at that time and the divorce and everything.

Q: Were you comfortable with the fact that she was a lesbian?

A: Well, I was comfortable with her, but I wasn't comfortable with her being out . . . my friends didn't know. I was afraid that I would be thought of as gay maybe too. I was scared to death that I would be included. So, I didn't tell anyone.

Q: When your parents got divorced, was it because your mother had come out?

A: Yes, that was one of the reasons. I mean one of the main reasons. Yes.

Q: Did you ever have the opportunity to ask your mother when she first knew she was gay? She must not have known right away since she married and had two children. Or is she bisexual?

A: No, I did not talk to my mom and become close to her until I was in tenth grade. I lived with my dad after 6th grade. And so I didn't have any contact with her . . . I basically thought I hated her. I just thought it was her fault they got a divorce, you know, I was really angry. And it took me a long time to get through that, but we are really close now. Talking with her about how she figured it out, she said that looking back on her life, she thinks that she might have always been that way, but because it wasn't discussed back then, she didn't recognize it. Because she always had a really strong feeling towards her girlfriends. And there would be certain girlfriends that she just really wanted to be with a lot. She felt really intensely close to them but she just thought, you know, that it was friendship. And she really couldn't pin a label on it. She says, looking back on it now, she can identify that maybe she was feeling something more than just friendship.

Q: So now you have worked through the stigma yourself, and you're okay with everything?

A: Oh, I'm wonderful with it. I have absolutely no problems with it. I almost am ashamed to talk about the way I used to be because it makes me so unhappy that I was like that but . . .

Q: Well you know our society has this feeling that if you, or someone close to you is a lesbian or gay, that they are going to draw you into that. Was that, or has that ever been part of the problem for you?

A: No, at first, earlier on, I thought that maybe my friends would think that but, mostly it was just mother/daughter problems. I just felt she was really unfair to me, that she favored my younger sister and what not. And I just had . . . we just had real big disagreements. And it really had nothing to do with her sexuality, although at one point I did strike out at her and say that I thought her lifestyle was disgusting. And I think I did that mainly just to hurt her.

Q: Well, it's neat that you have thought this all through and you guys have a relationship now. Did *her* sexuality have any effect on your sexuality?

A: Well, there have been times when I've had a boyfriend and I would start to lose feelings for boys and I wouldn't understand why. This was sexually, mostly. I was scared, really paranoid . . . like this was in high-school and I started thinking well, what if I'm gay. But this had nothing really to do with my mom. It was just that I knew more about the possibilities. I'd cry about it. Now in college I sometimes wonder . . . I've only had heterosexual relationships but I know that I find some women attractive. I don't know if I find them attractive in that way. I guess until I am ever attracted to a woman in that way I won't, you know, I can't say . . . but I wouldn't ever rule it out . . . I think people are attracted to all kinds of . . . you know . . . along the spectrum.

Q: One of my professors was saying the other day that it was her opinion that to some extent we are all bisexual. I think that some of what you are talking about is very normal and we all experience it somewhat. I just wanted you to know that. Now, do you have a dad and a step-mother, and then two moms? Is that kind of the way it is right now?

A: Actually, no. Right now my mom has separated from people that she was involved with when I was young. She is now involved with someone but, they are more like friends. The people she becomes involved with now are all her friends. Because she doesn't live with them. She decided after she broke up with the last person she lived with, that she would never put (because my sister still lives with her), that she would never put her child in that position again. Because my sister didn't get along with them either.

Q: Well, you know that's interesting. That is the same thing that can happen with your dad if he was married.

A: Oh yeah, Right! I know. Well my mom, she just decided until she really, *really* knows, she doesn't want to live with someone again. This is because it's so hard in the end when they end up breaking up . . . dividing everything out. She just would rather, I think, live in separate households. And also the woman she is involved with right now has a child also.

Q: How have your mother's parents handled this? Do they know? Has she been able to be open with them? Or really, either set of grandparents for that matter?

A: Well, *that's* a story in itself! My mother's mom recently died of cancer but, she was a very, very strong Catholic. So there of course were very conflicting ideas there. She never like, didn't want my mom in part of her life . . . but there was always a sort of disapproval. So for a time they went without speaking for quite a while. My mom was very disappointed she wasn't going to be accepted wholly. But when my grandma came down with cancer, my mom was there to take care of her, and I think that they resolved a lot of their problems. They just let everything go. They just accepted one another for who they were.

Q: Does your mom have any brothers or sisters?

A: No, she was an only child. And then my dad's mom basically hates my mom!

Q: Oh. Well, her son got hurt, so that's probably where that is coming from.

A: Right, right! So, that is about it.

Q: Okay. Well is there anything else you would like to add to this?

A: Yes, I really wish . . . because I remember how I felt when I was a kid. I was scared to death of what people would think if they found out. It was like this hideous secret. And it's not. I wish . . . I don't know, that there was some way I could get to kids who have a similar situation, talk to them or help them talk to each other. Because *I* thought I was the only one. And of course I couldn't have been the only one, you know. But I felt like, well who else in my entire school would have a gay parent?

Q: Yes, we know that's not the case but, the thing is, would kids feel secure enough with themselves and that some sort of support group could really help these children? I really see you being able to start something like that some day.

Interview conducted by Jamie Paige, social work student, University of Northern Iowa, May 20, 1997. Reprinted by permission of Stacy Wilson.

they were lesbians. Many of these women suffered great loneliness from the loss of family kinship, a loss that might have been related to their development of substance abuse problems. Effective treatment clearly requires a strong cultural sensitivity to deeply ingrained expectations concerning sexuality.

For lesbians of color, generally, there is often conflict with their communities of origin over their sexual orientation. Simultaneously, lesbians of color have to deal with racism in the gay and lesbian community. Most of these geographical communities, in fact, are overwhelmingly white. African American and Hispanic gays and lesbians tend to find their niche within their own racial and ethnic neighborhoods (Hunter & Mallon, 1998). Shernoff (1998) reports that professionally successful gay African American men in his practice have reported a significant degree of pain about the lack of acceptance for them as total human beings within either of their two communities. Nevertheless, it is not like the African American culture to disown discredited family members the way some but not most European Americans do.

Legal Hassles

Lesbian and gay couples in open relationships are demanding official recognition of their partners as spouses. The right to marry movement has broad social and legal implications for custody and visitation, second-parent adoptions, and foster-parent adoptions. A couple deprived of the right to have their relationship legally recognized are deprived of many of the basic rights that provide security to a family. Many court decisions, such as those depriving lesbian mothers of custody "for the good of the child," are based on pervasive myths concerning the lesbian family that foretell dire consequences for children raised in such nonnormative homes (Laird, 1995). Some of the trickiest cases legally and emotionally involve breakups of lesbian couples in which the nonbiological parent must sue for visitation rights. Even co-parenting agreements spelling out joint custody in cases of separation have questionable legal standing in the absence of marriage rights for the couple.

In even more progressive countries, the same myths prevail concerning the need for child protection. In Denmark, Norway, Sweden, Belgium, Iceland, and France, for example, couples can legally marry and have all the basic married rights except the right to adopt children or to have a child through artificial insemination provided through the national health plan. In the Netherlands, moreover, where public support for same-sex parents is high, legislation has been recently introduced to pave the way for full adoption rights for gay and lesbian couples. British Columbia recently has adopted the most advanced law of its kind in North America, essentially giving gay and lesbian couples the same rights and obligations as heterosexuals in the areas of child support, custody, and access (*Accessline,* 1998). Alberta, meanwhile, was held in violation of the Canadian Charter of Rights and Freedoms by failing to protect a gay teacher from being fired on the basis of sexual orientation. Already gay and lesbian couples have equal adoption rights with heterosexuals in that province.

In Norway where domestic partnerships are legal, an interesting news bulletin reveals:

> The incidence of divorce is three times greater among heterosexuals than among homosexuals. Since partnership was introduced in 1993, 377 homosexual couples have entered into partnerships in Oslo. Only six of these partnerships, i.e., 1.6% have ended in divorce.

Figures from Norway statistics show that 5.3 percent of heterosexual marriages are dissolved in the course of four years (*Norwaves,* 1997, item 13).

In early 1998, in another setback to gay/lesbian rights and family stability, legislators in Washington state and Iowa voted to make their states the twenty-seventh and twenty-eighth, respectively, to ban same-sex marriage. On a positive note, New Jersey became the first state in the nation to allow same-sex partners to *jointly* adopt children on the same basis as married couples. Meanwhile, people in more than forty U.S. cities, including Charlotte, North Carolina, and Dallas, Texas, celebrated Freedom to Marry Day (*The Advocate,* 1998a).

Gay-Headed Families

The same social and legal issues discussed previously pertain to gay families (or families headed by a male couple). If anything, the prejudice against them is more pronounced. Furthermore, there is far less information on the gay than lesbian family. The inclusion of a section on gay male parenting in *Encyclopedia of Social Work* is a first (Morales, 1995).

The most significant gender difference in gay versus lesbian parenting, obviously, is in how the children are conceived. Most children reared by gay couples are children from a previous marriage in which custody or visitation arrangements have been awarded to the biological father. An ad in *In the Family* (Ariel, 1997) reveals another possibility:

> SURROGATE MOTHERS wanted to give the gift of life. Healthy gay men who are committed to creating a family are waiting for surrogate mothers to help them. Women between ages 21–36 who are mothers will be spiritually and financially rewarded. Expenses paid. Professional support and guidance provided. (p. 25)

Benkov (1995) explores the gender difference in gay versus lesbian parenting. The gender difference, notes Benkov, corresponds to the different socialization of men and women toward parenting. Whereas women are socialized to be primary parents, men are socialized to play a more secondary role in the home. Two women may have problems sharing this role whereas men may have conflicts over who ends up "babysitting" and who gets to go out.

Because of biological restrictions, gay parents may look to foster parenting and adoption. Sometimes a gay father adopts a hard-to-place child as a single parent, concealing his sexual orientation initially. Then the roommate or friend moves in the house and a family is created. Another avenue open to gay parents is to openly seek to be foster or adoptive parents for a child who cannot be placed otherwise or for whom a gay couple would have a special advantage. Appleby and Anastas (1998) refer to evidence that child welfare agencies have been placing adolescents known to be gay in homes where they can have positive role models. The new constitution in South Africa, one of the most liberal in the world, guarantees gay/lesbian rights. Gays and lesbians are now adopting mixed-race and black children, a fact that antagonizes some blacks who perceive an element of discrimination here (Mabry, 1997). It is perceived to be a case of giving the unwanted to the undesirable.

In England, as a creative solution to twin problems, homeless youths who have been expelled from their homes because of their sexuality are being placed in the care of gay and lesbian couples. The Albert Kennedy Trust, which helps finance this arrangement, also maintains a national register of gay and lesbian "foster carers" widely used by social service departments (*Community Care,* 1996). The program is not without controversy, however, and the popular press has run headlines stirring up public opinion, as, for example, the one proclaiming, "Gay Homes for 100 Problem Children."

Singularly setting apart gay from lesbian parenting is the devastation sweeping the male gay community in connection with the AIDS epidemic. This sexually transmitted disease stigmatizes gay people and sets them up for societal victim blaming. Children reared in gay homes are sometimes thought by classmates to have AIDS themselves. And sometimes the fathers do have AIDS. As one young man described his childhood, "I got silence when I told friends my dad had AIDS. They were scared. Some feared I was somehow infected" (Shapiro, 1996, p. 79).

Another gender-specific aspect relevant to gay fathers is a certain hostility, even resentment, within the gay community to what Rofes (1997) calls the "dogged tyranny of family" (p. 155). As Acosta (1998) remarks:

> Being a father in the gay community has its challenges. Some of the people I met didn't like that I was, as they said, "tied down to my kids." Some men felt I put too much emphasis on spending time with my children. They thought I should be concentrating on being "a proud gay man." (p. 15)

Rofes (1997) argued vehemently against "the rising Queer quest for recognition of 'our families' " (p. 151), inasmuch as gay males violate the key tenets of established family life in the United States, namely, monogamy, nonsexualized friendship networks, and merging as one economic unit. Indeed, as Appleby and Anastas inform us, the lifestyles of parents and nonparents are so different on a daily basis that gay parents often feel a pull away from "their own" community. Certainly, there is less time for hanging around the gay bar or attending drag shows or engaging in political lobbying.

In sharp opposition to the antifamily sentiment, Wishon (1997), a gay pastor, is a strong believer in the "celebration of queer love" and the shift toward commitment. Wishon describes his own commitment ceremony with great fervor: "There were elders, pastors, deacons, rabbis, and priests. . . . All of them had come to witness the love between two men, celebrated in a holy union. One ceremony has touched hundreds of lives" (p. 113).

For a moving newspaper story of a gay couple from Eldora, Iowa, who were selected as the "Foster Parents of the Year," read Box 11.2.

Gay Male Friendships with Women

In an essay entitled, "Ties That Bind: Friendship between Lesbians and Gay Men," Jay (1997) explains the warm bonding between lesbians and their gay "brothers." Because gay men are generally not potential sex partners, friendship with them is free of the tensions that can arise in lesbian interactions. Women can talk openly about sexual preferences with gay men, Jay suggests, because such topics would not be taken as a "come on." In a similar vein, gay men can talk frankly to lesbian women. Another aspect of friendship that is special between lesbians and gay males is the way in which they can use one another for "cover," pairing up for a social event. Still due to gender differences in attitudes, Jay further suggests, lesbians are sometimes horrified by the way in which gay men fragment potential partners into body parts or express attraction for youths far younger than themselves. The most commonly heard complaint by lesbians, however, according to Jay, is that for all their spearheading of fundraising efforts for AIDS treatment, gay men have not reciprocated in support of lesbian health issues such as breast cancer, for example.

Straight women also find great solace and support in friendships with gay men. Wasserstein (1998), the screenwriter of the gay-centered movie *The Object of My Affection,* recounts

BOX 11.2

Gay Couple from Eldora, Foster Parents of the Year

The Iowa Foster and Adoptive Parents Association has startled the state by naming a gay couple from Eldora as Foster Parents of the Year of its Des Moines region. Gair Bridges and Ron Travis have served as foster parents since 1989, and have taken in 13 kids, mostly teen-agers. They've been a couple for 26 years.

The gift shop owners said they enjoy helping children in need of a home, but they don't hide their sexual orientation. "We were up-front from the very beginning," Travis said. "When we had our very first home study, we told them." They require the state to notify the natural parents and get their consent, but it's never been a problem. He said they do not "display homosexuality in front of people."

Local gay-rights supporters cheered the news, but those opposed to homosexuality expressed shock that youths are placed in openly gay households. The Iowa Department of Human Resources does not consider the parents' sexual orientation when making placements, even though the state does not recognize gay marriages. The Rev. Preston G. Smith of the Waterloo Church of the Nazarene considers homosexuality a grave sin. "We don't see any way that Christianity and active homosexuality are compatible," he said. "We preach that Christ can forgive any sin and can transform people." Smith said "it's a tragedy" that children are placed in gay households. "We wonder what's happening with our society, and we see this type of thing foisted upon us again and again, from all different angles," he said.

Among those cheering the news locally was Scot Morris, vice president of ACCESS, a Waterloo homosexual and bisexual support group. "I think the award goes to show that children can grow up in a homosexual household and come out on top of the world," Morris said. "Twenty-six years is a lot longer than many heterosexual marriages last."

DHS officials say the need for foster homes far outweighs the supply. The agency looks for a stable and safe environment, sufficient income, and it checks for criminal history.

Conservative lawmaker Rep. Bob Brunkhorst, R-Waverly, said the DHS rules should be changed to consider sexual orientation. He said it should give a weighting toward heterosexual couples. "I think this shows another step toward the breakdown of the traditional Christian family," he said.

Travis said he's gotten many phone calls and letters of support from around the state, since it was reported. "It took me a while to get through all the messages on the answering machine today," he said. "But it's been all positive."

the intense love between two friends—she's straight; he's gay. The basic theme of this romantic comedy is that the relationship between a gay man and straight woman can achieve a deeper intimacy than one can experience with a conventional romantic partner. A parallel theme, which perhaps makes a greater accomplishment of this film, is its presentation of the notion of harmonious extended family ties (the family includes relatives, friends, and ex-lovers).

Family Therapy

Family therapists can expect to have considerably less contact with gay families than with their lesbian counterparts. Fewer gay males are rearing children, for a start. Second, gay men are more reluctant than lesbians to seek counseling for family problems. Unwillingness to seek help for a relationship problem was indicated by 40 percent of the gay men versus 14 percent of the lesbians in an extensive survey conducted by Modrcin and Wyers (1990).

Gay family therapist Michael Shernoff (1997), in describing his work with gay couples, suggests that the issues they bring into treatment probably stem more from their gender socialization and the fact that two *men* are in a relationship than from the homosexuality aspect. Shernoff presents a typical case study: Paul and Tom are partners in an open relationship. Tom breaks off his affair with Paul to move in with one of his lovers. Paul enters therapy complaining not about the breakup but about being overwhelmed with depression. Therapy interventions need to be directed at building empathy ("How would you feel in Tom's place or the other lover's?") and mourning the loss of relationships. "Queer culture has been very rich and allowed us to experiment creatively with relationships," notes Shernoff, "but there are emotional casualties along the way that we have to begin to acknowledge and that we have to take responsibility for creating" (p. 10). To summarize Shernoff's essay in a nutshell, the connection between a man's emotional and sexual needs must be recognized. Given the reality described in this article, one wonders what the institution of marriage would do to the openness of these relationships. And what would be the impact on parenting?

Carron (1992) provides at least a partial answer in his essay, "On Being a Gay Father." Having adopted an infant daughter, Carron discovered that most of his dates lost interest as soon as they found out about the baby in the crib or as soon as romance was interrupted for diaper time. But then, after a few years, the perfect family-type man showed up and they ended up as a family of three.

Working with Children in Gay Families

Of all the issues facing gay parents, the most difficult may be dealing with societal disapproval and disbelief. Whether or not children's fathers are known to be gay, invariably their children will be exposed to antigay comments and jokes at school. Once the children know, they may then feel guilty if they don't speak out in defense of their fathers. They may need help through counseling in learning how to handle this situation and whom to tell what and when. Above all, they need to know the truth from their fathers before they hear it from someone else.

Two helpful books for children with gay fathers are *Daddy's Roommate* (Willhoite, 1990) and *How Would You Feel If Your Father Was Gay?* (Heron & Maran, 1991). These books, which are aimed at elementary school audiences, can be introduced by a therapist to help normalize the child's situation.

Social workers can refer children of lesbian/gay parents to an organization called COLAGE (Children of Lesbians and Gays Everywhere), which is headquartered in San Francisco. Today, with a membership of nearly 2,000, COLAGE runs more than twenty-five peer support groups and holds an annual conference in alternating locations (Metz, 1996).

Bisexual Families

One would expect the incidence of families with children in which one parent is bisexual to be quite large. Many bisexuals, of course, are married and mothers and fathers. Yet as a group that is neither claimed by those who are gay or straight and marginal in both groups, this population is rarely studied at all much less studied as parents. Because of the lack of support this group receives, and because of marital complications, married bisexuals may need special support from mental health professionals to help them sort things out. It is, therefore, vital that all therapists, and especially those with a sizable gay and lesbian clientele, familiarize themselves with bisexuality and with issues that arise in polyamorous relationships so that they can offer support not available elsewhere (Rust, 1996).

Children with one or more parents who are bisexual come from families that in no way seem odd or different on the surface. The children may not be aware of the bisexuality, nor are their peers or neighbors. The usual pattern would be to have a mother and father, one of whom has a series of same-sex relationships outside the marriage. These sexual liaisons may come to the child's attention if the heterosexual parent suddenly becomes aware of an affair going on and a fight ensues. Family therapist Matteson (1996), a self-identified bisexual, states that when bisexuality results in a breakup of the marriage, the bisexual parent may want to delay disclosure until custody or visitation arrangements are assured. However, children may overhear their parents' arguments and need some help in dealing with a situation made more difficult through earlier secrecy.

The family therapist needs to be flexible and nonjudgmental in dealing with bisexual situations. Because so many possible variations exist, each situation is relatively unique. Two facts to be aware of, according to Matteson, are that (1) monogamy is the exception in these situations, and (2) significantly, among bisexuals, both men and women tend to seek out male partners when they want recreational sex.

One variation is for two bisexuals to marry and have children in an open marriage situation, with each partner having same-sex relations on the side. Today's AIDS scare, however, has made women, especially, wary of such an arrangement. Moreover, if the husband does become HIV positive, his bisexuality is apt to become public at some point and to be extremely disturbing to children facing the loss of one or both of their parents.

Another variation explored by Matteson is for two lesbians to live in a marriage-like union with one of them seeking recreational sex with heterosexual men. Counselors may well find themselves working with such couples who come to therapy in need of mediation. They may need help, perhaps, in making a shift from a traditional commitment to monogamy to an open relationship allowing for sexual exploration or may need support in reaching an agreement to terminate the partnership. Bisexuals often express a desire for contact with both genders because, as they explain, they get something totally different out of each relationship.

In an extensive international survey of bisexuals' sexual behavior, sociologist Paula Rust (1996) reports that a large majority of bisexual men and women in the survey replied that they did not desire a relationship committed to lifetime monogamy. In contrast, a majority of gays and lesbians desired such a relationship. Many bisexuals in the study did engage in sexually monogamous relationships, however, while pursuing romantic relationships that did not involve active sex. In her survey of behaviorally bisexual men, Rust also found that whites are more likely to identify as homosexual and blacks as bisexual. Rust's explanation is that African American culture is more supportive of bisexuality than is European American culture.

The most frequently stated criticism concerning professionals' work with bisexuals and their families, according to Matteson, is that counselors get fixated on the uniqueness of the lifestyle and lose sight of the problem for which the client is seeking help. The problem may be organic (e.g., a mental disorder) or it may have to do with child-rearing matters that have no connection to sexual identity. Another major counselor stumbling block relates to the tendency in our society to dichotomize people and their behavior in rigid either/or categories. In such a milieu, the problems raised by bisexuality are obvious.

Transgender Families

There can be few shocks as jolting to the family as to have one of its members, especially a parent, declare himself or herself to be of the other sex. Because the sex of a person is our most central personality trait and considered inborn and unchangeable, the mere thought of someone we know going from a he to a she is apt to seem almost laughable. Most often it is the father who says he is really a woman, that he is a female imprisoned in a male body. Family denial is usually overwhelming. Gradually, however, after the individual takes physical measures to conduct a sex change (whether through taking hormones and/or surgery), reality begins to set in. Perhaps then, in recognition of their powerlessness in talking the person out of such a drastic course of action, the bewildered family will contact a family agency for counseling. What Cullen (1997) found in his informal survey of Canadian social work educators was a complete lack of familiarity with transgenderism. Social workers, therefore, are ill-prepared for work with families in which a member is a transsexual, as in the example, above, or a transvestite or drag queen. Social workers and other mental health professionals are apt to have negative, if any, associations with transsexualism due to its unfortunate inclusion as a mental disorder in the American Psychiatric Association's *DSM IV.* We must look elsewhere, therefore, to writers and academics, as Cullen notes, who celebrate the transgendered community and contribute to our understanding of it, writers such as lesbian-feminist-educator bell hooks (1994). Additionally, the journal *In the Family* is a positive and invaluable resource for social workers engaging in family therapy. *In the Family* draws on personal narratives from therapists and their clients to depict diverse family forms. The following selection from Buckwalter (1997) describes her ordeal in breaking the news to her seventeen-year-old son of her pending sex change:

> I try to find the words to tell Damon that his father has died, and that I am responsible for his death. I want to reassure him that in the place of that father will be a woman who will try to embody all the things that Damon had come to count on from the father I once was. (p. 17)

It took the author, as she tells us, forty-some years to completely accept herself and come to a decision as to who she was. It will be hard on her kids, especially her sons, she knows. Her children have seen her make a gradual transition from father to mother, from man to woman, and from heterosexual to lesbian. The woman she was once married to, not surprisingly, has never accepted this transition. Lori and her children now live with her partner, Sharon, and Sharon's daughter.

In an interview with gay psychiatrist Gary Sanders, director of the Human Sexuality Program at the University of Calgary, Markowitz (1995) unravels some of the facts about transsexuality: Almost one half of 1 percent of the population feel themselves to be of the opposite gender. Individuals attend the sexuality program because of an incongruity between their gender identity and their physical characteristics. Family members receive counseling in preparation for the sex change of a loved one. Generally the children have an easier time adjusting to such things as a name change and, more significantly, the switch in pronouns used than adults do, according to Sanders.

News reports often highlight the stories of persons in positions of authority, such as police officers or college professors who undergo surgery and/or hormone treatments to become women or, rather, to look like the women they are. Increasingly, in cities across the United States antidiscrimination laws are protecting the rights of transgendered people. British Columbia is likely to become the first Canadian province to extend human rights protections to the transgendered under a category dealing with gender identity.

Counseling Parents of Gay, Lesbian, and Bisexual Children

Unlike Chapter 4, which focused on adolescent homosexuality from the child's point of view—coming out to the self and the parents—this section will discuss the process of discovery that a child is gay or lesbian from the parent's standpoint. The road from the first initial shock and absolute denial to final wholehearted acceptance is a long one. Many get stuck somewhere along the way. The journey goes something like this:

Denial. "It's just a phase."
Bargaining. "Try dating someone of the opposite sex."
Self-blame. "It's because you and your mother were too close."
Grief. "How will I have grandchildren now?"
Acceptance. "I love you as you are."
Advocacy. "I will march in a PFLAG parade."

Parents, Families, and Friends of Lesbians and Gays (PFLAG) is an organization to promote the health and well-being of gay, lesbian, and bisexual persons, their families, and friends. PFLAG is a self-help group to help families, especially parents, adjust to the reality of having a gay or lesbian child.

Box 11.3 is a reconstruction based on notes taken by van Wormer immediately after a typical PFLAG meeting.

Founded in 1981, PFLAG is a national, grassroots family organization. PFLAG currently represents 65,000 member households and is organized in 410 communities representing every state and Canada and eleven other countries. The majority of members are the parents, family members, and friends of gay, lesbian, bisexual, and transgendered people.

Support, education, and advocacy are the keywords of this organization. Each year approximately 1,000 members attend a national conference consisting of workshops and recreational activities. PFLAG brings the family voice into play in bridging the gap between the straight and gay/lesbian communities. Their newsletter, *PFLAGpole,* reports on such activities as the more than twenty-five screening parties for the "coming out" of Ellen Morgan, the first lead character on television; a meeting between the head of PFLAG and President Clinton; and a speech given by a new member, the Hollywood celebrity, Cher.

Whereas PFLAG families are accepting their children and are lobbying for their civil rights, one out of four gay and lesbian teens, according to a recent *60 Minutes* segment (CBS,

BOX 11.3

PFLAG Meeting

I'm sitting in a circle of members of my local PFLAG group. We are meeting as usual at Paul's house, the first Monday of the month. His place is warm and cozy on this cold Iowa evening. We start out making small talk about the big, orange tabby cat who prances around the room, choosing one woman's lap. I've been attending these meetings for over a year now—we've done dinners, videos, and political organizing. Tonight we are snacking on chocolate cake and drinking tea and coffee. The leader, Paul, a gay activist and father of two daughters, suggests we go around telling a little bit about ourselves, our stories and how we came to get involved in PFLAG. Present are several middle-aged and elderly couples, and two unattached women, including myself. All our children are grown, their ages ranging from 18–35. A man sitting beside his wife begins:

First man: "We have a son who's gay and a son who's a Promise Keeper."

His wife: "I'm so proud of our gay son."

Second man: "Our daughter is a lesbian. We were shocked when we found out. . . . It threw us for a loop."

Third man: "I found out in 1987 that our son was gay. We had two years; then he was dead. We learned he was HIV positive and gay at the same time. So we had both issues to deal with at once. We didn't suspect a thing. He was a loner, but we thought nothing. We didn't recognize the symptoms."

I'm surprised the group leader doesn't object to the negative word, *symptoms.* But he is amazingly patient and seems to take no offense. Now it's my turn:

Me: "I first called a PFLAG number several years ago when my daughter announced she was a lesbian. I wanted some support. But when I asked about the group, I was told all the members were parents of gay sons. And the woman on the phone said her son had died of AIDS. So I didn't think I'd fit in the group. Not when my daughter is so healthy and happy. Then recently I heard Paul speak at a panel, in my social work class, in fact, and he invited me here, saying there were now some new members. I've worked through what I needed to work through, but I thought I'd like to join a group of parents."

Woman no. 1: "Our daughter's a lesbian. She's in her thirties."

Her husband: "She's very much in the closet, and living in Washington state. So we have to keep quiet too."

His wife: "She's a very private person, you see."

Woman no. 2: "Our daughter's a lesbian also. We just never suspected a thing."

Paul: "I never suspected my children were *straight*! But when I came out to them, they announced they were straight. (laughter) Recently John (his partner) and I, this was a first; we stayed over at my daughter's home. Everything seemed to be fine. She let us sleep in her bed. But when we got home, I got a letter. The letter said, "I love you Dad, but these things are off limits." Then she wrote a list—things such as no physical contact between John and me, no lovemaking when we are at her home, no gay lingo or risqué gay novels. No remarks about good looking men you pass on the street. . . . We won't go back. I don't know if it influenced her, but my ex-wife once told me that her psychologist said, "Just don't have anything to do with someone you disapprove of. . . . "

All of us: "Oh, no!"

Paul: "I guess my wife never really got over it. . . . There's never a good time to tell your wife you're gay. And it was a difficult time telling the kids. I've been to my son's home in Dallas only twice. When I used to visit, his house was always full of his friends. He hasn't told his friends about me, and he never brings them around."

Man no. 1: "People are so afraid of homosexuality. . . . We were asked to leave the church as our son was dying of AIDS."

His wife: "Yes, it all started when I went in to tell our minister about our son. And he said he would have to check with some others if we would be welcome at church. Later I got a call asking our family to leave the church."

Man no. 1: "So we found another church. . . . They were wonderful. But then I was discriminated against at the factory."

Group member: "Why?"

Man (angrily): "I'm the father of a FAGGOT. . . . Even after my son died . . . I've never had the kind of work I got before. Now I'm on the road crew."

Paul has quite a collection of short videos for us to watch. So after serving some more coffee and displaying some gay/lesbian books we can borrow, Paul puts on the video, *Families Come Out: The Process,* a 1992 film produced by PFLAG.

A lesbian introduces the film. "I prayed to God over an attraction for another woman," she says, "then decided God could not have given me these feelings for nothing. About three months later I started going to PFLAG. Over the years I've seen parents coming to meetings and crying, then years later the same people saying, 'I'm okay with this.' "

The camera closes in on a group session. A gay son puts his arm around his mother. "I cried because I wasn't going to have grandchildren," she says. Another parent speaks, "When your child comes out of the closet, the family goes *into* the closet."

A father of a gay son explains the process to viewers: "One of the things you go through is what did I do wrong? I tossed the ball with my son; he was not interested. Then my wife said, 'You should have tossed the ball.' "

The mother of a gay son chimes in, "You blame each other, the other parent. This was always in the back of my mind: Dominant mothers create homosexual sons. So I sent all my sons to live with their father. Then he (the son she was worried about) told me he was gay."

The film ends with PFLAG members, gay and lesbian children and their parents, expressing how they've all come to see how important family is. It's getting late, and the end of the video marks an appropriate ending for the meeting, so most of us make our excuses and collect our coats at this point. But not before agreeing to chip in the next time for a pizza and a viewing of the Hollywood gay film, *In and Out.*

Source: By Katherine van Wormer, February 2, 1998, meeting in Waterloo, Iowa.

1998), is thrown out of the house by his or her parents. And according to the same broadcast, fundamentalist Christian parents are organizing in groups such as PFOX (Parents and Friends of Ex-Gays) to force their children into conversion therapy. After a round of intense brainwashing treatment, one formerly gay-identified man married an ex-lesbian and had a child. "The old John Polk is no more," this man declared.

An encouraging development relevant to family diversity took place without fanfare in the form of the wording of an article. Writing a review in *Newsweek* of a new book by lesbian writer Dorothy Allison, Giles (1998) states that Allison and her female partner "live on a steep hill in San Francisco, along with their 5 year old son, Wolf" (p. 66). The image projected in the story is of a healthy, happy family living in a household that includes the boy's father in addition to the two mothers. The appreciative tone of the article and the lack of any qualifying statement regarding two women parenting a son mark a first in the mainstream press for a story of this kind. This fact gives the article a significance that goes beyond the content, which is the review of the book *Cavedweller.*

To bring some levity to this section, let us enjoy some of the dialogue from a relevant episode of the ABC show *Ellen.* Excerpts are from the segment "Ellen Tells Her Family" (ABC, 1997).

The scene is a white-tablecloth restaurant. After unsuccessfully trying to get her parents to order wine, Ellen tries to introduce The Topic by asking her parents if some people across the room look gay. Her parents ask her what's this to her—she's not gay. "Yes, I am gay," she says. Her parents throw themselves full force into frantic ordering from the menu.

Later the truth begins to sink in. Ellen's father says, "Your brother had exactly the same childhood, and he turned out perfectly normal."

"I *am* normal, Dad," Ellen replies. To her mother she says, "You always wanted me to be open and honest with you."

"Oh, honey, that's what *you* wanted. . . . We were always very happy keeping our feelings bottled up."

The scene shifts to a PFLAG meeting. The father, still in a state of denial, does not show up as expected. Ellen and her mother walk around awkwardly in a crowded room.

Her mother: "So what goes on around here?"

Ellen: "I think it's like any other group, you just blame each other and sit around and cry."

Soon they are seated in a circle, going around for introductions.

Ellen: "I'm Ellen, and I haven't had a heterosexual thought in eight days."

Group member to Ellen's mother: "And you are?"

Her mother: "I'm heartbroken, confused, sad."

Ellen: "No, I think they mean give your name."

Her mother: "I'm confused. What do two women do in bed together?"

As the introductions progress, an irate father jumps up and verbally attacks Ellen for being a lesbian. In walks Ellen's father to the rescue: "She's here, she's queer, get used to it! I read that on the bumper sticker," he explains.

Couples Counseling with Gays and Lesbians

When gays and lesbians fall in love and begin hanging around together, even moving in with each other, they will find themselves having some explaining to do to friends, relatives, and neighbors. This is just one of the many complications of long-term gay and lesbian relationships. An excellent sourcebook that should be read by every therapist preparing to work with gay and lesbian couples is *Lesbians and Gays in Couples and Families,* edited by Laird and Green (1996). Gender roles among Latino gay and bisexual men, lesbian couples and childhood trauma, parenting issues, and African American lesbians are among the topics addressed. The case history of a clinical intervention with an interracial lesbian couple is especially informative.

Relationship difficulties are common to all adult couples and are the fundamental disturbance bringing most couples into therapy. "This problem is bigger than we are" is often the opening comment by a troubled pair of individuals trying to sort things out. Whether the relationship consists of two men or of two women is, of course, a key determinant in the nature of the problems that bring a couple in for treatment and in the issues that emerge during the course of treatment.

The gender difference can be summed up in a sentence: "Women cling, men compete." When you have two of a kind in one relationship, instead of a blending of complementary roles, you are likely to get an exaggeration of relational patterns. The key issue, as Elise (1986) and Carl (1990) inform us, is not homosexuality but gender.

Appleby and Anastas (1998) pinpoint an important variable in male versus female relationships. For males, they suggest, it is same-gender sexual activity that is likely to precipitate questions about a gay or bisexual identity, whereas for females the emotional attachment comes first. With men, it is sex first, then love; with women, it is love first, then sex. Seeking out anonymous or casual sex is termed *cruising* in the gay male community. Getting beyond impersonal activity to a long-term relationship, both men may initiate sexual activity but fail to work to meet each other's emotional needs. Two women, socialized to be sexually passive, may take care of their domestic needs while the sexuality between them may wane over time.

Lesbian couples who are engaged in family therapy often are told they are *enmeshed.* Fusion among lesbians is a common theme throughout the literature (Appleby & Anastas, 1998; Laird & Green, 1996; Markowitz, 1991). The intensity in the close woman-to-woman partnership is viewed as both functional in its nurturance and protectiveness and problematic in that partners may be overly invested in each other and restricted in their individuality, rendering breakup extremely difficult to handle.

Therapists can help their clients have insights about relationship problems that may be less personal than gender based. Many such conflicts—such as man-to-man power struggles—can be resolved when the nature of the dynamics is understood. Talking it out with a well-informed and objective outsider, whether gay/lesbian or straight, can be immensely helpful.

A major task for the therapist is to help clients move toward positions of equal power in relationships. Power imbalance and excessive dependence lead to resentment in the person whose needs are not being met.

As with heterosexual couples, work on communication skills—how to say what and when—can be invaluable. Brief "fighting fair" schemes with rules directing them toward helpful rather than hurtful ways of putting things can be shared with couples. In his or her role of teacher, the therapist can illustrate the use of feeling words as an overture to resolving disputes. Sentences of the format, "When you . . . I feel . . . ," can be used as a model, as for example, "When you go to sleep without telling me good-night, I feel rejected." Sample rules for preventing arguments from escalating are:

Don't rehash the past.
No put-downs.
No personal threats.
No name-calling.
Respect each other's racial/ethnic background.

Couples can take copies of the rules home with them to consult in their dealings with each other. Then they can report back on their progress at the following therapy session.

Spouses of Gay Men

When a woman discovers that her husband is having an affair with a gay man, she or the married couple may choose to get counseling. The love between them is often very deep. An excellent video produced by 21st Century News, *Another Side of the Closet,* consists of interviews with three ex-wives of gay men. As one woman tells her story, "To save the friendship, I got a divorce. . . . Why did you get a divorce? everyone asked. I was in the closet about this."

"I was married twenty-four years," another woman says. "My husband became withdrawn. Then he said he was very actively gay and had repressed it for years. So we got a divorce but remained friends. I met the gay fathers. Why were their ex-wives so angry and I wasn't, they wanted to know. So I helped provide support, got their stories and wrote the book *The Other Side of the Closet.*" (This speaker and author is Amity Buxton, 1994.) "There can be healing. We [the wives] are the link. Our children are the children of gays."

"Most lesbians leave [the marriage] and most gay men stay," continues the author.

The first speaker describes her situation, "He wanted to stay in a nonsexual marriage. The gay man wants it both ways. In so many cases we love each other, so divorce is harder for us than for straight people."

In the rest of the video the wives describe their predicament, "We are guilty by association: How could you marry him? If you later start dating, it's thought maybe the woman has AIDS. Or we caused their homosexuality. Also there's voyeurism: What was it like?"

"For the parent when the child is out, it's a new relationship," another comments. "For the spouse, it's the end of the relationship."

"When I was in a support group [of wives in gay marriages], a woman said she wished he had died instead of coming out. Then she could have mourned. And the whole group said, 'Me too.' "

This excellent video shows the importance of a support group, but, unfortunately, only a large city would have such a specialized group. When the Waterloo, Iowa, PFLAG meeting viewed this film to help a gay/straight couple, Paul, the gay host said, "My wife said, 'You're going to be a very lonely old man.' I was not going to be. But I didn't know that then. Now she's the one who's alone. We (John and I) have mostly single friends. But married people have friends as couples. When you divorce, you lose those couples as friends."

The therapist would do well to share some of these insights with clients whose spouse has come out to them. Buxton's highly readable book *The Other Side of the Closet* can be a tremendous help to the woman who finds herself in this predicament. Shernoff (1998b), a gay therapist who does couples counseling, urges extreme sensitivity toward the straight spouse. Using a strengths approach, he describes how he would help a wife deal with her feelings of self-doubts due to her husband's lack of sexual interest in her. "Maybe it was because you are so attractive to him that he stayed in the marriage for so long," he might say, "even though he was attracted to men" (p. 24). In this situation, Shernoff concludes, we should not assume that we have to give priority to a client's coming out as gay without exploring the ramifications of such a disclosure. We need to help the gay or lesbian spouse be deliberate in his or her actions, to take things one step at a time.

Tapping into Strengths

Besieged by societal scorn and misunderstanding from family and friends, gays and lesbians often find fulfillment by developing compensatory strengths. Still they may feel "down" at times and seek professional help for the support and affirmation that the rest of society fails to provide. Gays and lesbians deserve recognition for a number of reasons, as Miley, O'Melia, and DuBois (1998) suggest, for the courage they demonstrate in coming out to others, in their ability to maintain long-lasting relationships in the absence of legal sanctions, and in their resourcefulness in creating families of choice.

The Spiritual Dimension

The strength that can come from religious faith should not be underestimated. Encouraging clients' spiritual awakening means helping them to feel loved, connected, and at one with the universe; it means exchanging the voice of oppression in their heads for a sense of unconditional love.

A common theme woven through the gay and lesbian narrative is an upbringing in which the church, synagogue, or mosque was a kind of sanctuary from the cruelties of childhood, especially the gay and lesbian childhood. A lesbian pastor, quoted in Markowitz (1998), recalls her early relationships with the African American church:

> Spirituality was the salvational force in our lives during slavery that allowed us to hold on, and often transcend, in the midst of tremendous oppression. When I finally came out at age 22, I didn't think about leaving the church; I thought about finding a church where I could be myself. (p. 8)

So many gays and lesbians sang in the choir, went to Sunday School, and considered entering the priesthood or becoming rabbis. And so many of these felt rejected by the orthodox religions of their childhoods. In the hearts of once deeply spiritual gays and lesbians, accordingly, there may be a painful sense of emptiness and loss.

A client's intense outburst of anger against his or her childhood religiosity is a clue to the need for some sort of resolution. The therapist who is knowledgeable of Biblical passages of love and acceptance can be a tremendous help to the client steeped in negative interpretations and out-of-context quotes. A focus on love, not condemnation, is the spirit transcending all the major religions. Markowitz (1998) provides the illustration of a gay man living with AIDS who had long since outgrown the judgmental religion of his childhood. Then, searching for meaning in his illness, he came to understand spirituality in a new light, spirituality as love toward himself and others, as an opening of the heart and an unraveling of the great mystery of life.

Referrals to gay and lesbian clergy can be a tremendous boon to clients in helping them reclaim the spirituality of their youth and to feel at peace with their sexuality. Metropolitan Community Churches are gay- and lesbian-oriented churches located in the large cities; their programs are televised on cable television across North America. The Quakers or Friends Meetings (those affiliated with Friends General Conference, unprogrammed meetings) are noted for their gay and lesbian advocacy. Gay and lesbian Quakers, in fact, often have their own meetings and weekend conferences. Unitarians, similarly, welcome gay and lesbian members. (See Religious Resources on p. 180 for more information.)

Transforming Gay and Lesbian Lives

Kaufman and Raphael (1996) who have shaped a whole book around the theme of shame—*Coming Out of Shame: Transforming Gay and Lesbian Lives*—offer a digest of helpful suggestions for affirmative couples counseling. Written from the perspectives of gays and lesbians, the major pathways from "gay shame to gay pride" follow.

Creating within Ourselves the Capacity for Self-Forgiveness and Affirmation. A good starting point, this pathway addresses internalized homophobia in the individual, the legacy of the gay/lesbian bashing of youth. We are using the word *forgive* here in the sense of withdrawing from someone the power to hurt. Forgiveness involves a restoration of peace and sanity. Its opposite is resentment and bitterness. Gays and lesbians, forever rebuffed by a heterosexist, heterocentric society, have a lot to forgive. And because of forced compromises with a blaming, homophobic society, gays and lesbians also may need to forgive themselves. As Kaufman and Raphael (1996) define the process of self-forgiveness: "Once we begin to come out of shame, we can forgive our past powerlessness, the years spent in the closet, the lies we told, the people we may have hurt by our dishonesty and fear" (p. 179). Being gay or lesbian is not wrong or bad, they reiterate; only shaming from others has made it seem to be this way.

A relevant intervention for the social worker is to help the client replace negative, self-blaming thoughts with positive, loving ones, and self-destructive acts (such as abusing substances or practicing unsafe sex) with healthier lifestyles.

Although extensive support services are in place to help a gay community ravaged by AIDS, no such support exists for men who do not have the virus, yet whose emotions are shattered by the ravages of the virus. Having accepted the fate of infection, gay men find themselves living in a wasteland of suffering and grief; like other survivors of mass tragedy, they are burdened with survivor guilt. Moreover, as gay family therapist Steven Ball (1995) notes, there is almost a taboo about not being HIV positive. Mental health workers tend to overlook the needs of uninfected gay men entirely, or to label them derogatorily as "the worried well."

To meet the needs of men who seem to feel they are "cursed" with good health, Ball conducts group therapy with HIV-negative gay men. "Why was I spared? Do I deserve to live?"—these are among the key issues dealt with in the group. The purpose of the group is twofold—to help the men develop positive, life-affirming strategies for coping with multiple loss, and to encourage the use of good common sense regarding present and new relationships.

Men who are suffering from feelings of guilt and low self-worth are at high risk for what could even be termed *suicidal sex.* Psychotherapist Michael Shernoff (1995) comments on the resurgence of unsafe sexual practices among gay men, in general, and of some of his clients, in particular: "One man told me he had to go out of town for business on New Year's Eve, which made him feel angry. He went to a bar, got drunk, and had oral sex with a stranger without using a condom. He has lived in fear that he has been infected ever since" (p. 16). Important tasks for therapists, according to Shernoff, are to help clients increase their self-esteem so they will take care of themselves; to emphasize the importance of closeness and intimacy; to perhaps redefine what they see as "good sex"; and, above all, to challenge the ethos that separates love from sex.

Counteracting the Sources of Shame by Transforming Powerlessness. The coming-out process for lesbians, gays, and bisexuals is one example of moving from a position of relative powerlessness to one of more equal power. In a survey of 124 lesbians involved in couple relationships, Caron and Ulin (1997) found that lesbians who were open about their relationship and whose partners were open reported higher scores of relationship quality. However, due to differences in work environment or family background, coming out may be easier for one member of the couple than the other. Still, in achieving openness, lesbian and gay couples are fundamentally transforming and empowering their relationships with others.

Sometimes breakup of a relationship is a healthy move toward personal growth, especially for relationships in which people stay together out of guilt or pity. Remien (1997) provides several clinical vignettes from his practice of breakups complicated by guilt feelings because one partner was HIV positive. In one of the case studies presented, a lesbian with AIDS was abusive in her behavior, pushing unprotected sex onto her partner and controlling her choice of friends. A second case study described how a gay man was held hostage by unnecessary guilt that kept him in a relationship long after the love had gone out of it.

Finding the Path to Gay/Lesbian Pride. Consciousness raising is a process that can be garnered by the therapist in helping clients transform self-shaming scripts into self-affirming ones. An empowerment exercise presented by Bricker-Jenkins (1995) uses personal imagery to raise awareness of personal hurt due to oppression in our society. The merit of the exercise is that a negative event—rejection by a parent of a child's homosexuality—can be a turning point toward a transformation or new beginning. In this exercise the participant is instructed to remember a disturbing event from long ago, one involving oppression, which was a learning experience in some way. The individual is then asked to close his or her eyes and to return to the scene as fully as possible, attending to every visceral sensation and to answer: What do you hear, see, smell, taste, feel, do? The conclusion can involve a transforming experience, for example, "I said no;" "I put my foot down;" "I decided to go for it."

Kaufman and Raphael demonstrate how we can relive the old scene of hurt or rejection and, in a sense, recreate who we are by giving ourselves new, nurturing messages. Clients can be encouraged to nurture the gay or lesbian aspects of themselves by prizing their erotic desires, by reading gay/lesbian books, watching gay/lesbian-positive films, and enjoying gay/lesbian music.

Consciousness raising arouses awareness of oppression and sometimes breeds anger, anger that may previously have been turned within. A process that we can call *externalizing anger* may be the first step toward personal liberation. Taking a stand to change the world helps give life purpose and results in inner change. Conversely, inner change can result in commitment to taking a stand. As people become bound by common experience and identity, collective pride enhances individual pride. The personal becomes political, and the political, personal with this step.

A unique strength can be found, as Kaufman and Raphael point out, in cross-gender collaboration. People linked in a joint struggle lose their sense of society-induced shame. One way to find solidarity and a lot of fun besides is by attending both gay male and lesbian events jointly—the musical pageants, comedies, drag shows, literary readings, and Halloween parties. In couples counseling, the therapist can help clients engage in such activities of celebration, celebrating the distinctive cultural, social, and spiritual aspects of the gay and lesbian communities. Much strength can be drawn from close ties among gay males and lesbians; through politics and celebration, such ties are being enhanced today.

Conclusion

Family therapy, as we have seen in this chapter, is highly relevant to direct practice with gay and lesbian clients. Family of origin issues from the past; extended family ties; newly created gay and lesbian families; the child-rearing dynamics of lesbian moms and gay dads; issues related to HIV status: All are issues skilled family therapists should be able to readily deal with. But can they?

The way a problem is defined affects the solution that is chosen. *Problem*-based assessments encourage individualistic rather than social environmental explanations of human problems. If homosexuality is defined as the problem, then homosexuality is both the centerpoint of the problem and its treatment. Conversion therapy might be the intervention of choice in hopes of changing the orientation; that failing, celibacy might be urged—the Catholic Church favors this approach. Or less radically, family therapists who take a problem-based, deficit orientation may "tolerate" various forms of sexual orientation or family lifestyles, but they may have very low expectations for happiness for gay and lesbian couples or their children. Their low expectations then can become a self-fulfilling prophecy.

A strengths perspective, as we have argued, is highly relevant for work with gay, lesbian, and bisexual families. Indeed, it is the only thing that ever does work. A positive, empowering approach can help people get control of their lives, and through collaboration with professionals, find a way to prevail over adversity. The social worker can play a pivotal role in helping family members realize the many resources available to them and to tap into those resources for a well-rounded family life. The basic strategies for successful work with sexual minorities, we can summarize succinctly: rename, reclaim, and reframe.

Rename refers to collaboration by the therapist and client on the positive words to use. When the father of a gay man used the term *symptom,* for example, as in symptoms of being gay, he might have been encouraged to substitute a more neutral word such as *sign.* Another example is that a client who says he is a *victim* of AIDS or of sexual abuse might be led in a direction of seeing himself or herself as a survivor.

Reclaim refers to the tendency by members of an oppressed group to take a negative name featured in name-calling (e.g., *queer* or *dyke*) and use the name with pride. One is reminded of prison inmates, who, in the progressive 1970s were called residents, yet insisted on calling themselves *convicts,* in the same way. Heterosexuals are frequently offended by this aspect of gay/lesbian pride, this forthrightness, often saying that *they* (heterosexuals) don't flaunt their sexuality. They fail to see that gay/lesbian pride is borne out of oppression and belittlement. They fail to see, furthermore, that public affirmation of one's gayness, lesbianism, or bisexuality is integral to the coming-out process. Although it is important for the social worker to help gay- and lesbian-headed families find a way to be as open as they can, given the particulars of their circumstances, it is also essential not to lose sight of client self-determination. If gay and lesbian families choose to be discreet, it is advisable to help them recognize the strengths inherent in making this life choice work as well. As always, the social worker should reveal the possibilities but recognize that it is the family members who will have to live with the choice.

The concept of *reframing* refers to a whole new way of construing reality. Thus, the social worker, drawing on the best traditions of the *social work imagination* (see van Wormer, 1997) and of what we can call African American power—"finding a way out of no way"—can lead clients into a realm of greater appreciation of who they are, what they have going for them, and how they can help make the world a better place. In so doing, the practitioner can help make the world a better place also.

REFERENCES

ABC. (1997, May 7). Ellen tells her family. *Ellen.*

Accessline. (1998, March/April). International news: British Columbia couples measure takes effect. *Accessline.* Waterloo, Iowa, p. 3.

Acosta, R. (1998, March). Winning season. *A&U: America's AIDS Magazine,* p. 15.

The Advocate. (1996, November 26). Well-mannered children. *The Advocate,* p. 18.

The Advocate. (1998a, March 31). Gay women are focus at new center. *The Advocate,* p. 18.

The Advocate. (1998b, March 17). The nation. *The Advocate,* p. 14.

Appleby, G., & Anastas, J. W. (1998). *Not just a passing phase: Social work with gay, lesbian, and bisexual people.* New York: Columbia University Press.

Ariel, J. (1997, October). Growing up in a lesbian household: A family conversation. *In the Family 3* (2), 7–9.

Ball, S. (1995, October). Positively negative. *In the Family 1* (2), 14–15.

Benkov, L. (1995). Lesbian and gay parents: From margin to center. *Journal of Feminist Family Therapy 7* (1/2), 49–64.

Bricker-Jenkins, M. (1995, June 17). Consciousness-raising presentation. Fem-School Gathering. Indianapolis, Indiana.

Buckwalter, L. (1997, January). Becoming trans-parent. *In the Family,* 16–19.

Burke, P. (1994). *Family values: A lesbian's fight for her son.* New York: Vintage Books.

Buxton, A. (1994). *The other side of the closet: The coming-out crisis for straight spouses and families.* New York: Wiley and Sons.

Cammermeyer, M. (1994). With Chris Fisher. *Serving in silence.* New York: Viking.

Carl, D. (1990). *Counseling same-sex couples.* New York: W. W. Norton.

Caron, S., & Ulin, M. (1997). Closeting and the quality of lesbian relationships. *Families in Society 78* (4), 413–419.

Carron, J. (1992). On being a gay father. In B. Berzon (Ed.), *Positively gay: New approaches to gay and lesbian life* (pp. 102–107). Berkeley: Celestial Arts.

CBS. (1998, March 1). *60 Minutes.* Exodus International.

Community Care. (1996, March 21–27). Handled with care. *Community Care 112,* 23.

Cullen, J. (1997). Transgenderism and social work: An experiential journey. *The Social Worker 65* (3), 46–54.

Dahlheimer, D., & Feigal, J. (1991). Bridging the gap. *The Family Therapy Networker 15* (1), 44–53.

Dwyer, V. (1997, May 19). Class action: Fighting homophobia in the school. *Maclean's,* pp. 52–54.

Elise, D. (1986). Lesbian couples: The implications of sex differences in separation-individuation. *Psychotherapy 23* (2), 305–310.

Garnett, B. (1994). Memoirs of a lesbian daughter. In K. Jay & A. Young, *Lavender culture* (pp. 315–324). New York: A Jove/HBJ Book.

Giles, J. (1998, March 30). Return of the rebel belle. *Newsweek,* p. 66.

Greene, B. (1994). Ethnic-minority lesbians and gay men: Mental health and treatment issues. *Journal of Consulting and Clinical Psychology 62,* 243–251.

Hardman, K. (1997). Social workers' attitudes to lesbian clients. *British Journal of Social Work 27,* 545–563.

Hardy, K. (1997, January). Not quite home: The psychological effects of oppression. *In the Family 6–8,* 26.

Hare, J. (1994). Concerns and issues faced by families headed by a lesbian couple. *Families in Society 75* (19), 27–35.

Heron, A., & Maran, M. (1991). *How would you feel if your father was gay?* Boston: Alyson.

hooks, b. (1994). *Outlaw culture: Resisting representations.* New York: Routledge.

Hunter, J., & Mallon, G. P. (1998). Social work practice with gay men and lesbians within communities. In G. Mallon (Ed.), *Foundations of social work practice with lesbian and gay persons* (pp. 229–248). Binghamton, NY: Haworth.

Jay, K. (1997). Ties that bind: Friendships between lesbians and gay men. *Harvard Gay and Lesbian Review 4* (2), 9–12.

Kantrowitz, B., & Senna, D. (1993, June 21). A town like no other. *Newsweek,* pp. 56–57.

Kaufman, G., & Raphael, L. (1996). *Coming out of shame: Transforming gay and lesbian lives.* New York: Doubleday.

Laird, J. (1993). Lesbians and lesbian families: Multiple reflection. *Smith College Studies in Social Work 64* (3), 263–296.

Laird, J. (1995). Lesbians: Parenting. In *Encyclopedia of Social Work* (pp. 1604–1616). Washington, DC: NASW Press.

Laird, J. (1996). Lesbians and their families of origins. In J. Laird & R. J. Greene (Eds.), *Lesbians and gays in couples and families* (pp. 89–121). San Francisco: Jossey-Bass.

Laird, J., & Greene, R. J. (1996). Introduction. In J. Laird & R. J. Greene, (Eds.), *Lesbians and gays in couples and families* (pp. 1–12). San Francisco: Jossey-Bass.

Laird, J., & Greene, R. J. (Eds.) (1996). *Lesbians and gays in couples and families.* San Francisco: Jossey-Bass.

Liddle, B. (1997). Gay and lesbian clients' selection of therapists and utilization of therapy. *Psychotherapy 34* (1), 11–18.

Mabry, M. (1997, April 14). Whose kids are they? *Newsweek,* p. 46.

Markowitz, C. (1991). Homosexuality: Are we still in the dark? *The Family Therapy Networker 15* (1), 26–35.

Markowitz, L. (1995, October). When the mirror is wrong. *In the Family,* 8–13.

Markowitz, L. (1998, January). Raising the sacred in therapy. *In the Family,* 7–13.

Matteson, D. R. (1996). Counseling and psychotherapy with bisexual and exploring clients. In B. Firestein (Ed.), *Bisexuality: The psychology and politics of an invisible minority* (pp. 185–213). Thousand Oaks, CA: Sage.

Metz, H. (1996). Support for kids of gay parents. *The Progressive 60* (1), 15.

Miley, K. K., O'Melia, M., & DuBois, B. (1998). *Generalist social work practice: An empowering approach.* Boston: Allyn and Bacon.

Modrcin, M., & Wyers, N. (1990). Lesbian and gay couples: Where they turn when help is needed. *Journal of Gay and Lesbian Psychotherapy 1* (3), 89–104.

Morales, J. (1995). Gay men: Parenting. In *Encyclopedia of social work* (pp. 1085–1094). Washington, DC: NASW Press.

Newman, L. (1994). *Heather has two mommies* (p. 30). Boston: Alyson Publications.

Norwaves (1997, July 29). Worth noting. *Norwaves 5* (29), electronic news of Norway, item 13.

Patterson, C. (1996). Contributions of lesbian and gay parents and their children to the prevention of heterosexism. In E. Rothblum & Z. Bond (Eds.), *Preventing heterosexism and homophobia* (pp. 184–201). Thousand Oaks, CA: Sage.

Remien, R. (1997). Three portraits of how HIV and AIDS can complicate break-up. *In the Family 3* (2), 18–19.

Reyes, M. (1998). Latina lesbians and alcohol and other drugs: Social work implications. *Alcohol Treatment Quarterly 16* (1–2), 179–192.

Rofes, E. (1997). Dancing bears, performing husbands, and the tyranny of the family. In R. E. Goss & A. A. Strongheart, *Our families, our values: Snapshots of queer kinship* (pp. 151–162). New York: Haworth.

Rust, P. (1996). Monogamy and polyamory: Relationship issues for bisexuals. In B. Firestein (Ed.), *Bisexuality: The psychology and politics of an invisible minority* (pp. 127–147). Thousand Oaks, CA: Sage.

Salholz, E. (1993, June 21). The power and the pride. *Newsweek,* pp. 54–60.

Sanders, G. (1993). The love that dares to speak its name: From secrecy to openness in gay and lesbian affiliations. In E. Imber-Black, *Secrets in families and family therapy* (pp. 215–242). New York: W. W. Norton.

Schope, R. (1998, March 5–8). Minority identity and locus of control among gay men. Paper presented at the Conference of the Council of Social Work Education, Orlando, Florida.

Shapiro, J. (1996, September 16). Kids with gay parents. *U.S. News & World Report,* pp. 75–79.

Shernoff, M. (1995, October). Death wish? *In the Family 1* (2), 16.

Shernoff, M. (1997, October). Unexamined loss: An expanded view of gay break-ups. *In the Family 3* (2), 10–13.

Shernoff, M. (1998a). Individual practice with gay men. In G. Mallon (Ed.), *Foundations of social work practice with lesbian and gay persons* (pp. 77–103). Binghamton, NY: Haworth.

Shernoff, M. (1998b, March/April). Coming out in therapy. *Family Networker,* pp. 23–24.

Tasker, F., & Golombok, S. (1997). *Growing up in a lesbian family: Effects on child development.* New York: Guilford.

Van Voorhis, R., & McClain, L. (1997). Accepting a lesbian mother. *Families in Society 78* (6), 642–650.

van Wormer, K. (1997). *Social welfare: A world view.* Chicago: Nelson-Hall.

Wasserstein, W. (1998, March 31). A deeper kind of love. *The Advocate,* pp. 59–61.

Weston, K. (1991). *Families we choose: Lesbians, gays, kinship.* New York: Columbia University Press.

Willhoite, M. (1990). *Daddy's roommate.* Boston: Alyson.

Wishon, B. (1997). The transforming power of queer love. In R. E. Goss & A. A. Strongheart (Eds.), *Our families, our values: Snapshots of queer kinship* (pp. 107–113). New York: Haworth Press.

GLOSSARY

ac/dc expression from electronics labels, current that goes both ways, means you can have sex with males or females.

ACT UP AIDS Coalition to Unleash Power; a highly militant group of gays and lesbians who have done many outrageous things to publicize their cause.

bareback sex unsafe anal sex without condoms.

berdache term coined by a French historian from the Persian term for "kept boy." This term is widely used for the ancient Native American institutionalized acceptance of transgendered people. *Two spirited* is the preferred Native American term.

biphobia fear of being bisexual or hatred of bisexuals who may be thought to be betraying their true gay or lesbian orientation.

bi or bisexual a person who is sexually attracted to people of both sexes.

bisexual symbol:

bisexual male

bisexual female

Boston marriage women who lived together as husband and wife in the early twentieth century, often in an asexual relationship.

black triangle Nazi symbol used in concentration camps for lesbians.

bugchaser gay man engaging in suicidal, high-risk sex.

buggery gay male anal sex, derived from "Bulgaria."

bull dyke slang term for a strong, warrior-like lesbian.

butch a lesbian who plays a masculine role in relation to femme.

The Castro gay neighborhood in San Francisco, the site of much political activity; includes the area near and on Castro Street.

coming out the developmental process through which gay and lesbian people disclose their sexual orientation to themselves and others.

dental dam mouthpiece used to practice safe oral sex.

diesel dyke a tough, masculine type of lesbian.

drag queen an individual, usually a gay male, who dresses as a female gender stereotype.

dyke formerly negative term used for masculine lesbian, now reclaimed by lesbians and used in a positive way for themselves.

fag hag a straight woman who keeps company with gay men.

faggot a gay man who participates in his gay culture in dress and mannerisms; used by heterosexuals as a derogatory term.

fairy slang for an effeminate gay man.

female genetic symbol intertwined identifies lesbian female. *See* lesbian.

femme French for woman, a lesbian who plays a feminine role in relation to butch.

freedom rings a chain of six aluminum rings, each of which is a different color of the rainbow to represent diversity, worn as a symbol of gay/lesbian pride.

gay homosexual; culturally the word applies to both women and men but is used more for men today. Symbolized as:

gaydar reported ability of gays and lesbians to detect each other, similar to radar.

gender identity disorder mental disorder listed in the *DSM:IV* (psychiatric handbook of mental disorders) for transgendered people.

granola dyke a masculine lesbian with hippie tendencies.

heterocentrism the assumption that everyone is heterosexual unless otherwise indicated, a world view through heterosexual lenses.

heterosexism discrimination against gays, lesbians, and bisexuals by heterosexual people or social institutions.

heterosexual privilege the rights and advantages that heterosexuals have and take for granted every day (e.g., the right to marry a person of the opposite sex or show affection in public).

homophobia the phenomenon of gays and lesbians absorbing the fears and prejudices of the society, turning these attitudes within.

homosexism term coined by the authors of this book to denote reverse heterosexism, seeing the world exclusively in gay or lesbian terms, a narrow, limited perspective, name-calling of heterosexuals or breeders, for example.

internalized homophobia the phenomenon of gays and lesbians absorbing the fears and prejudices of society, turning these attributes within.

lambda letter of the Greek alphabet used as a symbol of gay or lesbian sexual orientation.

lavender color identified with gay and lesbian culture, thought to be derived as a symbol from a mix of pink and blue.

lesbian a women who is sexually attracted to other women and whose orientation is acknowledged as such. Symbolized as: ⚢

l g b t stands for lesbian, gay, bisexual, transgender.

lipstick lesbian feminine, made-up lesbian.

male genetic symbol intertwined identifies gay male. *See* gay.

outing a controversial phenomenon of forcing gay men and lesbians out of the closet, or announcing a sexual orientation other than heterosexuality.

PFLAG Parents, Families, and Friends of Lesbians and Gays. Started as a support organization for parents of lesbians and gay men, PFLAG now boasts over 300 chapters, a quarterly newsletter, and extensive networking for political organizing.

pink triangle in Nazi Germany, homosexuals were forced to wear a pink triangle and were treated as the lowest status of people in the concentration camps.

queer formerly negative word for homosexuals, derived from the word *crooked;* recently reclaimed to refer affectionately to gay, lesbian, bisexual, and transgendered culture as queer theory, queer art, for example.

Queer Nation known for flyers, protests, and flamboyance, this organization stages impromptu fashion shows and demonstrations.

rainbow official six-colored (red, orange, yellow, green, blue, and purple) symbol of gay and lesbian pride.

salt and pepper sexual relationship across racial lines.

sexual continuum notion from Kinsey that sexuality occurs along a continuum with homosexuality at one end and heterosexuality at the other.

sexual minority a group term to identify a person who self-identifies as gay, lesbian, bisexual, transgender, or transsexual.

sexual orientation the scientific term for the direction of sexual attraction or affection. Examples of sexual orientation are heterosexuality, bisexuality, and homosexuality.

sodomy refers to anal penetration, most often between men, but may also include anal penetration of a woman; from Sodom, an inhospitable city destroyed in the Bible.

Stonewall the sight where, in 1969, gays and lesbians fought police for five days after a police raid at the Stonewall Inn; a symbol of rebellion, a turning point in gay/lesbian pride.

the strengths approach a traditional social work perspective, recently reclaimed, stressing a focus on client strengths rather than weaknesses; a view of the personal and political as intertwined.

transgenderism an umbrella term to refer to transsexuals, transvestites, cross-dressers, performance artists, and drag queens.

transvestite an individual who dresses in "opposite" gender clothing for a combination of reasons. Most transvestites are bisexual men.

transsexual a person who identifies his or her gender identity and biological sex with that of the "opposite" gender, a person who feels he or she is in the wrong body and may request a sex change through gender reassignment surgery.

two spirited Native American term to refer to a cultural acceptance of persons with characteristics of the opposite sex, revered for their special spiritual qualities.

RESOURCES

ACT UP New York
(http://www.interchg.ubc.ca/aidsll/aids96html)

AIDS Action Committee
(http://www.aac.org)

American Psychological Association
Committee on Lesbian & Gay Concerns
750 First Street, NE
Washington, DC 20002-4241
(202) 336-6052

Association for Gay, Lesbian and Bisexual Issues in Counseling
P.O. Box 216
Jenkintown, PA 19046

Black Gay and Lesbian Leadership Forum
3924 W. Sunset Boulevard
Los Angeles, CA 90029

Gay Teachers Association
Box 435 Van Brunt Station
Brooklyn, NY 11215

Black Gay and Lesbian Leadership Forum/AIDS Prevention Team
1219 S. La Brea Avenue
Los Angeles, CA 90010
(213) 964-7820
Fax (213) 964-7830

Gay and Lesbian Latinos Unidos
P.O. Box 85459
Los Angeles, CA 90072
(213) 660-9681

Gay Alcoholics Anonymous World Service Office
475 Riverside Drive
New York, NY 10115
(212) 777-1800

Gay Al-Anon Inter-group Referral
220 Park Avenue South
New York, NY 10003
(212) 254-7230

National Association of Social Workers
Gay and Lesbian Task Force
750 1st St., NE, Suite 700
Washington, DC 20002-4241

An arena for support and discussion of issues pertinent to queer individuals working within the field of psychology. To subscribe, send an e-mail to:
Listserve@Home.ease.lsoft.com.
In the body of the message type (exactly as shown):
SUBscribe QUEERPSYCH "your full name"
(without the quotes).

L/G/B/T THERAPISTS OF COLOR: Join a national conference and add your name to our growing directory. Contact *In the Family* for more information.
P.O. Box 5387
Takoma Park, MD 20913
phone (301) 270-4771
fax (301) 270-4660

In the Family: Gay/lesbian/transgender magazine. Order through LMarkowitz@aol.com or
ITF, P.O. Box 5387, Tacoma Park, MD 20913

Adovate Internet: www.advocate.com

Canada PFLAG
Mary Jones
35 Willis Dr.
Brampton, ON
L6W 1B2
ljones@pathcom.com

The Gay, Lesbian, and Straight Education Network: The only national organization whose mission is to combat antigay/lesbian prejudice in the schools.
121 West 27th St., Suite 804
New York, NY 10001
Glsenalerteglsen.org.

Lambda Rising: Large brochure but will send a free catalog of published works.
AT 1625 Connecticut Ave., NW
Washington, DC 20009-1013
lambarishingehis.com

Canadian information: Pink Triangle Service
71 Band St., 2nd Floor
Ottawa, ON KiP 6H6

Gaynet: majordomo@queernet.org

Sappho: sappho-request@fiesta.intercon.com

BISEXU-L: listserve brownvm.brown.edu

PFLAG
P.O. Box 27605
Washington, DC 20038

National Gay and Lesbian Task Force and Policy Institute
2320 17th St., NW
Washington, DC 20009

Religious Resources

Association of Welcoming and Affirming Baptists
(508) 226-1945
http://members.aol.com/wabaptists/

Catholics Speak Out
P.O. Box 5206
Hyattsville, MD 20782

Dignity—Gay and Lesbian Catholics
(800) 877-8797
http://abacus.oxy.edu/qrd/orgs/dignity

Friends for Lesbian and Gay Concerns (Quaker)
143 Campbell Ave.
Ithaca, NY 14850

Integrity—Gay and Lesbian Episcopalians
(603) 595-4245
http:/members.aol.com/natlinteg/home.htm

Interweave: Unitarian Universalists for Lesbian, Gay, Bisexual and Transgendered Concerns
(617) 742-2100

United Fellowship of Metropolitan Community Churches
(310) 360-8640
http://www.ufmcc.com

World Congress of Gay and Lesbian Jewish Organizations
P.O. Box 23379
Washington, DC 20026
http://www.dircon.co.uk/weglijo

INDEX